Design Research Now
Essays and Selected Projects

Ralf Michel
(ed.)

Design
Research
Now

Essays and Selected Projects

Birkhäuser
Basel · Boston · Berlin

Colophon

Editor, concept and editorial: Ralf Michel, Zurich
Concept and editorial: Janine Schiller, Zurich
Graphic Design: Formal, Christian Riis Ruggaber & Dorian Minnig, Zurich
Translation from German into English ("Design as Practice, Science and Research",
"The Uneasy Relationship between Design and Design Research", "Introduction" and
"Foreword", and the biographies of R. Michel and B. Schneider): Robin Benson, Berlin
Printer: Kösel GmbH & Co. KG, Altusried-Krugzell
Paper: MunkenPrint white, paper volume 1.5, 100g/m^2; LuxoArt silk, 115g/m^2
Typeface: Akkurat Light, Arnhem Blond

Library of Congress Control Number: 2007931249

Bibliographic information published by the German National Library
The German National Library lists this publication in the Deutsche Nationalbibliogra-
fie; detailed bibliographic data are available on the Internet at http://dnb.d-nb.de.

© 2007 Birkhäuser Verlag AG
Basel · Boston · Berlin
P.O. Box 133, CH-4010 Basel, Switzerland
Part of Springer Science+Business Media

Printed on acid-free paper produced from chlorine-free pulp. TCF ∞

Printed in Germany

ISBN: 978-3-7643-8471-5

9 8 7 6 5 4 3 2 1
www.birkhauser.ch

If international design research is to continue to develop, we need to have fundamental discussions, not only on what we understand design research to be, but also on the most important questions and issues, on exemplary design projects, and on the most promising subject areas now and in the future. Rather than asserting unilaterally that a particular conception of research is the only valid one, or that a single type of approach is exemplary, however, our aim should be to present a diversity of viewpoints and research projects to a wider audience of design researchers, introducing specific research areas and giving reference points for more extensive debate on the focus, issues, objectives, approaches and methods of design research.

The significance of *Design Research Now* by Ralf Michel in this context it is that it collects together a number of positions that have come to prominence over the past few years and are now repeatedly cited in discussions of design research. At the same time, it has the courage to present exemplary projects that are particularly exciting for contemporary discussion of design research. The selection here resulted from an evaluation procedure in which Ralf Michel compiled key positions on design research according to his own assessment of the research community. This compilation, then, is definitely not representative of BIRD's individual preferences but rather an attempt to show the state of design research today.

BIRD's various publication projects help to make the central positions in design research available to others by presenting interesting projects appropriately, publishing key reference books and anthologies in the original language and/or in translation, and compiling a set of reference points and materials that are vital for international design research. The aim is to illustrate the enormous heterogeneity of these key positions, to convey en idea of the vigorous and controversial research debate, and to encourage and stimulate further discussion.

For over forty years, design research has been considered an essential element in the emerging academic discipline of design. In the last decade in particular, it has been conducted more broadly than ever before. At the core of most, if not all, concepts of design research is the realisation that, in an age of increasingly complex conditions for practising and studying design, there are almost no systematic bases for the continued development of design as an academic discipline; systematic in the sense of scientific and thus independently arguable. Many people have come to realise that if design is to have a future as a socially, culturally or economically relevant discipline, it cannot dispense with the academic tools of the discipline's cognitive force and agency.

The teaching and research activities at the Hochschule für Gestaltung in Ulm (hfg ulm) are an important point of departure in the evolution of design into an academically grounded discipline supported by theoreticians, teachers and former students. Their number includes Tomás Maldonado, Gui Bonsiepe and Klaus Krippendorff, whose concepts and theories influence design discourse to this day. In his essay, 'The Uneasy Relationship between Design and Design Research', Gui Bonsiepe explicitly introduces the German term *Entwurf* as an alternative to Design (the current popularity of which has, in his opinion, rendered it misleading). This makes translation problematic because English, unlike the Romance languages, has no exact equivalent to *Entwurf*. In his essay, Bonsiepe notes that it is no longer possible to design in the same way as people did one or two generations ago. He therefore concludes that it is equally impossible to do research as people did one or two generations ago, 'i.e. orienting themselves primarily or exclusively on texts.' Bonsiepe summarises this approach in the phrase 'from discourses to viscourses.' In his postscript, he expresses the need for a debate between design and design research on the one hand, and the very real exclusive processes of a globalised economy on the other.

At the end of the present publication, Ezio Manzini returns to this theme and broadens the concept to include 'Design Research for Sustainable Social Innovation.' Manzini observes that in sustainable development, the role of the user changes, and that of the designer changes decisively. This process, he argues, must logically result in new design processes and have far-reaching consequences both for how design defines itself as a discipline and for design research too.

From the late 1960s to the present, the driving forces of design research have come from the English-speaking countries, especially the UK, and from colleges that encouraged and offered doctorates in design research, and whose exponents still engage in the debate on the development of independent positions within design science. In 2006, Nigel Cross's 'Designerly Ways of Knowing' [01] was republished in extended form as a book, which will be published jointly by BIRD and Birkhäuser this year as a reprint. In the essay included here,

01 |

01 | See de Vries, Cross and Grant [18]

he describes 'Understanding Designerly Ways of Knowing and Thinking' in the context of a shift from a design science to a design discipline.

02 |
More recently, the 'Research through Design' [02] approach has gained special epistemological significance. In 1993 Christopher Frayling proposed the integration of subjective experience-, activity- and image-based designer-artistic knowledge into the process of intersubjectively verifiable knowledge production. His position has far-reaching consequences: on the one hand, it opens up perspectives for independent design research, thus simultaneously provoking rigorous debates on the 'academic' significance of that approach. On the other hand, 'research through design' is usually pursued in the form of application-oriented research. As such, it is expected to produce useful – i.e. applicable – knowledge, in line with the growing significance of practice-oriented and application-related knowledge for 03 | science and society.[03]

In his essay, 'Design and its Meaning to the Methodological Development of the Discipline,' Wolfgang Jonas illustrates how research through design provides the epistemological concepts for the development of a genuine design research paradigm, which he considers a prerequisite for methodological development. His text compares inter alia the positions of Christopher Frayling and Alain Findeli [04] on the significance of 'research through design;' his own definition sides with Findeli, before concluding that: 'The Scientific Paradigm has to be embedded into the Design Paradigm...'

Richard Buchanan focuses in his essay on the strategy of design inquiry and its closely related branches of productive science and rhetorical inquiry, in order to demonstrate viable alternatives to the strategies of design science and dialectics.

Klaus Krippendorff asks whether the expression 'design research' is not, in fact, an oxymoron. He concludes more constructively that at any moment, the viability of a design depends on its stakeholders' conceptions, commitments and resources, which can be studied in order to inform design decisions. In his opinion, this is what the investigation of design needs to do.

Finally, Pieter Jan Stappers reports extensively on his experience with the theory and research of design engineering. He believes that it is possible for design research to make optimal use of designers' skills rather than forcing them into existing modes of disciplinary research. This approach lays greater emphasis on the appreciation of generative types of research. His essay is therefore entitled 'Doing Design as a Part of Doing Research.'

Susann Vihma advocates a 'semiotic Theory of Form' and examines current positions (such as Klaus Krippendorff's 'Semantic turn', 2006). She presents her thoughts in the institutional context of the School of Visual Culture, University of Art and Design Helsinki, which draws on a wealth of experience in research-oriented doctoral theses on design.

---

02 | Frayling C (1993) *Research in Art and Design*. Royal College of Art Research Papers 1(1): 1–5

03 | Gibbons M, Limoges C, Nowotny H, Schwartzman S, Scott P, Trow M (1994) *The New Production of Knowledge: The Dynamics of Science and Research in Contemporary Societies*. Sage, London

04 | Findeli A (1998) A Quest for Credibility: Doctoral Education and Research in Design at the University of Montreal. *Doctoral Education in Design*, Ohio, 8–11 October 1998

From his experience in setting up the Scientific Community of Design Research in Switzerland, Beat Schneider presents his views on design research in the context of an emerging academic discipline, and reveals design as differentiated practice, science and research.

This first volume on design research attempts to display the significant positions within design research, placing selected research projects slightly to one side; they stand alone and are not included as illustrations of the essays.

A glance at the table of contents alone shows that the book contains far more (nine) essays on design research than reports on finished research projects (four). There are several reasons for this. The two most important are:

— Current research projects often (still) do not satisfy the quality standards proposed by the pioneers of design research.
— BIRD – the Birkhäuser Board of International Research in Design – is still in an early stage of development. It is therefore possible that not enough relevant research projects were submitted (more than 80 proposals have arrived from Europe, North America, Asia, New Zealand and Australia).

The proposals received were first examined by experts. We then invited the best candidates to submit an article; this underwent double-blind peer review by international experts who then prepared a written report on it. We had decided in advance to publish only those articles that were accepted by the experts with no or only minor revision. The criteria for examining and reporting on the articles were the research topic's design autonomy, the quality and originality of the reported research project, the significance of the topic and the visual presentation of the results.

Articles by Anna Meroni on design and sustainability, Joep Frens on a research-through-design project, Paul Chamberlain's 'Shape of Things to Come,' and Ianus Keller's research on designer interaction with informal collections of visual material, made the grade and are published in this book.

The book does not contain any research projects or contributions from Asia and Scandinavia. However, in places where design research is a normal part of the development of design educational courses and the design discipline, hundreds of people are now doing research on topical questions. I hope that the next volume of *Design Research Now* will fill this gap.

Ralf Michel

Acknowledgements

I should first of all like to thank Janine Schiller, without whose academic experience and tireless work this book would not have been possible. I also wish to thank Beat Schneider for the many discussions we had on controversial topics, and for advancing the cause of design research in Switzerland. I would like to extend my thanks to Gui Bonsiepe for his constant support and for encouraging me to publish. And I want to express my gratitude to my colleagues on BIRD, the Birkhäuser Board of International Research in Design, for their kind assistance and for their critical support while I was preparing the concept. My thanks also go to the publishers for providing, within the framework of BIRD, a forum for discussion on design research.

I thank Dorian Minnig and Christian Riis Ruggaber of Formal for the graphic design, and finally, the editor, Véronique Hilfiker, whose patience we often taxed, for such a fine production.

Last but not least, I should like to thank the authors, without whom this work would never have been possible, for their great commitment, and the experts who participated in the review process.

The Uneasy Relationship between Design and Design Research 01

Themes:

— The unsubstantiated basis of design science
— The debasement of the word 'design'
— The indispensability of design research in our present time
— The part played by science in design
— Design as reflective practice
— A misinterpretation of design
— A map of design research
— Changes in the design discourse
— The characteristics of innovation in the fields of industrial design and graphic design
— The unanswered question about the foundations of design
— The iconic turn in the sciences
— Postscript on design practice in the age of globalisation

On the limits of design science

In 1848, a thin book appeared with the provocative-sounding title: *Die Wertlosigkeit der Jurisprudenz als Wissenschaft* [The worthlessness of jurisprudence as a science]. The author was the well-known lawyer Julius Hermann von Kirchmann.[01] In this work, he analysed the part played by jurisprudence in improving the practice of law and arrived at a conclusion that did not go down very well with lawyers. In order to allay any suspicions that he was trying to start a futile dispute, he began his exposition with the following sentence: 'The subject of my paper today might easily lead some to suspect that I am only interested in a piquant sentence, with no concern for the deeper truth of the matter.' [01]

He explains the ambiguity of the title, which may mean that jurisprudence is indeed a science, albeit one without any influence on everyday activity. Or, conversely, it may mean that jurisprudence is not a science, since – as he writes – it does not 'fulfil the requirements of a true concept of a science.'

01   Revised version of a paper given at the symposium of the Swiss Design Network, Basel, 13–14 May 2004

Why this reference to jurisprudence and legal practice? What do these concepts have to do with the dialectics of design, and the related question of design research, which are at issue here? For all their difference in content, parallels can be drawn. The conceptual model in Kirchmann's comment may, when transferred to design, mean that although design science is a genuine science, it has no influence on design practice; or that design science is not a science because (as the philosophers put it) it does not fulfil the requirements of a true concept of the latter. It is the task of science to 'understand its subject, discover its laws, with the aim of creating concepts, of identifying the relationship and connections between the various phenomena and, finally, of assembling its knowledge in a simple system', [01] p. 12.

We shall leave aside the question as to whether today's scientists (and this includes design researchers too) would accept so unreservedly the goal of amassing their discoveries in a simple system. Here, the first goal is to create free space for reflection and thus avoid making premature characterisations of what design research und design science are and what they ought to be doing. In this situation, a fluid physical state is preferable to a solid one.

'Designing' and projecting

The English term 'design' does not allow for the differentiation, made in German, between design and *Entwurf* (project). Consequently, it is difficult to grasp this distinction in the English language. It may even seem incomprehensible that the term 'design' (in contrast to 'project') is used in this context with a certain degree of detachment. However, there are reasons why the term 'design' should be used carefully in both languages. The popularisation of the term 'design' during the past decade – not only in English-speaking regions – and its more or less inflationary usage have turned the word design into a commonplace term that has freed itself from the category of projecting and has now attained a sort of autonomous existence. Everyone is entitled to call him- or herself a designer, especially as people generally equate design with the things they see in lifestyle magazines. Not everyone would suddenly call him/herself a project-maker (in Daniel Defoe's sense of the term[02]) because this carries an overtone of professionalism that the word design has lost. As an alternative, we could use the German expression *Gestaltung*. The only problem is, of course, that it has no equivalent in other languages. For although it refers to design, it does so primarily from the perspective of perception (Gestalt psychology) and aesthetics. However, the German term *Gestaltung* has taken a few blows, from which it has not yet recovered.

If we examine the relationship between design education und design science, it becomes apparent that they appeared almost simultaneously in the 1920s: in the Dutch De Stijl movement and at the Bauhaus. After the Second World War, design research gradually began to establish itself. There are various reasons why this happened; these will be considered later.

In 1981, Bruce Archer, who became well-known through the publication of his *Systematic Methods for Designers*, characterised design research as a form of systematic inquiry performed with the goal of generating knowledge of the form/embodiment of – or in – design, composition, structure, purpose, value and meaning of human-made things and systems.

This definition of design research is clearly tailored to industrial design and does not therefore touch on communication design. Archer then goes on to explain his definition, ending with the plausible conclusion that: 'Design research is a systematic search for and acquisition of knowledge related to design and design activity.' There ought to be no dispute about this, especially as the statement comes close to being tautological.

In English-speaking regions in particular, the main representatives of design research formerly came from the fields of engineering science and architecture. Interest correspondingly focused on developing rational design methods and on procedures for evaluating buildings and products. Graphic design was barely mentioned. It is hardly surprising then that practising industrial and graphic designers viewed events dealing with design methods and design science as well as any *papers* (if they registered the latter at all) published in this context as esoteric glass-bead games, played – with no noticeable impact on practice – on academic 'reservations' shielded from the constraints and exigencies of professional practice. As a result, discourse on design science found itself cast – rightly or wrongly – in a bad light, since it appeared to have been usurped by a network of concepts irrelevant to design practice. This may be due, in part, to the fact that design research was carried out under the aegis of systems theorists, computer scientists, operations research specialists and mechanical engineers, whose categorical conceptual systems bypassed industrial and graphic design. Furthermore, they often had no experience – or, at best, very little – in product design or visual communication. The autonomisation of method research thus also motivated Christopher Alexander at quite an early stage to distance himself from such research projects because he felt that they had either forgotten or lost sight of the goal of producing better designs.

How has the theme of design research/design science come to assume greater significance?

There are two possible reasons for this:

— First, complex design problems can no longer be solved without prior or parallel research. It should be noted that design research cannot be equated with consumer research or variations of it that take the form of ethno-methodology, i.e. an empirical science that examines the behaviour of consumers in their everyday environments and thus refrains from carrying out laboratory research. Whether or not we are prepared to designate such activity (which accompanies design) as 'research' is a question of judgement and depends on which criteria are applied to research. We cannot rule out in advance the possibility that design activity will raise questions that will, in turn, yield new knowledge as a result of the research involved in answering them.

— Second, the consolidation of design education at universities and colleges creates pressure to adapt to academic structures and traditions. Anyone who seeks to pursue an academic career is expected to acquire the appropriate qualifications in the form of a master's degree or doctorate. Anyone who does not possess this 'symbolic capital' (Bourdieu) may find him/herself unable to fill certain key positions in hierarchically structured institutions. In Turkey, for example, it is impossible to gain a professional qualification in architecture or industrial design without a doctorate.

We can therefore identify two reasons for the emergence of design research: one linked to professional practice and the other to academic activity. The tension between the two can and does lead to controversies and divergences.

Designing is initially a free and independent form of activity unconcerned with the existence of design science. However, this form of design has a provisional character. After all, it is quite possible that this activity will increasingly come to depend on the existence of design science: in other words, that design science will become the precondition for practising design. This trend will obviously have dramatic consequences for design courses, especially in the case of industrial and communication design, as well as all the new fields of study, such as interaction design and information design, which have arisen and are arising in the wake of digitisation.

Science and design

In general, scientific activity and design activity are – rightly – distinguished from one another, for each pursues its own mundane interests. The designer observes the world with an eye to its designability, unlike the scientist who regards it from the perspective of cognition. It is thus a question of divergent points of view with different contents in terms of innovation. The scientist and the researcher generate new knowledge. The designer gives people an opportunity to have new experiences in their everyday lives in society, as well as with products, symbols and services; experiences of an aesthetic character, which, in turn, are subject to socio-cultural dynamics.

The tension between cognitively related activity (research) and non-cognitively related activity (designing) becomes apparent here. To avoid any misunderstandings, however, it should be pointed out here that design activity is increasingly permeated by cognitive processes. This also raises the issue of mediating between these two areas, something that has been done with varying degrees of success since the 1920s. The unavoidable revision and updating, which are now on the agenda, of traditional study courses in the field of design and planning, inevitably raises the question of how students' cognitive competence can be improved. And this also touches on the intimately linked part played by language in the teaching of design, among other things.

Despite the difference between design and science, there is also a hidden affinity and structural similarity between the approaches of the innovative scientist and the innovative designer: both are engaged in 'tinkering', as the American philosopher Kantorovich puts it.[03] They both try things out in accordance with the motto: let's see what happens when we do this or that. Both proceed experimentally.

A glance at contemporary design problems clearly shows that the cognitive demands on design have grown. For this reason, neither design studies nor design practice can ignore the sciences and research. One example should make this clear: nowadays, when an industrial designer is commissioned to design sustainable packaging for a carton of milk for a client, she or he will need access to scientific information about energy profiles and *ecological footprints* and, if necessary, to systematic experiments on material combinations to place design activities on a scientific footing. It is no longer possible to tackle a task of this nature intuitively. As an example from the field of communication design shows, it is impossible to develop an interface for courseware without engaging in subject-related research. Anyone who relies on their inner voice and supposed creativity will go to the dogs.

Reflection/theory and design

With the introduction of design courses at universities of applied science, education programmes are now expected to stimulate students' capacity for reflection. In other words, design students must learn to think – a demand that may sound totally normal, but has by no means been fulfilled. As an American graphic designer wrote: 'Design has no heritage of or belief in criticism. Design education programs continue to emphasise visual articulation, not verbal or written. The goal is to sell your idea to a client and/or a hypothetical audience. Design in relation to culture and society is rarely confronted.'[04]

Reflective behaviour is discursive thinking: thinking that manifests itself in language. Although the idea of including language in design courses goes back to the 1950s, teaching programmes generally have a lot to catch up on when it comes to language and texts, especially in the field of visual communication. The anti-discursive tradition and predisposition of design education remains powerful. We need to admit and recognise that design's image frequently attracts the wrong students. Hip-hop and cool are qualities to which design – fortunately – cannot be reduced.

What is reflection? Reflection means establishing distance to our own activities and thematising our interdependences and contradictions, especially those of a social nature. Theory points beyond what exists. With regard to the emphasis on design research, it should be noted that free space must be set aside for theoretical activity in the future as well: anyone who only considers the direct application of an idea will suffer from a narrowing of their horizon and the degeneration of their speculative consciousness. In *Lob der Theorie* Gadamer mentions '... the closeness of theory to the realm of pure play, to purely contemplating and marvelling, far removed from all customs and uses and serious business.' Furthermore, he establishes a relationship between theory and those 'things..., that are "free" from all the calculating attitudes associated with need and use.'[05] When we speak of theoretical activities in the field of design, we are certainly not issuing a kind of *carte blanche* for people to start speculating about designing and design in a manner that is totally alien to design, in which speculation occasionally serves scientists as a welcome vehicle for distinguishing themselves academically when they treat design as an object of research. Such strategies are quite tempting, because the subject of design, with its complex ramifications and interconnections, is virgin territory for scientific activity. It seems that people easily forget that talking about a subject demands a minimum degree of knowledge about it, and that, no matter how good people's intentions, speculative theoretical studies are no substitute for specialised knowledge. Hence, when such discussion contributions on design – which are frequently full of pre-conceived ideas and interpretation models – serve as norms aimed at standardising practice in the guise of scientific dignity, then it is time to cut those displaying such presumptuousness down to size.

Design as an object of criticism

For many decades, design was not thematised in scientific discourse. It was a non-issue. Despite its presence in everyday life, it hardly awoke the interest of scientific disciplines. Now that design has become a media topic, however, the situation has changed so much that there is no lack of critical discussion on the subject. One pertinent publication worth mentioning here is the latest work by the art theoretician Hal Foster, entitled *Design and Crime*.[06] Foster argues from an anti-conservative, culturally critical perspective. The title of Foster's book alone, an allusion to Adolf Loos' *Ornament und Verbrechen*, [07] which attained fame because of its polemical tone, speaks volumes. Foster writes:

> *'The old debate (infuse art into the utilitarian object) takes on a new resonance today, when the aesthetic and the utilitarian are not only conflated but all but subsumed in the commercial, and everything – not only architectural projects and art exhibitions but everything from jeans to genes – seems to be regarded as so much design.' [emphasis in the original].* [06]

To which we can only reply: all of this *is* design, even though the author himself evidently finds no pleasure in saying this. Foster continues:

'... the old project to reconnect Art and Life, endorsed in different ways by Art Nouveau, the Bauhaus and many other movements, was eventually accomplished, but according to the spectacular dictates of the culture industry, not the liberatory ambitions of the avant-garde. And a primary form of this perverse reconciliation on our time is design.'[06]

Here we find a distinct example of a mistaken understanding of design (applied art). Design has long since ceased to involve the aestheticisation of everyday life, if it ever did in the first place. We can hardly get to the roots of design using art-theoretical concepts. Design is an independent category. Located at the interface of industry, the market, technology and culture (living practice), design is eminently suited for engaging in culturally critical exercises that focus on the symbolic function of products. Foster uncritically adopts a theorem formulated by Baudrillard that asserts that design is basically limited to the symbolic dimension of objects, to the 'political economy of symbols'. Design is thus dematerialised and degraded to a *sign exchange value*. Those very positions that view themselves as anti-conformist show a remarkable tendency to pour blanket criticism on modern design for being pure ideology. There were times in which avant-garde positions in philosophy (the Vienna circle, for example) and modern design regarded one another with mutual respect. Nowadays, such an attitude is rare indeed. Today, design serves as the compliant stooge for critics of the commodity society: for critics of pan-capitalism.

Research in class

When and how should students be taught how to reflect and do research? So far, universities and colleges have failed to provide a unanimous answer to this question. Reflection and research should not be reserved for students in the more advanced classes but should be taught and practised from the beginning of the first year. Design studies would then no longer be limited to master's degree courses but encouraged and required in bachelor courses too. This does, of course, also entail risks. Every design instructor has experienced students who try to steal their way out of doing designs by performing rhetorical acrobatics and concealing weaknesses in the field of design with the aid of verbal gymnastics. Such discourse, which is a strategy for avoiding design, must be prevented. It has nothing to do with the kind of cognitive competence envisaged here, which is anchored in design. Teaching programmes must take into account cognitive competence, especially if students display theoretical interests that have hitherto been tolerated, at best, but not explicitly encouraged; for this defect is one of the reasons for the oft-criticised speechlessness of designers.

In the field of design, it is possible to distinguish between two different approaches to research:

1.   Endogenous design research, i.e. research initiated spontaneously from within the field of design. This primarily proceeds from concrete experiences in designing and is frequently integrated into the design process, thus signifying a primarily instrumental interest. It may be hoped, however, that in the future a form of endogenous design research will be pursued that goes beyond its immediate application in the design process. This would create a pool of knowledge that the field of design still lacks. (The complaint about the lack of a pool of knowledge specifically related to design is well known.) Designers should definitely be involved in this kind of research in order to counteract the danger of other-directedness in design discourse. Should the profession fail to address this need, it would put the future of industrial designers and graphic designers in doubt. These two professions might then find themselves members of a dying species.

2.   Exogenous design research, which views design as an object of research and other disciplines as meta-discourses, so to speak. We should proceed with caution here, however: for the further removed texts and research exogenous to design are from concrete experience with the contradictions, paradoxes and the aporia of design, the greater the danger that they will be at the mercy of sweeping judgements. The last thing that designers need are scientific high inquisitors who, with one finger raised, try to drum norms into their students' heads, telling them what they should and should not do.

As far as the content of research work is concerned, a rhizome table can be drawn to illustrate the broad range of themes and arrange them in a distinct order. It goes without saying that this classification, like every other, contains subjective moments and is subject, above all, to certain plausibility criteria. The map outlined here is subdivided into six thematic groups:

—   History
—   Technology
—   Form/structure
—   Media
—   Design/daily practice
—   Globalisation/the market

Each of these themes is, in turn, subdivided into a series of sub-themes.

Within the framework of a historical research project, it would be possible to draw a timeline of the subjects of the discourse on design that shows the emergence and duration of certain themes that appear in design discourse. The timeline would show the ups and downs of the discourse too. Certain themes vanish and new ones – whether under familiar or novel names – appear, while old ones may experience a revival. (This would make a fruitful field for research on design history.) As far as design education is concerned, it would be very interesting to examine how the dominance of discourse subjects has left its mark on diverse curricula. The following timeline merely serves illustrative purposes. It needs to be verified by detailed empirical analysis.

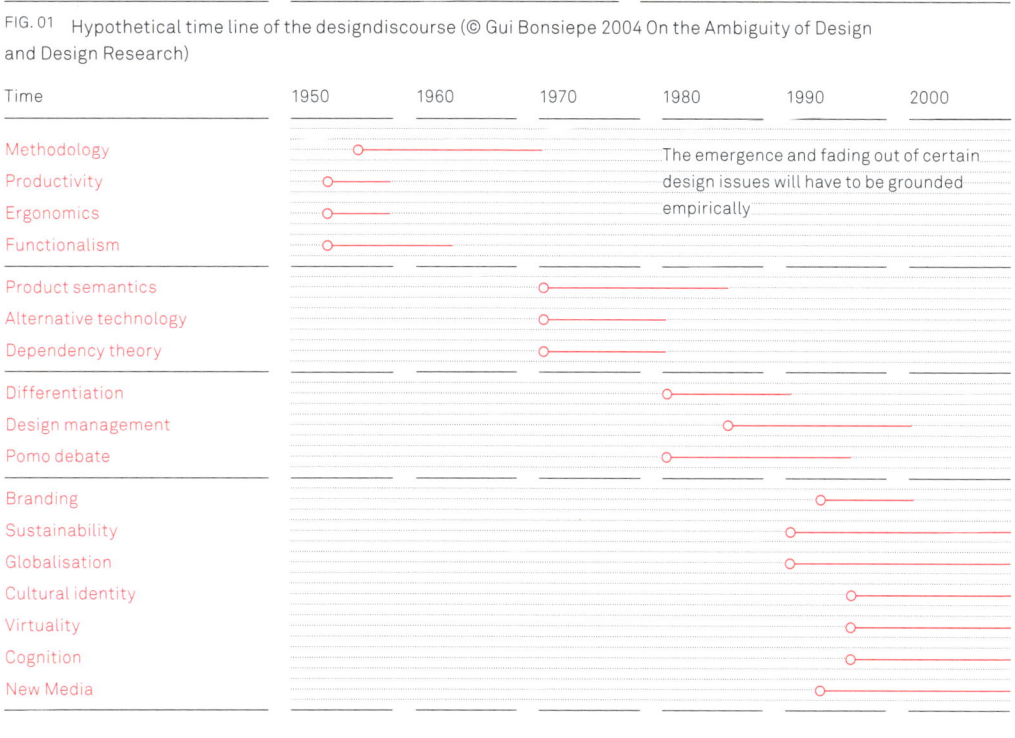

FIG. 01   Hypothetical time line of the designdiscourse (© Gui Bonsiepe 2004 On the Ambiguity of Design and Design Research)

Innovation and Entwerfen

The various branches of economics distinguish different strategies that a company can pursue to assert itself in competitive markets are:

1.   Technical innovation (e.g. a new chip)
2.   Quality (reliability, durability, finish)
3.   Rapid delivery
4.   Design

There is, of course, also the strategy of competing via lower prices. However, this is likely to play an ever-smaller role. Markets demand quality products, technically advanced products and products with high-quality designs.

How is innovation manifested in industrial design and communications design? How does innovation differ in the fields of engineering science, management and the applied sciences? In other words, what is design innovation?

How do the results of design activity look in terms of product design and visual communication, inasmuch as the latter are intended to be innovative? Before this question can be answered, the main characteristics of design must be outlined, concretised – from an integrational perspective – with the aid of non-propositional knowledge. The following list shows areas in which innovative design leaves its mark:

— Innovation in the form of improving the useful quality of a product or information
— Innovation in the form of improving the production process for manufacturing a product
— Innovation in the form of inventing new *affordances*
— Innovation in the form of sustainability
— Innovation in the form of the accessibility of information or a product (social and non-exclusive design)
— Innovation in the form of finding possible applications for new materials and technologies (solutions looking for a problem)
— Innovation in the form of greater comprehensibility in dealing with information or a product
— Innovation in the area of formal aesthetic quality (socio-cultural dynamics)
— Innovation in the sense of strategically extending a company's product range (for example, citing a manufacturer of agricultural machinery who has broadened his range – as part of strategic branding – to include services in the form of optimal fodder compositions)

From an economic point of view, there is evidently a relationship between an economy's competitiveness and its design ranking at an international level. A survey by the New Zealand Institute of Economic Research reveals that the 25 countries with the world's most competitive economies are also world leaders in design.[08] The survey is quite instructive, despite reservations about the marketing criteria underlying the ranking system. The survey could be broadened to find out which countries are leaders in the field of design research and whether there is a correlation between this and general economic competitiveness.

_____

The foundations of design

Another unanswered question in design education concerns the foundations of design and related research into the foundations of design. Very divergent views prevail on this matter among design instructors. There is, for example, the question as to what actually constitutes the foundations of design, and, taking this a step further, whether design can be said to have foundations in the first place, i.e. whether design isn't an activity without foundations. To anyone who subscribes to this position, any insistence on foundations would indicate nothing other than a pious, outmoded and unfounded wish. In this context, the sciences are often cited for the purpose of comparison, as they are generally considered to rest on foundations, and are therefore upheld to serve as a model and benchmark for design.

If we consult the sciences, however, we learn otherwise: that the sciences do not rest on foundations either. In a lecture in 1941, Max Planck said:

> *'... if we ... subject the structure of the exact sciences to precise analysis, we very soon become aware that the edifice has a dangerously weak spot, and this spot is the foundation. ... for the exact sciences there is no principle of such general validity and, at the same time, of such great importance with respect to content that it can serve science as an adequate basis. ... We can, therefore, reasonably draw only one conclusion from this, namely, that it is absolutely impossible to place the exact sciences on a general foundation composed of definitively conclusive content.'* [09]

No matter what position we adopt regarding whether design has foundations or not, it must be noted that, in the field of design education, the teaching of foundations has always aimed to solve an undeniable problem: providing the students with a formal aesthetic education that seeks to cultivate not only their receptive differentiation skills but also, and above all, their generative differentiation skills. A glance at the history of design education reveals that heated controversies raged over the Bauhaus basic course, on which design courses across the globe would subsequently model their identity (distinguishing them from courses in other fields of study). When the basic course was being developed, there was a debate on whether formal-aesthetic generative competence should be allowed to develop independently and as an organisational unit within the curriculum, or whether the basic course should be simply abolished as a relic from a hazy, romantic period of design education. Terms such as 'basic course' and 'basic design course' sometimes irritate people and cause them to adopt rigid positions that block all discussion from the start. Hence it might be advisable to refrain from using these terms. Such a move would not do away with the problem of educating students to develop formal aesthetic competence, but it would at least diffuse the situation. Instead of talking of basic courses and foundations of design, we could use Christopher Alexander's term *patterns*, which refers to recurring phenomena that exist in a context relatively free of the influence of economic factors, production technology issues etc. This would make it possible to avoid the immanent danger of academicising basic courses and thereby transforming design exercises into formal recipes that assume the form of canons or 'style bibles'.

From discourses to viscourses

For some years now, there has been talk within the social sciences of an *iconic turn*. This notion denotes a new epistemological constellation that ends the primacy of discoursivity as the privileged domain of cognition. The term iconic turn signifies the recognition of the visual plane as a cognitive domain in contrast to the centuries-old tradition of verbo-centrism. This turn is determined by technological innovations, especially in digital technology, which have made possible the new processes of image generation and image production. In the words of Günter Abel: 'Here (in the basic processing of the images) it is not a question of merely passively, illustratively or graphically reproducing something that already exists in finished form, but of an original, active process of revealing or showing something visually [*Ins-Bild-Setzen*].' [10]

It is well known that training the ability to reveal or present an object or an idea visually is central to graphic design and visual communication courses. Thanks to the *iconic turn* in the sciences and to digital technology, it is now possible to explore the cognitive potential of visual design and adequately to characterise the indispensable role that visual design plays in the cognitive process. This opens up a fascinating new field of activity and research for traditional graphic design. Even so, it is difficult – in the beginning at least – for a mode of thinking in which the discursive tradition has been dominant to acknowledge the cognitive status of images and, above all, of visuality. The deeply rooted prejudice against images is evident in the fact that they are so often downgraded with the adjective 'beautiful', revealing a visceral distrust of anything that betrays even a trace of aesthetic sensitivity. The anti-aesthetic attitude, or at least the indifference of a scientific tradition that is fixated on language, is sufficiently well known. For centuries, Plato's allegory of the cave contributed to the contempt for visuality and its being situated outside the mainstream. The epistemological constellation based on enmity towards pictures is the counterpart to a design tradition that adheres exclusively to images and disdains language. Günter Abel characterises visual knowledge thus:

> *'In contrast, non-linguistic and non-propositional knowledge refers to a form of knowledge that one can possess without having the corresponding linguistic predicates and concepts and without having learned these.'* [10]

Digital technology will bring about far-reaching changes in epistemological traditions and indicate a new role for visual design. One media analyst wrote in this context:

> *'Writing and reading will certainly not lose their meaning immediately; however, they will be come to occupy a less-central position among the broad range of cultural performances.'* He went on to say that the claim: *'that only a printed monograph can represent, for instance, the standard of knowledge achieved by a scientific discipline is generally viewed as one of the 'myths of book culture' these days.'* [11]

If it is true that designers can no longer design the way they did one or two generations ago, then it must also be acknowledged that researchers can no longer do research as they did one or two generations ago – i.e. orienting themselves primarily or exclusively by texts. This newly emerging trend can be summarised in four words: from discourses to viscourses. Under these circumstances, an iconic turn in the sciences might correspond to a cognitive turn in the design disciplines. It is still the early stages.

Postscript

Since the 1980s, when the term globalisation found its way into the social sciences, design, too, has been called upon to reconsider its role vis-à-vis this process. However, the term itself must be treated with a pinch of salt, especially in view of the fact that the alternative is not between globalisation fundamentalists and globalisation phobics (the expression unjustly used by critics in the conservative media to stigmatise them). In a recent interview, Kenneth Galbraith criticised the naïve use of this term, which he exposed as a means of camouflaging the process in which world economic policy was subjected to the hegemonic economic interests of the United States of America. That said, there are purely practical reasons why it will not be so easy to exclude the term from discourse. If we consider the adverse impacts of this development, we cannot avoid seeing a tendency towards social exclusion and the ruthless plundering of our planet's resources. Considering design in this context, we are entitled to ask after design practices that oppose this trend and refuse to unthinkingly fall in line with or subordinate them-

FIG. 02 (WEF, NZIER 2002)

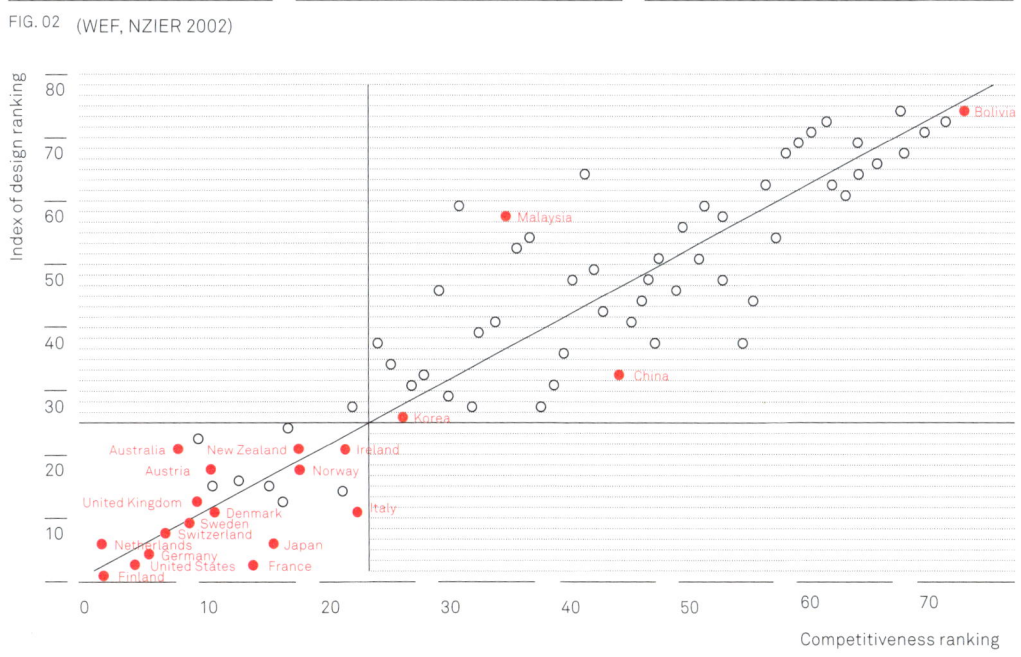

selves to this process. Of course, not everyone wants to occupy themselves with these questions. How would a design practice look that presented an alternative to a form of design that excludes people; if it no longer restricted itself to addressing a mere 10 or 20 per cent of the world's population in the highly industrialised countries, or in enclaves within zones formerly known as the Third World? It seems that there has been no unanimous answer to this question so far, especially as it is a highly explosive issue with an inescapably political character. Design research could certainly find a very relevant subject here if it aimed to reduce the gap between the different societies, assuming, of course, that we consider this at all meaningful and do not dismiss it as the perpetuation of the status quo of a social value system that has no future and needs to be radically renewed and turned upside down.

References / Bibliography

[01]   Kirchmann JH von (2000) *Die Wertlosigkeit der Jurisprudenz als Wissenschaft.*
         Manutius Verlag, Heidelberg

[02]   Maldonado T (2007) Das Zeitalter des Entwurfs und Daniel Defoe. In: *Digitale Welt und*
         Gestaltung, Birkhäuser Verlag, Basel, 257–268

[03]   Kantorovich A (1993) *Scientific Discovery – Logic and Tinkering.* State University of
         New York Press, New York

[04]   FitzGerald K (2003) Quietude. *Emigre* 64: 15–32

[05]   Gadamer, H-G (1991) *Lob der Theorie.* Suhrkamp Verlag, Frankfurt

[06]   Foster H (2002) *Design and Crime.* Verso, London

[07]   Loos A (1982, 1908[1]) Ornament und Verbrechen. In: *Trotzdem. Gesammelte Schriften*
         1900–1930. Prachner Verlag, Vienna, new edition 1997, 78–88

[08]   Building a Case for Added Value through Design. Report to Industry New Zealand
         February 2003. New Zealand Institute of Economic Research (NZIER). This report
         is based on indicators from the World Economic Forum's Global Competitiveness
         Report.

[09]   Planck M (1942) *Sinn und Grenzen der exakten Wissenschaft.* Johann Ambrosius
         Barth, Leipzig

[10]   Abel G (2003) Zeichen- und Interpretationsphilosophie der Bilder. In: Bredekamp H,
         Werner G (eds): *Bildwelten des Wissens. Kunsthistorisches Jahrbuch für Bildkritik.*
         Vol. 1,1. Akademie Verlag, Berlin, 89–102

[11]   Hartmann F (2003) *Mediologie – Ansätze einer Medientheorie der Kulturwissenschaften.*
         Facultas Verlag, Vienna

From a Design Science to a Design Discipline: Understanding Designerly Ways of Knowing and Thinking

In the past couple of decades we have seen a significant shift in focus within the field of design research. It is a shift from the aim of creating a 'design science' to that of creating a 'design discipline'. The focus is now on understanding the design process through an understanding of design cognition, or the 'designerly' ways of knowing and thinking.

Design and science

A desire to 'scientise' design emerged in the 20th-century Modern movement of design. For example, in the early 1920s, the De Stijl protagonist Theo van Doesburg expressed this perception of a new spirit in art and design:

'Our epoch is hostile to every subjective speculation in art, science, technology etc. The new spirit, which already governs almost all modern life, is opposed to animal spontaneity, to nature's domination, to artistic flummery. In order to construct a new object we need a method, that is to say, an objective system.' [01]

A little later, the architect Le Corbusier wrote about the house as an objectively designed 'machine for living':

'The use of the house consists of a regular sequence of definite functions. The regular sequence of these functions is a traffic phenomenon. To render that traffic exact, economical and rapid is the key effort of modern architectural science.' [02]

In both of these comments, and throughout much of the Modern Movement, we see a desire to produce works of art and design based on objectivity and rationality; that is, on the values of science.

These aspirations to scientise design surfaced strongly again in the 'design methods movement' of the 1960s. The Conference on Design Methods, held in London in September 1962, [03] is generally regarded as the event that marked the launch of design methodology as a subject or field of enquiry. The desire of the new movement was even more strongly than before to base the design process (as well as the products of design) on objectivity and rationality. The origins of this emergence of new design methods in the 1960s lay in the application of novel, scientific and computational methods to the novel and pressing problems of the Second World War – from which came civilian developments such as operations research and management decision-making techniques.

The 1960s was heralded as the 'design science decade' by the radical technologist Richard Buckminster Fuller, who called for a 'design science revolution', based on science, technology and rationalism, to overcome the human and environmental problems that he believed could not be solved by politics and economics. From this perspective, the decade culminated with Herbert Simon's outline of 'the sciences of the artificial' and his specific plea for the development of 'a science of design' in the universities: 'a body of intellectually tough, analytic, partly formalisable, partly empirical, teachable doctrine about the design process.' [04]

However, in the 1970s came a backlash against design methodology and a rejection of its underlying values, notably by some of the early pioneers of the movement. Christopher Alexander, who had originated a rational method for architecture and planning, [05] now said:

'I've disassociated myself from the field... There is so little in what is called "design methods" that has anything useful to say about how to design buildings that I never even read the literature anymore... I would say forget it, forget the whole thing.' [06]

Another leading pioneer, J. Christopher Jones said:

'In the 1970s I reacted against design methods. I dislike the machine language, the behaviourism, the continual attempt to fix the whole of life into a logical framework.' [07]

To put the quotations of Alexander and Jones into context it may be necessary to recall the social/cultural climate of the late 1960s – the campus revolutions and radical political movements, the new liberal humanism and rejection of conservative values. But it also has to be acknowledged that there had been a lack of success in the application of 'scientific' methods to everyday design practice. Fundamental issues were also raised by Rittel and Webber, who characterised design and planning problems as 'wicked' problems, essentially un-amenable to the techniques of science and engineering, which dealt with 'tame' problems. [08]

Nevertheless, design methodology continued to develop strongly, especially in engineering and some branches of industrial design (although there may still have been very limited evidence of practical applications and results). The fruits of this work emerged in a series of books on engineering design methods and methodology in the 1980s. To mention just some English-language ones, these included Tjalve, [09] Hubka, [10] Pahl and Beitz, [11] French [12] and Cross. [13] Another significant development throughout the 1980s and into the 1990s was the emergence of new journals of design research, theory and methodology.

To refer, again, to English-language publications, these included *Design Studies* in 1979, *Design Issues* in 1984, *Research in Engineering Design* in 1989, the *Journal of Engineering Design* in 1990, *Languages of Design* in 1993, and the *Design Journal* in 1997.

Despite the apparent scientific basis (or bias) of much of their work, design methodologists also sought from the earliest days to make distinctions between design and science, as reflected in the following quotations:

Alexander: *'Scientists try to identify the components of existing structures, designers try to shape the components of new structures.'* [05]

Gregory: *'The scientific method is a pattern of problem-solving behaviour employed in finding out the nature of what exists, whereas the design method is a pattern of behaviour employed in inventing things ... which do not yet exist. Science is analytic; design is constructive.'* [14]

There may indeed be a critical distinction to be made: method may be vital to the practice of science (where it validates the results) but not to the practice of design (where results do not have to be repeatable, and in most cases must *not* be repeated, or copied). The Design Research Society's 1980 conference 'Design:Science:Method' provided an opportunity to air many of these considerations.[15] The general feeling from that conference was perhaps that it was time to move on from making simplistic comparisons and distinctions between science and design; that perhaps there was not so much for design to learn from science after all, and rather that perhaps science had something to learn from design. Cross *et al.* further claimed that the epistemology of science was, in any case, in disarray, and therefore had little to offer an epistemology of design.[16] Glynn later suggested that 'it is the epistemology of design that has inherited the task of developing the logic of creativity, hypothesis innovation or invention that has proved so elusive to the philosophers of science.' [17]

01 |

Despite several attempts at clarification [01] there remains some confusion about the design-science relationship. Let us at least try to clarify three different interpretations of this concern with the relationship between science and design: (a) scientific design, (b) design science, and (c) a science of design.

Scientific design

As I noted above, the origins of design methods lay in 'scientific' methods, similar to decision theory and the methods of operational research. The originators of the 'design methods movement' also realised that there had been a change from

01 | See de Vries, Cross and Grant [18]

the craftwork of pre-industrial design to the mechanisation of industrial design – and perhaps some even foresaw the emergence of a post-industrial design. The reasons advanced for developing new methods were often based on the assumption that modern, industrial design had become too complex for intuitive methods.

The first half of the 20th century had seen the rapid growth of scientific underpinnings in many types of design – e.g. materials science, engineering science, building science, behavioural science. One view of the design-science relationship is that, through this reliance of modern design upon scientific knowledge, through the application of scientific knowledge in practical tasks, design 'makes science visible'. [19]

So we might agree that *scientific design* refers to modern, industrialised design – as distinct from pre-industrial, craft-oriented design – based on scientific knowledge but utilising a mix of both intuitive and non-intuitive design methods. 'Scientific design' is probably not a controversial concept, but merely a reflection of the reality of modern design practice.

Design science

'Design Science' was a term perhaps first used by Buckminster Fuller, but it was adapted by Gregory into the context of the 1965 conference on 'The Design Method'. [14] The concern to develop a design science thus led to attempts to formulate *the* design method – a single rationalised method, as 'the scientific method' was supposed to be. Others, too, have had the development of a 'design science' as their aim; for example, Hubka and Eder, [20] originators of the *Workshop Design Konstruction* (WDK) and a major series of international conferences on engineering design (ICED), also formed 'The International Society for Design Science'. Earlier, Hansen had stated the aim of design science as being to 'recognise laws of design and its activities, and develop rules'. [21] This would seem to be design science constituted simply as 'systematic design' – the procedures of designing organised in a systematic way. Hubka and Eder regarded this as a narrower interpretation of design science than their own, which was:

> '*Design science comprises a collection (a system) of logically connected knowledge in the area of design, and contains concepts of technical information and of design methodology... Design science addresses the problem of determining and categorising all regular phenomena of the systems to be designed, and of the design process. Design science is also concerned with deriving from the applied knowledge of the natural sciences appropriate information in a form suitable for the designer's use.*' [20]

This definition extends beyond 'scientific design', in including systematic knowledge of design process and methodology as well as the scientific/technological underpinnings of the design of artefacts.

So we might conclude that *design science* refers to an explicitly organised, rational and wholly systematic approach to design; not just the utilisation of scientific knowledge of artefacts, but design being in some sense a scientific activity itself. This is certainly a controversial concept, challenged by many designers and design theorists. As Grant wrote: 'Most opinion among design methodologists and among designers holds that the act of designing itself is not and will not ever be a scientific activity; that is, that designing is itself a non-scientific or a-scientific activity.' [22]

Science of design

However, Grant also made it clear that 'the study of designing may be a scientific activity; that is, design as an activity may be the subject of scientific investigation.' There remains some confusion between concepts of design science and of a science of design, since a 'science of design' seems to imply (or for some people has an aim of) the development of a 'design science'. But the concept of a science of design has been clearly stated by Gasparski and Strzalecki: 'The science of design (should be) understood, just like the science of science, as a federation of subdisciplines having design as the subject of their cognitive interests'. [23]

In this latter view, therefore, the science of design is the *study* of design – something similar to what I have elsewhere defined as 'design methodology' – the study of the principles, practices and procedures of design. For me, design methodology 'includes the study of how designers work and think, the establishment of appropriate structures for the design process, the development and application of new design methods, techniques and procedures, and reflection on the nature and extent of design knowledge and its application to design problems'. [24] The *study* of design leaves open the interpretation of the *nature* of design.

So let us agree here that the *science of design* refers to that body of work which attempts to improve our understanding of design through 'scientific' (i.e. systematic, reliable) methods of investigation. And let us be clear that a 'science of design' is not the same as a 'design science', and that it opens the way to developing a discipline of design in its own right.

Design as a discipline

Donald Schön explicitly challenged the positivist doctrine underlying much of the 'design science' movement, and offered instead a constructivist paradigm. [25] He criticised Simon's 'science of design' for being based on approaches to solving well-formed problems, whereas professional practice throughout design and technology and elsewhere has to face and deal with 'messy, problematic situations'. Schön proposed instead to search for 'an epistemology of practice implicit in the artistic, intuitive processes which some practitioners do bring to situations of uncertainty, instability, uniqueness, and value conflict,' and which he characterised as 'reflective practice'. Schön appeared to be more prepared than his positivist predecessors to put trust in the abilities displayed by competent practitioners, and to try to explicate those competencies rather than to supplant them. This approach has been developed particularly in the series of workshops and conferences known as the 'Design Thinking Research Symposia', beginning in 1991.[26, 27, 28]

Despite the positivist, technical-rationality basis of *The Sciences of the Artificial*, Simon did propose that 'the science of design' could form a fundamental, common ground of intellectual endeavour and communication across the arts, sciences and technology. What he suggested was that the study of design could be an interdisciplinary study accessible to all those involved in the creative activity of making the artificial world (which effectively includes all humankind). For example, Simon wrote that,

> '*Few engineers and composers … can carry on a mutually rewarding conversation about the content of each other's professional work. What I am suggesting is that they can carry on such a conversation about design, can begin to perceive the common creative activity in which they are both engaged, can begin to share their experiences of the creative, professional design process.*'[04]

This, it seems to me, is the challenge for a broad and catholic approach to design research – to construct a way of conversing about design that is at the same time interdisciplinary and disciplined. We do not want conversations that fail to connect between sub-disciplines, that fail to reach common understanding, and that fail to create new knowledge and perceptions of design. It is the paradoxical task of creating an interdisciplinary discipline – design as a discipline, rather than design as a science. This discipline seeks to develop domain-independent approaches to theory and research in design. The underlying axiom of this discipline is that there are forms of knowledge peculiar to the awareness and ability of a designer, independent of the different professional domains of design practice. Just as the other intellectual cultures in the sciences and the arts concentrate on the underlying forms of knowledge peculiar to the scientist or the artist, so we must concentrate on the 'designerly' ways of knowing, thinking and acting.

Many researchers in the design world have been realising that design practice does indeed have its own strong and appropriate intellectual culture, and that we must avoid swamping our design research with different cultures imported from either the sciences or the arts. This does not mean that we completely ignore these other cultures. On the contrary, they have much stronger histories of enquiry, scholarship and research than we have in design. We need to draw upon those histories and traditions where appropriate, while building our own intellectual culture, acceptable and defensible in the world on its own terms. We have to be able to demonstrate that standards of rigour in our intellectual culture at least match those of the others.

Design research

At the 1980 'Design:Science:Method' conference of the Design Research Society, Archer gave a simple but useful definition of research, which is that '[R]esearch is systematic enquiry, the goal of which is knowledge'.[29] Our concern in design research has to be the development, articulation and communication of design knowledge. Where do we look for this knowledge? I believe that it has three sources: people, processes and products.

Design knowledge resides firstly in *people*: in designers especially, but also in everyone to some extent. Designing is a natural human ability. Other animals do not do it, and machines (so far) do not do it. We often overlook the fact that people are naturally very good at design. We should not underplay our abilities as designers: many of the most valued achievements of humankind are works of design, including anonymous, vernacular design as well as the 'high design' of professionals.

One immediate subject of design research, therefore, is the investigation of this human ability – of how people design. This suggests, for example, empirical studies of design behaviour, but it also includes theoretical deliberation and reflection on the nature of design ability. It also relates strongly to considerations of how people learn to design, to studies of the development of design ability in individuals, and how that development might best be nurtured in design education.

Design knowledge resides secondly in *processes*: in the tactics and strategies of designing. A major area of design research is methodology: the study of the processes of design, and the development and application of techniques that aid the designer. Much of this research revolves around the study of modelling for design purposes. Modelling is the 'language' of design. Traditional models are the sketches and drawings of proposed design solutions, but in contemporary terms they now extend to 'virtual reality' models. The use of computers has stimulated a wealth of research into design processes.

Third, we must not forget that design knowledge resides in *products* themselves: in the forms and materials and finishes that embody design attributes. Much everyday design work entails the use of precedents or previous exemplars – not because of laziness by the designer but because the exemplars actually contain knowledge of what the product should be. This is certainly true in craft-based design: traditional crafts are based on the knowledge implicit within the object itself of how best to shape, make and use it. This is why craft-made products are usually copied very literally from one example to the next, from one generation to the next.

As with the design knowledge that resides in people, we would be foolish to disregard or overlook this informal product knowledge simply because it has not been made explicit yet – that is a task for design research. So too is the development of more formal knowledge of shape and configuration – theoretical studies of design morphology. These may be concerned as much with the semantics as with the syntax of form, or may be concerned with prosaic matters of efficiency and economy, or with relationships between form and context – whether ergonomics or environment.

My own taxonomy of the field of design research would therefore fall into three main categories, based on people, process and products:

Design epistemology – study of designerly ways of knowing
Design praxiology – study of the practices and processes of design
Design phenomenology – study of the form and configuration of artefacts

What has been happening in the field of design research is that there has been a growing awareness of the intrinsic strengths and appropriateness of design thinking within its own context, of the validity of 'design intelligence'.[30] There has been a growing acceptance of design on its own terms, a growing acknowledgement and articulation of design as a discipline. We have come to realise that we do not have to turn design into an imitation of science; neither do we have to treat design as a mysterious, ineffable art. We recognise that design has its own distinct intellectual culture.

But there is also some confusion and controversy over the nature of design research. I believe that examples of 'best practice' in design research have in common the following characteristics:

The research is:

Purposive – based on identification of an issue or problem worthy and capable of investigation
Inquisitive – seeking to acquire new knowledge
Informed – conducted from an awareness of previous, related research
Methodical – planned and carried out in a disciplined manner
Communicable – generating and reporting results that are testable and accessible by others

These characteristics are normal features of good research in any discipline. I do not think that such normal criteria inhibit or preclude research that is 'designerly' in its origins and intentions. However, they would exclude works of so-called research that fail to communicate, are undisciplined or ill-informed, and therefore add nothing to the body of knowledge of the discipline.

We also need to draw a distinction between works of practice and works of research. I do not see how normal works of practice can be regarded as works of research. The whole point of doing research is to extract reliable knowledge from either the natural or the artificial world, and to make that knowledge available to others in re-usable form. This does not mean that works of design practice must be wholly excluded from design research, but it does mean that, to qualify as research, there must be reflection by the practitioner on the work, and the communication of some re-usable results from that reflection.

One of the dangers in this new field of design research is that researchers from other, non-design, disciplines will import methods and approaches that are inappropriate to developing the understanding of design. Researchers from psychology or computer science, for example, have tended to assume that there is 'nothing special' about design as an activity for investigation, that it is just another form of 'problem solving' or 'information processing'. However, developments in artificial intelligence and other computer modelling in design have perhaps served mainly to demonstrate just how high-level and complex is the cognitive ability of designers, and how much more research is needed to understand it. Better progress seems to be made by designer-researchers, and for this reason the recent growth of conferences, workshops and symposia, featuring a new generation of designer-researchers, is proving extremely useful in developing the methodology of design research. As design grows as a discipline with its own research base, so we can hope that there will be a growth in the number of emerging designer-researchers.

Another of the dangers is that researchers adhere to underlying paradigms of which they are only vaguely aware. We need to develop this intellectual awareness within our community. An example of developing this awareness is the work of Dorst, in making an explicit analysis and comparison of the paradigms underlying the approach of Herbert Simon, on the one hand, and Donald Schön on the other. [31] Simon's positivism leads to a view of design as 'rational problem solving', and Schön's constructivism leads to a view of design as 'reflective practice'. These two might appear to be in conflict, but Dorst's use of the two paradigms in analysing design activity leads him to the view that the different paradigms have complementary strengths for gaining an overview of the whole range of activities in design.

We are still building the appropriate paradigm for design research. I have made it clear that my personal 'touchstone' theory for this paradigm is that there are 'designerly ways of knowing'. [32, 33] I believe that building such a paradigm will be helpful, in the long run, to design practice and design education, and to the broader development of the intellectual culture of our world of design.

Designerly ways of knowing

If the design research community wishes to pursue the case for design as a discipline of scholarship, research and practice, then it is necessary to establish a solid basis for the claims of expert, designerly ways of knowing, thinking and acting.

In the field of design epistemology there has been a rapidly growing series of studies of design cognition. However, many studies of designer behaviour are based on novices (e.g. students) or, at best, designers of relatively modest talents. This is because of the easier availability of such subjects for study. It is difficult to gain access to designers of outstanding ability, but studying such designers gives us different insights and understanding of design activity. It is like studying chess masters rather than chess novices in order to gain insight of expert cognitive strategies in chess playing.

The aim of studying outstanding designers is to gain knowledge of design activity at the highest levels at which it is practised. This knowledge might enable us to transfer and diffuse 'best practice' more widely across the design professions, thus raising general levels of performance. It could be useful for education, in guiding pedagogy towards the development of better-than-average designers. It could aid the design of support tools, not only for the outstanding designers themselves, but also in providing enhanced methods of practice for all designers.

Outstanding designers can be expected to work and operate in ways that are at the boundaries of normal practice. Studying such 'boundary conditions' may provide more significant results and an extension of understanding that is not available from studying average designers. Exceptional cases may provide a clearer view on differences between working practices, rather than the everyday commonalities.

Outstanding individuals in any field can often provide insights that are more extensive and informative than those of average-ability individuals. They are therefore a rich source of new ideas and alternative perspectives. Studying average and novice designers may well limit our understanding of design activity, holding back progress in design methodology, and leading to weak or even inappropriate models of design cognition.

Studying outstanding designers falls into the more general field of studying expertise. Generic models of expertise generally define a progressive series of levels of attainment. In such models performing at the lower levels is seen as a prerequisite for moving on to the higher levels. Thus the development of expertise within an individual passes through different phases. A novice undergoes training and education in their chosen field, and then at some later point becomes an expert. For some people, the 'expert' level of achievement is where they remain, perhaps with some continued moderate improvement before reaching their peak and beginning their decline. A few manage to go beyond the level of their peers, into a further phase of development, reaching outstanding levels of achievement and eminence.

The levels of achievement are usually seen as plateaux in the time versus performance curve. An important reason for this plateau-plus-increment series of phases is probably because the acquisition of a certain amount of knowledge or experience enables insight to a new way of operating or perceiving. The acquisition of skills seems generally to proceed in this way. Thus these models suggest that operating at higher levels of expertise is not just a matter of working harder, better or faster, but of working differently. To understand expertise fully, therefore, we need to study these 'different' ways of working at the highest levels.

Studying outstanding designers is particularly problematic because of their limited availability as participants. The majority of studies of outstanding designers are based on interviews, because that seems the only way to gain access. However, this technique does have its advantages – it gives a 'rich picture' rather than formalised data, enables cross-project comparisons to be discussed, and enables insights to emerge that were not in the researcher's prior assumptions. Shortcomings of the interview method include being very time-consuming (in post-interview transcription, etc.), a lack of strict comparability between studies, and sometimes there are problems of attributability and commercial confidentiality relating to the design projects that are discussed. The personal recollections of the participants are sometimes poor on time sequences of events, and may be influenced by a variety of factors that may be incidental to the researcher's purposes (e.g. difficult relationships with clients, or financial problems of projects). Participants may post-rationalise their accounts or attempt to fit them to conventional (or idiosyncratic) wisdoms or philosophies of design activity.

Lawson[34] and Cross,[35, 36, 37] amongst a few others, have conducted separate studies of outstanding designers – one set of studies in architecture, and the other in engineering and industrial design. Here I attempt to bring these studies together, to form a more general overview of design cognition at its highest levels.

Lawson made a series of interview and observational studies of outstanding architects.[34] He found many similarities in their ways of working, and also some differences. For example, some of the architects prefer to generate a range of alternative solution concepts, while others will focus on a narrow range or just one concept. Something they all seem to have is an ability to work along 'parallel lines of thought' – that is, to maintain an openness, even an ambiguity, about features and aspects of the design at different levels of detail, and to consider these levels simultaneously, as the designing proceeds. One message that recurred from these studies was the extremely demanding standards set by the designers themselves – outstanding expertise is fuelled by personal commitment.

Many findings in Lawson's studies of outstanding architects resonate with those from studies of outstanding designers in the fields of engineering and industrial design by Cross.[35, 36, 37] These are based on protocol and interview studies with three outstanding designers, and draw conclusions on the common aspects of design strategies. First, all three designers either explicitly or implicitly relied upon 'first principles' in both the origination of their concepts and in the detailed development of those concepts. Second, all three designers explored the problem space from a particular perspective in order to frame the problem in a way that stimulated and pre-structured the emergence of design concepts. In some cases, this perspective was a personal one that the designers seem to bring to most of their designing. Finally, it appeared from these three examples that creative design solutions arise especially when there is a conflict to be resolved between the designer's own high-level problem goals (their personal commitment) and the criteria for an acceptable solution established by client or other requirements. The outstanding designers are able to draw upon a high-level, or more systemic view of the problematic in which their actions are situated.

These cognitive strategies identified by Cross overlap significantly with those features of expertise in design identified by Lawson as the reliance upon guiding principles, the ability to 'recognise' situations in a seemingly intuitive way, and the possession of a repertoire of 'tricks' or design gambits.[38] Working at the highest levels of performance in design, outstanding designers aim to produce not just satisfactory solutions, but innovative responses to situations that could – and would – be treated in conventional ways even by 'expert' designers. Outstanding designers produce work that goes beyond the solving of the 'given' problem. They produce valuable precedent upon which others can come to depend. They generate new gambits that eventually may become standard or common practice.

Conventional wisdom about the nature of problem-solving expertise seems often to be contradicted by the behaviour of expert designers. In design education we must therefore be wary of importing models of behaviour from other fields. Studies of design activity have frequently found 'intuitive' features of design behaviour to be the most effective and relevant to the intrinsic nature of design. We still need a much better understanding of what constitutes expertise in design, and how we might assist novice students to gain that expertise.

It seems possible to conclude that there are enough commonalities in the behaviours of outstanding designers to suggest a view of expertise in design that has its own particular features, with some differences from generic models of expertise, which have been mainly drawn from studies in more conventional types of problem solving. More studies of exceptional designers might lead to a more informed consensus about how design skills are exercised by experts, and on the true nature of designerly ways of knowing and thinking.

References / Bibliography

[01]   van Doesberg T (1923) Towards a Collective Construction. *De Stijl* (Quoted by Naylor G in: *The Bauhaus* Studio Vista, London, 1968)

[02]   Le Corbusier (1929) *CIAM 2nd Congress*, Frankfurt

[03]   Jones JC, Thornley DG (eds) (1963) *Conference on Design Methods*. Pergamon, Oxford

[04]   Simon HA (1969) *The Sciences of the Artificial*. MIT Press, Cambridge, MA

[05]   Alexander C (1964) *Notes on the Synthesis of Form*. Harvard University Press, Cambridge, MA

[06]   Alexander C (1971) The State of the Art in Design Methods. *DMG Newsletter* 5(3) 3-7

[07]   Jones JC (1977) How my Thoughts about Design Methods Have Changed during the Years. *Design Methods and Theories* 11(1) 48-62

[08]   Rittel H, Webber M (1973) Dilemmas in a General Theory of Planning. *Policy Sciences* 4: 155–169

[09]   Tjalve E (1979) *A Short Course in Industrial Design*. Newnes-Butterworth, London

[10]   Hubka V (1982) *Principles of Engineering Design*. Butterworth, Guildford

[11]   Pahl G, Beitz W (1984) *Engineering Design: a Systematic Approach*. Springer/Design Council, London

[12]   French MJ (1985) *Conceptual Design for Engineers*. Design Council, London

[13]   Cross N (1989) *Engineering Design Methods*. Wiley, Chichester

[14]   Gregory SA (1966) Design Science. In: Gregory SA (ed.): *The Design Method*. Butterworth, London

[15]   Jacques R, Powell J (eds) (1981) *Design:Science: Method*. Westbury House, Guildford

[16]   Cross N, Naughton J, Walker D (1981) Design Method and Scientific Method. In: Jacques R, Powell J (eds): *Design:Science:Method*. Westbury House, Guildford

[17]   Glynn S (1985) Science and Perception as Design. *Design Studies* 6(3) 122-133

[18]   de Vries M, Cross N, Grant D (eds) (1993) *Design Methodology and Relationships with Science*. Kluwer, Dordrecht

[19]   Willem RA (1990) Design and Science. *Design Studies* 11(1) 43-47

[20]   Hubka V, Eder WE (1987) A Scientific Approach to Engineering Design. *Design Studies* 8(3) 123-137

[21]   Hansen F (1974) *Konstruktionswissenschaft*. Hanser, Munich

[22]   Grant D (1979) Design Methodology and Design Methods. *Design Methods and Theories: Journal of the DMG* 13(1) 46-47

[23]   Gasparski W, Strzalecki A (1990) Contributions to Design Science: Praxeological Perspective. *Design Methods and Theories: Journal of the DMG* 24(2) 1186-1194

[24]   Cross N (1984) *Developments in Design Methodology.* Wiley, Chichester

[25]   Schön D (1983) *The Reflective Practitioner.* Temple-Smith, London

[26]   Cross N, Dorst K, Roozenburg N (eds) (1992) *Research in Design Thinking.* Delft University Press, Delft

[27]   Cross N, Christiaans H, Dorst K (eds) (1996) *Analysing Design Activity.* Wiley, Chichester

[28]   Cross N, Edmonds E (eds) (2003) *Expertise in Design.* Creativity and Cognition Press, University of Technology, Sydney, Australia

[29]   Archer B (1981) A View of the Nature of Design Research. In: Jacques R, Powell J (eds): *Design:Science:Method.* Westbury House, Guildford

[30]   Cross N (1999) Natural Intelligence in Design. *Design Studies* 20(1) 25-39

[31]   Dorst K, Dijkhuis J (1995) Comparing Paradigms for Describing Design Activity. *Design Studies* 16(2) 261-274

[32]   Cross N (1982) Designerly Ways of Knowing. *Design Studies* 3(4) 221-227

[33]   Cross N (2006) *Designerly Ways of Knowing.* Springer, London

[34]   Lawson B (1994) *Design in Mind.* Butterworth-Heinemann, Oxford, UK

[35]   Cross N, Clayburn Cross A (1996) Winning by Design: the Methods of Gordon Murray, Racing Car Designer. *Design Studies* 17(1) 91-107

[36]   Cross N (2001) Achieving Pleasure from Purpose: the Methods of Kenneth Grange, Product Designer. *The Design Journal* 4(1) 48-58

[37]   Cross N (2002) Creative Cognition in Design: Processes of Exceptional Designers. In: Hewett T, Kavanagh T (eds) *Creativity and Cognition.* ACM Press, New York, 14–19

[38]   Lawson B (2004) What Designers Know. Elsevier Architectural Press, Oxford, UK

Richard Buchanan

Strategies of Design Research: Productive Science and Rhetorical Inquiry

'We make subject matters to fit the examination and resolution of problems, and the solution of problems brings to our attention further consequent problems, which frequently require the setting up and examination of new fields.'
Richard McKeon, 'The Uses of Rhetoric in a Technological Age' [01]

Introduction

The history of design is a history of evolving problems. The earliest problems were those of practice and production, and the solution of those problems led to further problems of practice and production, as well as problems of philosophy and theory that were consequent upon the existence of new products. In the ancient world, there was little need to distinguish design from the making of products, because the craftsperson and the master-builder carried within themselves both the ability to conceive products and the ability to embody their conceptions in tangible form. Technical treatises were written to solve the problem of education, passing on accumulated knowledge of practice and production to individuals who would continue the work of making. Even before such treatises were written, however, there were already theoretical and philosophical speculations on the nature of products and their effects on human life. Those speculations were typically embedded in treatises on other subjects and problems, but they provided the distant foundations for what is now regarded as the field of design and design research. They characterised the subject matter of human-made products or the artificial, developed the fundamental strategies of inquiry into the nature of products and making, and explored possible principles of making and use that would later turn design from a trade practice into a domain of many professions and, subsequently, into a field of research encompassing history, criticism and theory, supported by empirical research and further philosophic speculation. This field did not emerge in recognisable form until the 20th century, when the problems of design and technology became so complex that their resolution required new thinking. However, the threads of design research emerged much earlier.

After the Industrial Revolution, when the work of design was effectively distinguished from the manner of production, the cumulative effect of mass production and products on human life gained increasing attention. One line of inquiry led into economics, political theory and social philosophy, supported by the diverse emerging social sciences. Another led into the natural sciences, first deepening the knowledge of natural laws and the ability to manipulate nature in new products, and then, by the 20th century, beginning to assess the effects of products on the environment, leading to questions about the sustainability of our cultural commitment to mass production and consumption. Finally, there was a third line of inquiry, directed toward design itself, leading to the establishment of a new field of inquiry, the field of design practice and design research.

The early steps in creating the field of design research in the late 19th and early 20th centuries were hardly noticed. Even at the beginning of the 21st century, there are few narratives that adequately explain the early developments in a coherent account. But the problems were, again, problems of practice and production, education, and the consequent effect of products on individual, social and cultural life. In the 20th century, these problems led to histories of design to address the past, various forms of design criticism to address the present, and diverse theories and philosophies of design and design education to address the future. Indeed, the pluralism of design and design research is one of the fundamental characteristics of the field. It is a characteristic that we may ignore at the peril of gross misunderstanding of the richness and complexity of the field. It is a characteristic that is one of the deeper philosophic problems in understanding design or any other field of human activity. Many investigators are tempted with the prospect of a single, monistic vision of design, but the diversity of potential monisms suggests that pluralism is an unavoidable reality. The pluralism of design research suggests that design is a field comprised of many fields, each shaped by its own problems and lines of investigation.

Such diversity is both strength and weakness in the field. It is a weakness because the diversity of work makes it difficult to present a clear, unified explanation of the advance of design research to those outside the field. Moreover, the diversity makes it difficult for those working within the field to take advantage of the contributions of others. Until the basis of the diversity is well understood – so that contributions are assessed and appreciated on their own terms – the field will remain in a somewhat naïve state, entrapped in unproductive self-criticism and disputes over the validity of different lines of investigation. From a broader perspective, design research is healthy, with advances on many fronts.

Strategies of inquiry

In every field of inquiry, the investigation and solution of problems leads to the discovery of new problems that require the same or new strategies of inquiry. After the early steps in establishing the field of design research, three major strategies of inquiry emerged in the 20th century to move the field forward. Each strategy had its successes and disappointments, but the diversity widened and deepened our understanding of design. These strategies continue to shape the field of design research, although they have undergone many variations. They have risen and declined popularity, but they have all persisted and been available when one or another embodiment of a strategy has temporarily run dry or has suggested further problems for which a different strategy was needed. Their interplay accounts for much of the vitality of the field of design research.

The strategies may be easily characterised, though their variations are many and diverse even within themselves. The first strategy is to explain design and the products of design within a larger whole or system. It begins with contradictions and conflicts in everyday experience – for example, the conflict of user requirements or the values of designers and their clients – and seeks unifying ideas and a larger context within which differences may be overcome in theory and in practice, often with specific methods of participation, analysis and synthesis, and creative thinking. It emphasises the social and cultural context of design, and typically draws attention to the limitations of the individual designer in seeking sustainable solutions to problems. This is the strategy of Dialectic, whether in an idealist, materialist or sceptical variation. In each variation, technical issues are assimilated into a broader context, and the perspectives or opinions of individuals are as much a part of understanding design as any technical analysis.

The second strategy is to explain design and the products of design by seeking the basic elements that underlie the complexities of the material world and the workings of the mind. It emphasises analysis of the processes and mechanisms by which those basic elements, once they are identified and analysed, are then combined and synthesised to yield the world of experience and the cognitive processes of designing and decision-making. This is the strategy of Design Science, whether in the form of cognitive science, psychology and computer simulation, or in related variations of the study of consumer and user behaviour. In this strategy, Design Science is often complemented by knowledge gained from other sciences, but the perspective of individuals is strictly limited, since the proper method of analysis is objective and independent of opinion and personal perspective.

FIG.01

DIALECTIC
Holistic Systems &
Unifying Ideas

EXPERIENCE OF
PRODUCTS & DESIGNING

DESIGN SCIENCE
Underlying Elements &
Mechanisms of
Combination

The strategy of Design Science had a wider following than other strategies in the 1970s, 1980s and 1990s, particularly in Europe and North America. However, there are ample signs that the strategies of Dialectic, as well as other strategies, are once again rising in popularity because of new problems that are not adequately addressed by Design Science. Both Design Science and Dialectic have led to sustained conversations that have advanced our understanding of design and technology, though the strategies tend to be mutually distrustful. Significantly, both of these strategies may also make claim to being scientific. A vivid example occurs in Asian design research programmes that follow the trend of Design Science in western nations but also infuse their research agendas with dialectical considerations that follow the intellectual traditions of eastern cultures – a feature that is often neglected, dismissed, or misunderstood by western design researchers who follow for example, the work reported in the Japanese Society for the Science of Design. To illustrate the point, the Sixth Asian Design Conference, held in Tsukuba, Japan, in 2003, was organised around the theme of 'Integration of Knowledge, *Kansei* and Industrial Power', which is clearly a dialectical theme of assimilation and integration within a holistic concept. To an unbiased observer, the claim to being 'scientific' by both Design Science and Dialectic suggests that 'science' is an ambiguous term that has diverse meanings. Science may be integrative in holistic systems or it may be reductive in the study of underlying elements. However, there are other possibilities for the meaning of science and the strategy of design research.

The third strategy lies midway between Dialectic and Design Science. Instead of seeking to understand design and the products of design by reference to something else – the context of a holistic system or the basic elements that underlie the complexity of experience – the third strategy seeks an explanation in the experience of designers and those who use products, without recourse to the theoretical abstractions of Dialectic or Design Science. On the one hand, it may emphasise the *inventive and creative power* of the designer and his or her ability to effect social change through argument and communication, whether in words or in products. On the other, it may emphasise the *discipline of designing*, based on analysis of the essential elements of products and the creative synthesis of these elements in the various branches of design, with appropriate regard for how products are produced and distributed as well as for how products evolve in human use within a community. This is the strategy of Design Inquiry, unfolding in two closely related but distinct lines of investigation. The lines are closely related because they both emphasise human experience as the basis for explanation. However, they may be distinguished by their emphasis and point of focus. One line focuses on communication and the imaginative power of the designer, while the other focuses on the discipline of making, within the framework of products and their use. One is a strategy of Rhetorical Inquiry; the other is a strategy of Productive Science or Poetics – from *poeisis,* the ancient Greek word for all activities of human making, and from Aristotle's specific use of the term for the science of made-things or the artificial.

FIG.02

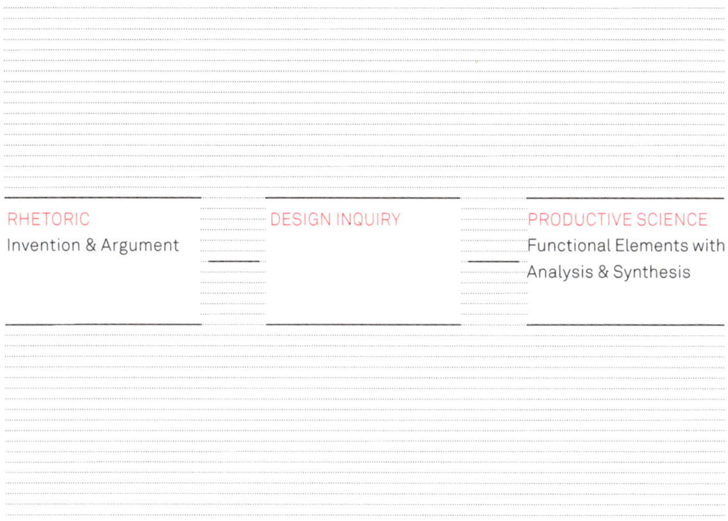

RHETORIC
Invention & Argument

DESIGN INQUIRY

PRODUCTIVE SCIENCE
Functional Elements with
Analysis & Synthesis

The strategies that we have discussed are 'strategic' in the sense that they offer broad perspectives on design and products – and any other subject of investigation, since they are strategies that may be applied to all areas of human inquiry. What distinguish the strategies are the characteristic relationships and connections to which they draw attention. It is the connections, not what is connected, that signifies a strategy. Better understanding of what is connected and why it is significantly connected is the goal of inquiry – the goal toward which the three strategies offer alternative approaches. As connections are explored in research, the inquiry becomes progressively more tactical and may involve a wide variety of particular methods and techniques that are shared by different investigators. Indeed, the strategies guide the use of methods and techniques that may be common to many or all forms of design and design research. For example, drawing is a method of design that involves many techniques, but drawing may be guided by quite different strategic considerations, both in manner of execution and in purpose. The strategies provide the potential lines of investigation that shape design research, leading in different directions.

The strategies of Dialectic and Design Science require comparison and discussion within the community of design researchers, but it may be useful to prepare the ground for such a discussion by considering some of the most important features of Design Inquiry and its branches of Productive Science and Rhetorical Inquiry. Design Inquiry offers a mediating middle between the other strategies, because it brings our attention back from the sometimes abstract issues of the other strategies, reminding us that design is a concrete human activity grounded in human experience and what we choose to make of our world.

FIG. 03

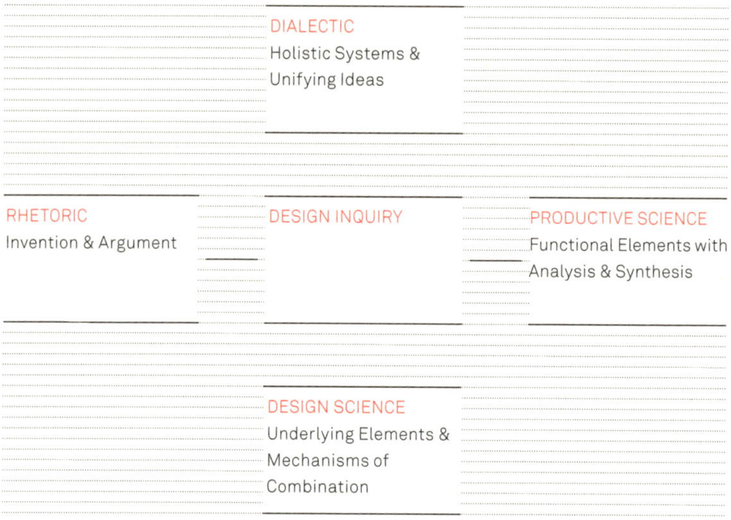

DIALECTIC
Holistic Systems &
Unifying Ideas

RHETORIC
Invention & Argument

DESIGN INQUIRY

PRODUCTIVE SCIENCE
Functional Elements with
Analysis & Synthesis

DESIGN SCIENCE
Underlying Elements &
Mechanisms of
Combination

The strategy of productive science

Like Design Science, the strategy of Productive Science employs a strong distinction between analysis and synthesis. However, the analysis of Productive Science is not directed toward the *underlying elements* or parts of complex phenomena. Rather, it focuses on the *functional elements* of effective products. This is an important distinction, indicating two different directions for investigation. Design Science typically regards the product as an aggregation of parts that are additively combined to result in a complex whole. In contrast, Productive Science begins with the idea of a whole product, the potential of which is progressively realised or made actual by refinement of the essential functional elements that are necessary for effective performance.

Typically, the analysis of Productive Science recognises four elements. The first is the manner of designing, producing, distributing, maintaining and recycling or disposing of products. Each branch of design has its characteristic way of working, with some practices shared between many branches. For example, there are many books in the literature that focus on the discipline of one or another branch of design, but the development of collaborative design and participatory design, to select only one example, is an important aspect of the manner of design work in many branches.[01] Research into the manner of designing and the variety of ways that designers work is an important consideration.

The second element is the material employed in a design. Different kinds of products use different kinds of materials, and advances in science and technology have provided a

01 | See CoDesign: International Journal of CoCreation in Design and the Arts

wide range of new materials for designers. The materials may be tangible or intangible, as in digital products. In each case, however, it is important to understand the nature of the materials to be used in designing. Research into materials and their actual or potential use in design is an important consideration.

The third element is product form. Form may be static or dynamic, but understanding the form of existing products is essential for the designer if he or she is to develop new forms that are suited to new technological developments or to different circumstances of product use. Research into product form and the dimensions of product form in usefulness, usability, and desirability is an important consideration.

Finally, the fourth element of any effective product is its purpose or function in supporting human activity. A careful analysis of the task that a product performs is essential for the designer. Analysis of existing products provides many insights into the situation of use or the designer's interpretation and understanding of such situations. Analysis of function extends beyond the formal structure of a product. It extends into the individual, social and cultural life of human beings in all of their varied circumstances of experience. Research into the expanded meaning of function and new product possibilities is an important consideration, particularly when connected with the issues of ethics and politics that surround products.

One aspect of Productive Science is the study of existing products and how designers work. Thus, it has both historical and critical components. However, it is also an empirical and theoretical science in the sense that it provides insight into the nature of design as a whole, the products of design, and the activities of designing. In this sense, it may contribute to new or improved design practices, broadening the theory of design and supporting practice. Nonetheless, Productive Science is distinct from the practical art of design and the individual practices of designers. That is, the creative and synthetic art of design presents its own problem, distinct from the analytic problems addressed by Productive Science.

John Dewey provides keen insight into this distinction in his discussion of inquiry. He defines inquiry as 'the directed or controlled transformation of an indeterminate situation into a determinately unified one'.[02] However, he also distinguishes between formal inquiries and inquiries of 'common sense'. Formal inquiries are scientific, and may include the natural sciences, the social and behavioural sciences, and productive science. In contrast, the inquiries of common sense are practical inquiries, typical of design itself, as well as all of the other forms of practical and professional activity, ranging from medicine and farming to any other form of human problem-solving in action.

Dewey's distinction between common sense and formal or scientific inquiries, and his idea of a shared core definition of inquiry, echo in Herbert Simon's more widely familiar definition of design as 'changing existing situations into preferred ones'.[03] While Simon subsequently turns this idea into the central feature of his version of Design Science – reducing all design activities to underlying cognitive mechanisms of decision-making for devising courses of action – his most important work on design, *The Sciences of the Artificial*, has its roots in the pragmatic concept of inquiry and productive science. Dewey's distinction also echoes in the work of Donald A. Schön, who argues that the technical rationality of Simon's positivist and reductive approach through Design Science is inadequate in accounting for the reflective practice of designers.[04] Schön's reflective practitioner, while more widely familiar as a concept in the design research community, is best understood as a popularised version of Dewey's concept of common-sense inquiry. Indeed, Dewey provides the stronger arguments and concepts for this kind of activity, well grounded in the philosophy of pragmatism and the nature of inquiry. Where Schön's exposition begins to falter and become vague, Dewey's line of argument offers a more sustainable strategy for development.

Productive Science does offer this insight into design practice: the struggle of the designer is to synthesise the functional elements of *manner of design and production*, *materials*, *form* and *function*. Productive Science may offer insight into these elements, but it does not offer prescriptions, simple steps of method, or a formula to the practising designer. Instead, it offers a different account of the work of designing. Rather than reducing design practice to Productive Science, it points toward design as a creative inquiry in its own right that involves thinking, feeling, and concrete practical action. Practice may be idiosyncratic, with personal variations of many kinds – hence the common reality of the design community is that every designer offers a different personal account of successful practice, each with favourite practices, methods and techniques. However, there is the possibility of a shared discipline of designing that may be captured not in Productive Science but in a formal art of the discipline of design.

Aristotle provides an interesting insight into this matter. Writing in the *Poetics*, his example of Productive Science directed toward the study of drama and tragedy, he pauses from the analysis of the elements of tragedy to discuss how a writer of tragedies may visualise the action of a story in the course of writing. This is a practical suggestion that departs from the main line of analysis, but points toward the discipline that an artist employs in solving the problem of creation. At another point, he pauses even more significantly to suggest that someone who wants to write a tragedy should study the discipline of rhetoric in order to craft the actual speeches of characters in a drama. These suggestions confirm what is already well known in the design community and in design research. For all of our advances in technical knowledge, there remains the central task of creative synthesis that characterises design thinking and practice.

Donald Schön's approach may be dissatisfying and vague in many ways, but it achieved popularity in the design community because it expressed a common doubt about the practical value of Design Science. Schön drew attention to a problem that required a new strategy of investigation. In fact, his writing served to bring design and design research back from the strategy of Design Science, turning toward alternative strategies of research. One alternative approach is the idea of 'practice-based' research. Although this is still a somewhat loose and vague concept, it is perhaps best understood as an expression of Dewey's idea of inquiry, because it points toward the idea that the work of the designer is itself an ongoing inquiry that is similar to Dewey's idea of common-sense inquiry. Investigating the nature of design through the practice of design involves reflection on the functional element of *manner* that we have discussed as one of the central features of Productive Science. In Schön's case, however, the alternative is somewhat different. It is based on a 'conversation' with the concrete problematic situation faced by the designer. The theme of conversation suggests a turn toward rhetoric and dialectic – strategies which had already entered the design research community but required new development and focus. However, Schön is unable to carry the discussion forward into a serious investigation of the uses of rhetoric and dialectic in design, and his argument falters, leaving it for others to find a way forward.

The strategy of rhetorical inquiry

Rhetorical inquiry has a natural affinity with the study of *manner* in Productive Science, since both manner and rhetoric focus on the activities of the designer and the experience of designing. Nonetheless, rhetorical inquiry is different from the strategy of inquiry in Productive Science. Rhetoric is an art of invention and discovery. In the past it was applied to discovering persuasive speech, but in the 20th century rhetorical thinking expanded into all areas of human activity, including the creation of all types of products, ranging from communications and artefacts to interactions and organisations. In some cases, the formal devices of rhetoric are explicitly discussed in design research; in others, discussion may avoid the traditional terms and devices of rhetoric while still pursing rhetorical themes in the treatment of design. In general, rhetorical inquiry allows greater and greater refinement and focus within the activities of the designer, the response and action of those who use products, and the communicative power of products themselves.

Rhetorical inquiry takes many forms, but the common theme is a relationship between the intentions of the designer and the expectations of those who will use a product.[05] The product itself is the reconciliation of intention and expectation, a record of the negotiation that takes place directly or indirectly between the designer and the community of use. Some research focuses on the practical design process of negotiation. It draws attention to the conflicting interests, values and goals of designers and their clients as well as those who will ultimately buy and use a product. It seeks to explore the characteristic reasoning and argumentation of designers – the mental activities and operations that are needed to cope with the essential creative freedom of the design situation. This approach is well illustrated in the work of Horst Rittel.[06] He is more interested in 'issues' than in 'problems', because issues are the place where different perspectives and values meet. He is also interested in the 'patterns' and 'figures' of reasoning, and, in general, the great variety of ways that designers reason in dealing with their creative freedom.

Rhetorical inquiry also may focus on other elements beyond the design process. For example, it may focus on the life and career of individual designers, assessing their perspective on design and the human-made world and their creative activity or influence. This is a well-known approach in design history, and it emerges in some case studies of design. In turn, rhetorical inquiry may focus on the career of products in social life: how people are persuaded to buy products and how they use them in daily living; how products reflect or shape beliefs, customs and practices; and in general, how products communicate to people and how people use products to communicate in social life.

The formal issues of rhetorical inquiry are distinctly different from the functional elements of Productive Science. A rhetorical account of design begins with issues in existing situations that require or would benefit from human action. The situation itself is indeterminate, because it is open to different interpretations and, particularly, is shaped by different perspectives on desired outcomes. This is different from a situation that is 'undetermined' or 'underdetermined'. In rhetorical inquiry, there is a radical indeterminacy at the heart of all design problems. The challenge is not merely to 'discover' what is underdetermined. The challenge for the designer is to bring focus and agreement on the course of action to be pursued in product development. This is an activity of 'discovery as invention', because the challenge is to find, amid all of the existing indeterminacies of the situation, an *argument* with which all or many of those with a stake in the outcome can agree. The argument is partly in words, because the designer must communicate and encourage communication in the beginning. But it is also in non-verbal materials. It is in the sketches, models, and prototypes that are characteristic of design work. These non-verbal expressions have a remarkable power to move discussion beyond the sometimes rigidly fixed positions and ideologies of participants and bring progressively stronger agreement on the direction for a solution. However, there is a profound sense in which the initial situation remains indeterminate at its core, even when a designer creates an acceptable argument. This is why later projects may revisit the initial situation and later product development may depart significantly from a previous solution.

Designing is a cascade of issues moving toward a final argument expressed in a product strategy and then in the concrete resolution of a specific product, whether this product is a tangible artefact or any of the other forms that a product may take. After the initial issues surrounding the indeterminacy of the existing situation, there are subsequent issues that move design forward. The issues are issues of argument in product form, issues of material embodiment and expression, and issues of delivery and implementation. The product itself will be an argument for its use. Rhetorical inquiry asks what aspects of products are persuasive for the members of a particular community. It answers that products are persuasive in three ways that are intimately related and interconnected. First, products are persuasive when they can do a job of work. That is, the product must be effective in the task for which it is designed. In tangible artefacts, this involves an appropriate level of technological reasoning, with proper and logical uses of electrical and mechanical principles. Other types of products, of course, involve other kinds of reasoning. When this aspect of a product is successfully discovered, we say that the product is *useful*. Second, products are persuasive when they are easily used. Discovering this aspect of the product involves such matters as ergonomics, cognitive study, and cultural factors, all of which help to shape usability. When this aspect of a product is successfully discovered, we say that a product is *usable*. Third, products are persuasive when users can identify with the product and are willing to take it into their lives as an extension of their identify and self-image. Discovering this aspect of a product involves finding an appropriate 'voice' or ethos of a product – a character that is consistent with the perceived character of the intended user or community of use. When this aspect of a product is successfully discovered, we say that a product is *desirable*.

Rhetorical inquiry seeks to understand the balance of these three considerations that is appropriate for a given product and a given situation of use. In some products, technological reasoning is paramount and the other considerations, while important, are secondary. In other products, voice and ethos may be paramount and other considerations are secondary – for example, in fashion design, as distinct from clothing design. The strategy of Rhetorical Inquiry in design research would explore these matters in depth, seeking to understand the resolutions that designers have reached and the possibilities for other resolutions in the future, whether in traditional products or entirely new kinds of products. 02 |

Conclusion

We have identified fundamental strategies of design research in the hope of clarifying the diversity of work in the field of design. The goal has not been to elevate one or another of these strategies above the others. All are valuable and productive for advancing the understanding and practice of design. However, the tendency of design researchers to prefer a monism instead of understanding the pluralism of research strategies is a tendency that hinders the field at the beginning of the 21st century. We have focused on the strategy of Design Inquiry and its closely related branches of Productive Science and Rhetorical Inquiry in order to demonstrate viable alternatives to the strategies of Design Science and Dialectic. Better understanding of the kind of problems characteristically addressed by each of these strategies may lead to productive and sustained conversations. In turn, these conversations may demonstrate to those outside the field of design that the investigation of design is a unified and coherent inquiry into the nature of the human made world that will ultimately serve all people.

02 | For further discussion of the devices and themes of rhetoric in design, see [05]

References / Bibliography

[01]   McKeon R (1987) The Uses of Rhetoric in a Technological Age: Architectonic Productive Arts. In: Backman M (ed.): *Rhetoric: Essays in Invention and Discovery.* Ox Bow Press, Woodbridge, CT, 1–24

[02]   Dewey J (1964) *Logic: the Theory of Inquiry.* Holt, Rinehart and Winston, New York, 117

[03]   Simon HA (2001) *The Sciences of the Artificial.* MIT Press, Cambridge, MA, 111

[04]   Schön DA (1983) *The Reflective Practitioner: How Professionals Think in Action.* Basic Books, New York

[05]   Buchanan R (2001) Design and the New Rhetoric: Productive Arts in the Philosophy of Culture. *Philosophy and Rhetoric* 34/3: 183–206

[06]   Rittel HWJ (1987) *The Reasoning of Designers.* Working Paper for the International Congress on Planning and Design Theory, Boston, August 1987

Design Research, an Oxymoron?

Why oxymoron?

An oxymoron is a figure of speech that combines two contradictory terms. The word *oxymoron* is of Greek origin. It combines the word *oxy* (= sharp) and *moron* (= dull). Thus, *oxymoron* not only names a contradiction in terms, it is an oxymoron as well. Oxymorons may be used for achieving rhetorical effects, as in *working vacation* and *uninvited guest.* They may also result from conceptual sloppiness, as in *extremely average, original copy,* or *same difference.* Oxymorons may remain unnoticed when the meanings of the contradictory parts are not distinguished, as in *spendthrift, virtual reality,* and *Artificial Intelligence.* Typically, contradictions of this kind are resolved by taking one term as the inferior attribute of a superior concept. For example, *unbiased opinion* is a kind of opinion, *accurate estimate* is a kind of estimate, and the reply "no comment" is not taken as a comment.

Oxymorons are not mere linguistic oddities. Words are far from neutral bystanders of what happens in the world. They can shape their users' perceptions and direct their actions. For this very reason, and to enhance its academic respectability, the design community has begun to adopt vocabularies from the more established disciplines, without noticing, I suggest, the implicit importation of paradigms that are essentially alien to it. One aim of this essay is to show that *design research* is an oxymoron whose contradictions, because they are not obvious to everyone, can lead its naïve users into thinking of it as a kind of research similar to what reputable scientists do.

What do science researchers (claim they) do?

Science is said to validate propositions that state facts. Research is the process by which this is accomplished, ultimately revealing the nature of what exists from what was observed, starting with simple hypotheses, going to more general theories, and ultimately reaching laws of nature. Since nature does not talk, the process of uncovering its secrets is not an easy matter. Scientists talk among themselves, but their talk is not considered science. Science starts with data – records of observations, measurements or texts – that can decide among competing hypotheses and validate or invalidate theories concerning them.

Why are data essential to research? Experiences are hard to study. Happenings come and go away like thunderstorms and spoken words. Witnessing historical events, watching a game of sports, or being aware of designing something, is not inter-subjectively analysable as such. To be sure that our observations are not entirely subjective, irreproducible illusions, scientists rely on other scientists who, when agreeing on what they see, are willing to conclude that the phenomena of interest existed independent of their subjectivities. Excluding observers' subjectivities from propositions about the observed world is a defining feature of scientific research. However, agreement on what happened can be established only if the phenomena of interest have been observed jointly and records of them are contemporary in order to be compared side by side and examined by many. This is what data are expected to do. They must represent the phenomena of interest, survive the conditions that gave rise to them, and remain sufficiently durable to withstand their analysis. Researchers take great care to assure themselves and others that their data are reliable in this sense and worthy of their trust, which means assuring everybody that nobody has tampered with them.

This tangible nature of data is also implied in the uncritical use of metaphors that implicitly absolve researchers from the responsibilities for their creation. For example, claiming that data were discovered, found, collected, or sampled entails that they were there to begin with and that the researcher merely picked them up to look at them. This metaphorical description of how data came into the hands of the researcher, and only that, is what makes critical assessments of their representativeness unnecessary, assures researchers of having nothing to do with the data they are analysing, and justifies describing research results as *findings* – as if they were merely uncovered in or extracted from available data. I will return to this point later.

But what is research? Fundamentally, it is – just as the English word suggests – *re-search*, a process of *re*peated *search*ing for patterns that are manifest in available data. In other languages, the English *research* may focus on different aspects of scientific work, for example, the German *Forschung* emphasises rigorous inquiry into truth, but this too involves recurring searches. Scientists are trained to be systematic and careful, systematic by leaving nothing out from what was observed, and careful by going through their data, again and again, until they are sure that what they find is unquestionably evident, not the result of spurious causes or flighty imagination. Re-search involves sorting, rearranging, tabulating, weighting and comparing data in place of the phenomena of interest – much like tangible objects can be handled – but systematically. Processes of scientific research are institutionalised, which encourages researchers to publish their results in the hope that colleagues will confirm their findings, or build on them.

The re-searched patterns are necessarily simpler and more abstract than the data in which they occur. For one thing, re-search findings are stated in language, which cannot but omit what escapes the researcher's vocabulary. But they also ignore details considered irrelevant – irrelevant to the researcher's theory or hypothesis. For example, statistical analyses can extract regression equations, clusters, networks or causal chains from available data. What does not fit these patterns is considered unexplained variation or noise. Pearson's product moment correlation coefficient, for example, measures the degree to which data conform to a linear relationship between two variables. That degree is the ratio of what fits to what fits plus what does not.

What about predictive theories? We can speculate about the future, but data from the future are never presently available. Scientific theories are predictive by generalising patterns found in data that are currently available to data that do not yet exist. (Note that predictions anticipate additional observations, including, but not exclusively, of future phenomena.) For example, when statistical hypotheses are considered, tests of the statistical significance of findings measure the generalisability of patterns found in a sample of data to a population of possible data, of which the sample was a part. Significance is expressed in probabilistic terms, the probability of the continued existence of the observed patterns. This seems entirely unproblematic until we realise that predictions (a) are intrinsically conservative by assuming that the patterns observed in the past will continue to explain future observations, and (b) leave no space for human agency by regarding future observations as necessarily following from past findings.

Finally, re-search is considered applicable to any subject matter. Scientists re-search the working of a machine, just as they study the performance of an economy, a play, or what designers do. Consumer researchers may generalise the performance of one product to all products that came from the same assembly line. Economists derive their predictions by extrapolating past trends into the future. Likewise, the theories of design that emerge from observations of what designers commonly do account only for what they did, not for how they might redesign the theory they were following. It is well established that scientific forecasts of technological developments are notoriously unsuccessful, largely because design escapes the conservatism of the re-search process – but this foreshadows what will be discussed next.

What do designers do by comparison?

The etymology of design goes back to the Latin *de+signare*, marking out, setting apart, giving significance by assigning it to a use, user, maker or owner. Sixteenth-century English emphasised the purposiveness of design, and because design often involves drawing, or 'marking out', while 17th-century English moved design closer to art. Based on these original meanings, we could say: *Design is making sense of things (to others)*.

The phrase can be read as 'design is a sense making activity', claiming perception, experience, and perhaps appearance as its fundamental concern, and this reading is quite acceptable. It can also mean that 'the products of design are to make sense to their users', and this interpretation is the central focus of *The Semantic Turn*.[01] It puts the creation of artefacts for future use by others into the centre of all design activities.

For Herbert Simon (1969) design is both broader and narrower.[02] He suggests:

'Everyone designs who devises courses of action aimed at changing existing situations into preferred ones. The intellectual activity that produces material artefacts is no different fundamentally from the one that prescribes remedies for a sick patient or the one that devises a new sales plan for a company or a social welfare policy for a state. Design, so construed, is the core of all professional training; it is the principal mark that distinguishes the professions from the sciences. Schools of engineering, as well as schools of architecture, business, education, law, medicine, are all centrally concerned with the process of design. (pp. 55–56)

Simon's account could be a starting point, except – and this may be due to the period in which he wrote these lines – he reduces design to rational problem solving, which begins with defining a problem in terms of how something ought to function, proceeds to enumerating alternative solutions to that problem, and ends with methods of selecting the optimal or satisfactory solution from among them. My own experiences lead me to depart from Simon's rational paradigm in two ways. First, I observe that designers, including myself, are motivated in at least three ways, by

— *Challenges*, troublesome conditions, problems, or conflicts that have escaped (re)-solution. Challenges arise from the perception of presently undesirable conditions that seem to defy routine improvement. Simon problem solving would be one example of this.
— *Opportunities* not seen by others to do something, to improve one own or other people lives. Opportunities do not imply the presence of problematic conditions, rather, they offer choices to move into something new and exciting without having been a problem at the time.
— *Possibilities of introducing variations* into the world that others may not realise or do not dare to consider. From the perspective of evolution, these variations are random mutations, without apparent purpose or plan, and they may prove to be successful or not. Just being different moves many poets, painters, and composers. There is no rational explanation for doing something different, except perhaps personal satisfaction.

To me, rational problem solving is just one way of designing and I do not wish to limit design to what Horst Rittel (1984) call 'tame problems'.[03]

Second and more importantly, the kind of design that occupies my attention is human-centred. If design is to encourage artefacts that are meaningful to others, to users or stakeholders, it must at least acknowledge, if not support, their conceptions and desires. This requires (a) listening to how other people think and justify their actions in worlds they always are in the process of constructing to live in, or (b) inviting the stakeholders of a design to participate actively in the design process. So conceived, design is an essentially social activity, one that cannot be separated or abstracted from the context of people's lives and certainly not be replaced by a deontic logic or algorithms for optimisation, discussed by Simon, which might well be appropriate to engineering design.

Let me suggest five activities that define human-centred design.

— Designers invent or conceive *possible futures*, including its artefacts that they may be able to bring about, imaginable worlds that would not come about naturally. A causally determined world and future, by contrast, would be evidence of nature work and of the absence (or irrelevance) of design activity. Artefacts are products of human agency. They do not grow on trees. Design is fundamentally tied to conceiving futures that could not come about without human effort.

— Designers need to know *how desirable these futures are* to those who might inhabit them, and whether they afford diverse communities the spaces they require to make a home in them. Desirable futures reside in language, in communication, particularly between designers and the likely inhabitants of these futures. Evidence about understanding these worlds consists of the ability to articulate and rearticulate these futures for designers to take note.

— Designers *experiment with what is variable or could be changed,* in view of the opportunities that variability could open up for them and others. Laws in the natural sciences, by contrast, state what does not vary–cannot be varied or has not been varied. The variability of interest to designers has more to do with people cultural commitments, habits, and values. Some variabilities are just not recognised, habits and values, some are actively resisted, and some are eagerly embraced. Probably the most important task for designers is to create possibilities that nobody has thought of and would not have considered without rhetorical interventions by a designer. These variables define a space of possible actions, a design space, as Phil Agre calls it.[04] A design space is an artefact, a human creation, not observed in nature.

— Designers *work out realistic paths*, plans to proceed towards desirable futures. By realistic I mean that these paths include sufficient details and take account of currently available technologies and material resources, as well as the abilities of those who might pursue them.

— Designers *make proposals* (of realistic paths) to those who could bring a design to fruition, to the stakeholders of a design. Proposals are stated in language. However, they go beyond mere suggestions for what to do or the policies to follow. They must offer their addressees possibilities to realise their desires and coordinate their actions towards something worthwhile. As such, proposals *must enrol stakeholders into a designer's project.* The ends that designers may have in mind do not need to be the same as the ones that stakeholders pursue as long as the latter stay involved, at least part of the way. Without a network of supportive and creative stakeholders, a design cannot be realised.

Some of the contradictions between what scientific researchers claim they do and what designers do are as follows.

— Simon already recognised that the disciplines of the sciences are concerned with what exists whereas the disciplines of design are concerned with what, in his words, ought to be.[02] In terms of this essay, whereas scientific theories are based only on what existed and could be observed prior to an analysis, design concerns artefacts that are not yet in use and could not have been observed in use, for which data are constitutively lacking, and experiences can at best be anticipated.

— Whereas predictive theories that arise from scientific research conserve the status quo constitutively assuming that the forces that operated in the past continue into the future designers need to break with the determinisms of the past, proposing novel and untested paths into alternative futures, especially by involving the stakeholders' creativity in realising a design.

— Whereas researchers in the natural sciences privilege causal explanations, which excludes them as originators or contributors of the phenomena they observe, designers intend to affect something by their own actions, something that could not result from natural causes, thus defying the causal explanations of scientific discourse.

— Whereas scientists celebrate generalisations, abstract theories or general laws, supported by evidence in the form of observational data, designers suggest courses of action that must ultimately work in all of their necessary details and in the future. Artefacts never work in the abstract. This contradiction is also manifest in scientists' preference for abstract mathematical explanations, and designers' preference for images, figurative models and prototypes.

— Whereas researchers theorise invariancies, treating unexplained variations as undesirable noise, designers are concerned with variabilities, conditions that could be changed by design. Something analogue to Werner Heisenberg uncertainty principle applies to this incompatibility. By focusing on what exists, researchers cannot possibly observe what could but has not yet been altered; by focusing on what could be altered, designers have no reason to care for why something had stayed the same. For these reasons scientific theories are not particularly interesting to designers unless the theory describes something that designers do not care to change or need to build on.

— Whereas researchers are concerned with the truth of their propositions, established by observational evidence, designers are concerned with the plausibility and compellingness of their proposals, which resides in stakeholders ability to rearticulate them in the context of the futures they desire and various paths to reach them.

— Whereas scientific researchers seek knowledge for its own sake, value-free, and without regard to their utility, designers value knowledge that improves the world, at least in the dimensions related to their designs.

— Whereas theories in science describe nature as unable to understand how it is being investigated, theories of design address the activities of designers who can understand not only what they are doing but also theories about what they are doing. As Wolfgang Jonas notes: ny theory of designing has to include the generation of theories of designing as followed by its practitioners and xplain its own emergence its own change,[05] p. 184. Thus, a research-based theory of designing could never keep up with the changes that designers introduce into their own subject matter.

Obviously, design and research are incommensurable in conception. They pursue unlike epistemologies, at least in regard to the above. 'Design research' is an oxymoron without question. As a subspecies of research, design research suppresses design.

As re-search stifles design, what inquiries could improve design practices?

Unquestionably, design re-search cannot support what designers need to practise. But what would be a more appropriate alternative? How and into what should designers inquire? *The Semantic Turn* (p. 209ff) proposes a *science for design*, which is meant to support what designers need to do to make their claims compelling.[01] A science for design is distinct from a 'science of design, …that body of work which attempts to improve our understanding of design through 'scientific' (i.e. systematic and reliable) methods of investigation',[06] p. 96. The latter is exemplified by the scholarship of art historians, sociologists of design, or theorists of technology, all of whom generalise dominant features of design, historical trends, psychological predispositions, or socio-cultural contingencies. Observing from outside the process, a science of design depicts designers as being causally determined by forces not under their control, and can contribute little to the practice of designing. A science for design is also not to be confused with a 'design science … an explicitly organised, rational and wholly systematic approach to design; not just the utilisation of scientific knowledge of artefacts, but design in some sense a scientific activity itself'.[06] A science for design raises questions from within the practices of design. I will spell out some of them.

First and fundamentally, designers *create possibilities*. Possibilities relate to what humans *can* do. Possibilities are not part of and cannot be observed in a nature void of humans. A science for design must nurture ways that enlarge the design space within which designers act. Some of these ways are psychological, freeing oneself from blind spots and cognitive traps. Some are social, making use of conceptions held by others, when brainstorming, for instance. Some are technological, expanding a design space combinatorially, using computers, to generate alternatives that easily escape cognition. Some are perspectival, approaching a design from multiple disciplinary perspectives, and some are morphological, suggesting transformations into alternative representations with different qualities. All of these ways expand the range of choices available to designers (before narrowing them to a workable proposal). Re-search, as discussed above, is driven by extracting certainties from diverse data. Design, by contrast, thrives on uncertainty that designers can create and handle.

Designers must be non-dogmatic and anti-authoritarian in order to *question the 'findings' of scientific re-search.* Blindly accepting scientific authority means surrendering to what existed in the past. Undoubtedly, there are limits to what design can accomplish. For example, I would be hesitant to invest in a proposal for a perpetual motion machine. It violates the second law of thermodynamics. But even laws of nature are human artefacts. They may have withstood the test of time, but we can never know whether the findings of the natural sciences are valid in the time frame of a design. The history of design is full of examples where scientists claimed impossibilities that designers managed to circumvent or prove wrong. Scientists once assured us that it was impossible for humans to fly and now we do. Engineers calculated that the steel wheels of locomotives on steel tracks would not have enough traction to pull a train, and they were wrong. In the 1950s, IBM researchers are reputed to have concluded that the world would need no more than five computers. This did not discourage Steve Wozniak and Steve Jobs, working in a California garage, to develop the first personal computer. In effect, designers need to question prevailing ontological beliefs. Being afraid of undermining common convictions makes for timid designs. Proposing what everyone knows or already uses is not design at all.

Designers must *vigorously examine their own methods.* Design science, as Cross defines it, institutes design methods, supposed to be scientific, and hence unquestionable.[06] Legitimising some practices and delegitimising others is the mark of a discipline. Disciplines discipline their disciples. Design, however, is an *undiscipline*, one that should be able to question anything and be allowed to try everything – provided its products are useful, work, and benefit others. But it should especially apply to itself.

Designers must inquire into how to *create variables*, things that can be altered by design. They need to learn to create what scientists mostly abhor: changes that cannot be explained by natural causes. Variability, the ability to vary something, is an exclusively human ability. Just as J.J. Gibson's 'affordances',[07] variability is a relational concept, relating human agency to the environment; to what can be done with something. As already mentioned, inquiries into variables render knowledge of what exists less relevant than the options that variations open up. There are physical constraints, of course. Artefacts may 'object' to how they are treated by falling apart or just not doing what their users had in mind for them. When invariancies are social or cultural, designers need to explore what it takes to unfreeze cherished habits or convictions, or to get people to learn something new. Inquiries into variability require interactions with people, not more observations. They differ from ethnographic fieldwork of what users do, market research of user preferences, and ergonomic studies of the efficiency of human interfaces with technology. The latter describe what people do, not what they *can* do.

Above all, designers *participate in stakeholder networks* and need to know how to support such networks and energise them with *compelling proposals.* I have already suggested that design must remain undisciplined but it cannot be totally free when it intends to succeed. For designers, success means enrolling stakeholders into the project of their design. This is what keeps design responsive to the conceptions, desires and capabilities of others, and it 'disciplines' the necessarily unruly design professionals – but not from within the profession. Unable to rely on data from a desirable future and without real experience of what is being proposed, designers need to know what makes their proposals compelling. Elsewhere, I have outlined several approaches to this effect.[01] I cannot reiterate them here except to say that designers need to inquire into the conceptual abilities of diverse stakeholders through processes of exchanging narratives with them about possible futures. Consequently, because design become real in communication with others, inquiries into what makes a proposal compelling are inquiries into how people understand and act on narratives pertaining to desirable worlds. Some scholars have suggested that design is an ethical enterprise. If designers realise that they cannot go alone, cannot force their conceptions onto others, and that whatever they propose must resonate with stakeholder conceptions,[08] the questions that designers need to ask are implicitly ethical. The only ethical principle I would add is to avoid monopolising design in a profession and instead delegate the practice to as many stakeholders as possible. Design is a basic human activity to which everyone should have access. Professional designers must not usurp the ability of other stakeholders to design their own futures. Proposals for designs may fail for all kinds of reasons, and systematically studying why they failed is an important source of changing design practices from within.

I suppose most of these suggestions for inquiries in preparation of design activity do not conform to what traditional designers do when they say they do research. Let me mention three traditional kinds and explore their value.

First, *surveying useful ideas* for how a particular problem might be solved. Genrich Altshuller *et al.* surveyed some 200'000 patents and found 77 per cent utilised something already existing within the inventor's field.[09] Eighteen per cent imported ideas from other areas. 4 per cent realised new concepts, and only 1 per cent pioneered landmark inventions. The problem of the first 95 per cent is to find something that already exists but elsewhere. While surveys of this kind might prevent reinventions or enable designers to creatively deviate from what is already known, they do not say anything about how these ideas could be utilised and are, hence, not about design practices.

Second, designers often start by trying to *understand how an artefact is to function.* Indeed, designers tend to spend much time exploring what they are asked to do, for example, by taking the current version of a product apart, observing how it is used in different situations, visiting the manufacturer, talking to sales representatives etc. Louis Sullivan's widely cited slogan *form follows function* abbreviates the common but naive belief that the form of a product that designers need to find automatically follows from a thorough understanding of its function. However, understanding is not what re-search can provide, and deep understanding does not automatically lead to ideal forms. In fact, that deeper understanding of how something needs to work can limit a designer's attention to the cosmetics of what already exists a rather minimal design contribution. Sometimes, starting naively or from scratch can prevent one from being boxed into what clients and users expect designers to deliver.

Third, there is one area where re-search in the sense described above can make valuable contributions and that is by *pretesting a design*. In the context of designers having to make proposals to those who matter, we need to realise that proposals are linguistic constructions whose compellingness usually depends on extralinguistic devices: sketches, models, diagrams and demonstrations, but they can also be enhanced by empirical evidence that a design works as claimed. Approximations to that future evidence may be obtained by observing prototypes in action, how targeted users respond to and benefit from a design. Valuable as this kind of re-search is, it can be conducted only after a design is at least provisionally complete. Pretesting is necessarily limited to parts of a stakeholder network, perceived bottlenecks, typically users. Pretests merely approximate the ultimate realisation of a design.

Hiding design in the process of scientific inquiries

What researchers claim they do is not the whole story and what is missing reveals their blind spots. Let me discuss two and end by suggesting a less delusionary epistemology for scientific inquiry, including research design.

First, the *metaphorical language* of the accepted accounts of scientific research *prevents acknowledgements of the researchers' agency*. As above noted, researchers speak of research results as findings, discoveries, or truths – as if the phenomena they describe had been there to begin with, theories were hiding themselves in the data, laws would govern nature, making the task of scientific research one of uncovering what is behind the observable surface of nature. But patterns must be recognised before their pervasiveness can be tested. Re-cognition – cognising something again – implicates a long history of the researchers' conceptions. Researchers' conceptual involvement cannot be avoided by delegating pattern recognition to mechanical devices, to systematic analyses or statistical tests. Such mechanisms, meant to assure objectivity, are always designed by someone and, hence, are representative of its designers' conceptual repertoire, and what they indicate must be re-cognisable as well.

It follows that re-search results are not the properties of data alone, as claimed, but of how the data fit a researcher's conceptual and linguistic vocabulary. The difference between outstanding and normal scientists lies in the former's ability to ask interesting questions, generate relevant data, and describe their implications in convincing terms. This is not to suggest that research results are subjective, but that so-called findings are the product of interactions between the data and their treatment. Privileging the properties of data at the expense of the researchers' role as the creators of hypotheses, proponents of theories, and designers of systems of analysis denies human agency in the products of science. The skilful design of research by scientists thus becomes the victim of the epistemological commitment to objectivity, the illusion of being able to observe without an observer[10] or to re-search without the cognitive and linguistic histories of the researchers.

Second, in order to preserve the abstract-objectivist[11] or representational[12] conception of scientific (propositional) language, the accepted accounts of scientific research deny or *omit the context in which re-search takes place.* This may be demonstrated with Bruno Latour and Steve Woolgar's (1986) five-stage model of scientific discoveries,[13] schematically stated as follows:

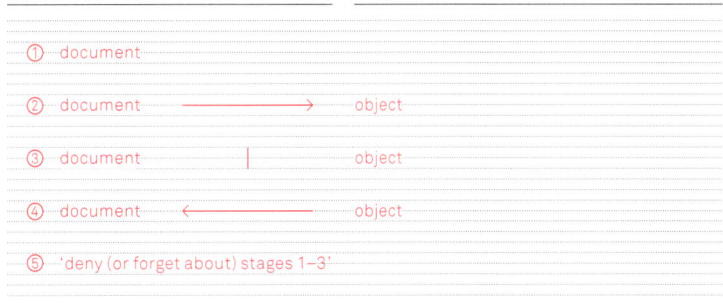

Based on ethnographic studies of scientific practices in research laboratories, astronomical observatories and other scientific enterprises, Latour and Woolgar noted that virtually all research starts with *(1) document*s: the literature of the discipline in which problems are identified as legitimate targets of investigation; lucrative requests for research proposals; or puzzling gaps in research results published by colleagues.

In a second step, such verbal matter gives rise to and defines an object of investigation: *(2) document → object.* In statistics, this step means identifying a population that can be sampled with suitable instruments. In physics, it nowadays means building very expensive apparatus to run theory-informed experiments that yield novel observations. In psychology, experiments with subjects are typical. They induce individual behaviours pertaining to a research question that might not occur in everyday life. Public opinion researchers design surveys and interview schedules through which publics are constructed that are of interest to candidates for political office or policy makers in government.[14] This step generates data that would not exist otherwise. Researchers do not merely stumble upon data. Data are made, which prompts Herminia Alfonso to call them *poieta.*[15] Scientific literature is full of how-to books on the design of experiments, of measuring instruments, of questionnaires, of coding instructions, and of transcription conventions. Even when data are produced by a process not controlled by the scientist, recognising them as data makes all the difference.

The third step involves separating the data from what caused them: *(3) document | object.* To justify this split, a variety of devices are in use, for example, for preventing experimenter biases from polluting the data, relying on objective measuring instruments, or admitting data to an analysis only when their inter-coder agreement is high. While such devices assure that the data are reproducible, that the method of generating them is not affected by spurious causes, none of these precautions can change the fact that the data could not exist without the application of a design that generates these data.

The fourth step inverses the original direction of the causality: *(4) document ← object,* now treating the data as selecting among hypotheses or judging the validity of a theory of interest to the researcher. This is the step that researchers in the sciences treat methodologically, and also the step described above as the re-search process.

The fifth and final step, *(5) 'deny (or forget about) stages 1–3,'* leaves step (4), research, as the accepted way of describing scientific research, effectively supporting the claim that research results represent phenomena existing in nature. Woolgar 1993 suggests:[16]

'Step (5) rewrites history so as to give the discovered object its ontological foundation. Construing the prior existence of the object entails the portrayal of the observer as passive rather than active. We thus see the rhetorical importance of the antecedence of the object in the way it implicates a particular conception of the agent (as) merely peripheral and transitory. It is as if observers merely stumble upon a pre-existing scene.' (p. 69)

One might be lenient and argue that steps (1) to (3) take less time or are easier to perform than step (4). However, ignoring the design phase of scientific research and the agency of the researcher/observer is no oversight. It is necessary to preserve the idea of representation, the belief that research probes reality the way it is. I take this the primary motivation of step (5).

Suppose we were to ignore the devious step (5) instead of (1) to (3). What difference would this make? Obviously, it would acknowledge the history of the re-search process. More importantly, it would require a significant shift in the epistemology of science from a representational enterprise to a constructive one. I want to build on Heisenberg's famous assertion: 'What we observe is not nature itself, but nature exposed to our method of questioning.' Our method of questioning points to the discourse in which we construct our worlds and ask our questions about these worlds. The answers we obtain reveal nothing other than whether our own actions, taken in view of our constructions, are afforded or fail to be afforded by whatever resides outside of us. Consequently, scientific work does not reveal what exists (in perpetuity or in fact), but what our constructions of the world had enabled us to do – the data we were able to generate to test the hypotheses we designed. While this brings science and design closer to each other, the past tense in the last sentence is of utmost importance in distinguishing between the two. Science articulates the constructions that worked so far. Design articulates constructions that might work in the future – but not without human intervention.

Conclusion

Re-search as practised today cannot possibly serve as a model for generating knowledge about design or to improve design. In fact, relying on re-search, being necessarily conservative, would condemn design to elaborations of the past. Even my modest proposal to acknowledge scientists as designers of research processes does not go far enough.

Inquiries that could inform design practices would have to start by acknowledging the simple fact that design is concerned with how we may want to live in future worlds. At any one moment in time, these futures reside in narratives that are sufficiently compelling to coordinate the stakeholders in these futures and encourage them to do their best to make them real. Whereas science concerns conceptions that worked so far, design concerns what could work in the future, a future that is more interesting than what we know today. A design is always a proposal, a conjecture. Whether it delivers what it promises, whether it will work in the foreseeable future, cannot be known until it ceases to be a design and becomes part of its users' history. At any one moment in time, the viability of a design depends on its stakeholders' conceptions, commitments and resources, which can be studied in order to inform design decisions. This is what inquiries in support of design need to do. They must not become entrapped by a debilitating oxymoron.

References / Bibliography

[01]   Krippendorff K (2006) *The Semantic Turn; a New Foundation for Design*. Taylor & Francis, Boca Raton, London, New York

[02]   Simon HA (1969) *The Sciences of the Artificial*. MIT Press, Cambridge, MA

[03]   Rittel HWJ, Webber MM (1984) Planning Problems Are Wicked Problems. In: Cross N (ed.): *Developments in Design Methodology*. Wiley, New York, 135–144

[04]   Agre PE (2000) *Notes on the New Design Space*. http://polaris.gseis.ucla.edu/pagre/design-space.html (accessed 5 June 2007)

[05]   Jonas W (2004) A Theory of what? In: Jonas W, Meyer-Veden J (eds): *Mind the Gap! On Knowing and Not-knowing in Design*. HM Hauschild, Bremen, 178–211

[06]   Cross N (2000) Design as a Discipline. In: Durling D, Friedman K (eds): *Doctoral Education in Design: Foundations for the Future*. Staffordshire University Press, Staffordshire, 93–100

[07]   Gibson JJ (1979) *The Ecological Approach to Visual Perception*. Houghton Mifflin, Boston, MA

[08]   Krippendorff K (2007) The Cybernetics of Design and the Design of Cybernetics. *Kybernetes*; *in press*

[09]   Altshuller G (2000) *The Innovation Algorithm: TRIZ, Systematic Innovation and Technical Creativity*. Trans. and ed. Shulyak L, Rodman S. Technical Innovation Center, Worchester, MA [original Russian publication in 1973]

[10]   Foerster H von (1995) From a public lecture, confirmed in personal communication

[11]   Volosinov VN (1986) *Marxism and the Philosophy of Language*. Harvard University Press, Cambridge, MA

[12]   Rorty R (1979) *Philosophy and the Mirror of Nature*. Princeton University Press, Princeton, NJ

[13]   Latour B, Woolgar S (1986) *Laboratory Life: The Construction of Scientific Facts*, 2nd edition. Princeton University Press, Princeton, NJ

[14]   Krippendorff K (2005) The Social Construction of Public Opinion. In: Wienand E, Westerbarkey J, Scholl A (eds): *Kommunikation über Kommunikation. Theorie, Methoden und Praxis. Festschrift für Klaus Merten*. VS-Verlag, Wiesbaden, 129–149

[15]   Alfonso HCM (2001) *Socially Shared Inquiry; a Self-reflexive Emancipatory Communication Approach to Social Re-search*. Great Books Trading, Sikatuna Village, Quezon City

[16]   Woolgar S (1993) *Science, the Very Idea*. Routledge, New York

Pieter Jan Stappers

Doing Design as a Part of Doing Research

Preface

The increasing complexity of modern technologies in products has led to the establishment of design as an academic discipline, and a rapid growth in the connections between science, engineering and design. As part of this development, the relation between design and research is dynamically changing toward a tighter coupling. University-based design courses are beginning to include scientific theory and research skills as part of their curricula, and designers are playing a part in research projects. In many places, the need to establish a PhD or other doctoral programme for designers has been discussed, with some hesitation, as the traditional backgrounds of designers and researchers has been quite different.

In fact, the introduction of research has been a difficult one in general. At engineering universities, doing a PhD was widely considered a waste of skill and time until well into the 1970s. And at present, there is considerable resistance from the arts arena against being dominated by 'uninspiring activities with tally tables and test tubes'. On the other hand, successful examples, both from industry (XEROX PARC's media experiments) and academia (MIT MediaLab) have provided well-recognised examples that appeal to both scientists and designers.

Currently, doctoral programmes in design are growing[01] and new journals targeting the 'middle ground' of design research are emerging.[02]

A lot of debate has been devoted to the relation between design and research, and a consensus outcome has not been established. One problem is that there always is a silent undercurrent underlying the rational (issues of status and politics and funding), and the debate is often carried on a level of abstraction that tends to confuse rather than enlighten, because generic terms such as 'research' and 'design' carry more implicit than explicit connotations. It may well be that the inspiring examples mentioned above were recognised as such because they could demonstrate concrete examples in the world (prototypes) and indicate their ramifications in theories.

I am not interested in settling these debates on an abstract level, but rather want to focus on what I (trained as an experimental physicist, but having worked in multidisciplinary design research for twenty years) have experienced as the most exciting part of having designers do research.

My experience and view may not be representative of the whole breadth of the field of design from which they were sampled. In the past twenty years I have worked within a specific school (within an internationally oriented engineering university), and on specific topics (human-centred design tools for supporting creativity and concept development) within a specific research approach (with an emphasis on human perception and experience and on developing prototypes of design tools as means of inquiry). Still, I believe that the lessons I encountered hold a wider value.

What are 'design' and 'research'?

As I stated, I am not about to treat in depth the many meanings that the short words 'design' and 'research' must have, because I believe that their instantiations in design research projects better convey the argument than word-play, sophisticated or not. But it is good to show some of the connotations.

Both research and design are endeavours that improve the understanding of or control over the human condition. They are carried out by (often passionate) individuals and groups, require talent and hard work, and come with sets of methods and techniques (which can be as disputed as the results that are claimed to come out of them).

The differences between design and research have often been highlighted, sometimes as prejudice, sometimes as overgeneralisations, in confrontations between designers 'from practice' and researchers 'from adjacent disciplines'. Research is perceived as seeking to understand of the past or present state of the world, and to establish explanations of why it must be so. Its methods and publication channels put great value on issues of validity and proof, by logical reasoning and empirical measurement. Its core structures are the theories that create the overall structure of its knowledge.

Design is seen as being concerned with establishing a working effect (creating a product) in a possible future, realising successful instantiations in a world that does not yet exist and is not yet known. Its methods and manifestations emphasise inspiration (findings must be useful, not merely true), realisation in-the-world, and proof by demonstration.

It is not strange that these two worlds are seen to conflict, as they seem to harbour different values and methods, and their communities, both indeed passionate, are driven by different cultures. To summarise the contrast, Frayling's rendering of the 'Hollywood' view on artists/designers and scientists/researchers is helpful, where the former are seen as 'self-conscious strivers for effect', the latter as 'rational developers of abstract theory from 'a crazy idea'.[03] But, as Frayling goes on to stress, '*[D]oing* science is much more like *doing* design' [my emphasis]. Sanders compares research approaches in science and design in their emphasis on informing versus than inspiring application.[04] Both design and research are characterised by iterative cycles of generating ideas and confronting them with the world. Designers do not just haphazardly generate ideas without evaluation (although they are prouder of having their ideas than of testing them). And neither do researchers just rationally test and refine ideas (although their journals tend to downplay the ways by which their new ideas came into being). Yet these supposed differences distract the discussion.

It is in the similarities of doing design/research that I believe the interesting way forward lies, and in this essay I want to focus on the designer who combines design and research in the process of generating new insights and artefacts. In recent decades, university-based design curricula, such as the one in Delft, have included theoretical knowledge and research skills as essentials for the industrial design engineer. Another, slower, process was the inclusion of design skills and methods in research programmes. This was slower both because prejudices had to be overcome and appropriate types of research had to be developed, and also because at first, PhD research projects (such as my own) were conducted by students with backgrounds in disciplines that had long-established research training. But over the past decade, with new generations of design students with research skills and attitude, pursuing a PhD, appropriate ways of research have been developed. But what are these types of research, where designers can employ their specific strengths most beneficially for the general academic and industrial research effort?

Designing as a cognitive activity

What abilities make designers different from other engineers or scientists? Our school, with its multidisciplinary design curriculum, integrates designing with inputs from marketing, engineering, aesthetics (*vormgeving* in Dutch; *Gestaltung* in German) and ergonomics. In several appraisals of the programme,[05] we came up with the following list of our students' characteristics that were most valued by their future industrial employers:

— They can *communicate* with all specialisms and specialists involved
— They can *integrate* the (often mismatching) inputs from specialisms
— They can *act* in the absence of complete information
— *They retain focus* on realising the product throughout the process

In these skills, the Industrial Design Engineers were seen to excel above other engineering disciplines. But these skills are as important for research as they are for design, especially in multidisciplinary or explorative research, where much of the landscape is *terra incognita*.

Moreover, designers (in our school and at many places elsewhere) are aware of and are trained in the different modes of generative and evaluative thinking. Traditional academic accounts have stressed evaluative thinking, which is characterised by logic, deduction, strict and explicit definitions and verbal notation, and converging by ruling out the impossible. Designers are also strong on generative thinking, which is often associative, inductive, using loose definitions, and supported by visual notations as sketching, gesturing, modelmaking, and diverging by conjecturing the possible. Creative processes make use of both these types, often in the diverge/converge or generate/evaluate spiral, as shown in figure 1. Within research, the logical skills are emphasised and the creative ones left to some part of personal intuition, or sometimes left to chance. Fostering the interplay of both styles is important for research, but a place where designers can be of special value.

FIG: 01　The iterative spiral of generative and evaluative cycles in design/research. The vertical arrow indicates a central 'product', which can be a prototype or a piece of theory. The sheets at the bottom indicate how there is always a varied set of inputs from different disciplines at the base of a project. The sheets with arrows indicate that, during its progress, the project draws in new knowledge from adjacent disciplines and may likewise return insights to those disciplines. [06]

Designing as a part of research

If we see research not as a domain claimed by a certain profession, but as 'endeavours that grow knowledge', the place of these design skills within research becomes clearer. Through realising 'products', designers absorb knowledge from different directions and confront, integrate and contextualise this knowledge. In this confrontation, much happens that may be of value for the home bases of this disciplinary knowledge, because its theories and hypotheses are put to a kind of test, producing insights. The confrontation happens in most knowledge-intensive design projects, but remains implicit, hidden and undocumented, because only the 'product' emerges and the decisions are kept silent. If such activities are to contribute to the growth of our ability to understand and act in the world, their outcomes need to be fed back to the disciplinary sources. This is as much a problem of motivation as of method, as most designers are more interested in creating effect than in writing about it.

But let us look at a historical example from engineering. The Wright brothers are well known for realising an effect: a working prototype of an aeroplane. They have most often been referred to as inventors, or engineers/designers (and bicycle repairmen). Yet, in the process of 'inventing flight' they developed typical 'research methods' such as a bicycle-mounted 'wind tunnel' *avant la lettre* for testing wing shapes; and their success is said to be due to their reshaping the paradigm of understanding flight by redefining the problem of attaining it as a problem of *controlling* flight (by the pilot), rather than of *powering* elevation. Now, their work is seen as having a profound and fundamental importance for a variety of disciplines.[07] But connecting back to these disciplines is difficult.

How does this fit in a general scheme of research?

FIG: 02

The need to reduce the separation between 'design' and 'science' can be found back in recent developments in the philosophy and policy of research. Not just in design, but also in wider areas of engineering and science, the field is wrestling with the question of what research can or should be. One of the most insightful breaks with prejudice – one that helps me to place designers on the research map – is Stokes's four-quadrant model of research.FIG: 02 [08] Stokes used this model to overcome the limitations of the ruling research paradigm of the second half of the 20th century, Vannevar Bush's linear model with 'basic' ('fundamental') and 'applied' science at its poles. In the linear model, basic science was where new knowledge originated, in a context of pure theory with no practical concern; applied science was where products were made, using scientific knowledge, but not producing new insights. Stokes labels the two extremes with quantum physicist Niels Bohr, who dealt with only basic problems and inventor Edison, who was so focused on application that he even forbade his staff to meddle with science. There are two problems with the model: it indicates that an increase of applicability of research by necessity entails a decrease in its fundamental quality. I personally remember one of my physics professors exclaiming that he was proud nobody could apply his work, because that proved that it was fundamental research. There seemed to be some intellectual status issues involved in being on the left-hand side of the diagram…

The second problem Stokes identified was that valuable work, such as that of Louis Pasteur, could not be given a single place on the line, because it was both fundamental (established new theories) and applied (resulted in vaccines). In the four-quadrant model, the two poles have become two independent dimensions, and the possibility of doing research that generates both generalisable knowledge and applications is given a place. In this quadrant we find many of the scientists who formed the basic theories we now take for established: Newton, Huygens and Archimedes worked on practical applications (e.g. making clocks for ships) as well as on producing fundamental models for parts of our world (e.g. mechanics and wave theory). Harré [09] presents a beautiful overview on how varied science can be and, like Feyerabend,[10] argues and illustrates that there is not just a single way of conducting research, but that insight progresses through many forms, all requiring substantial creativity, sensitivity and hard work.

I think it is in Pasteur's quadrant where designer's research can be at the most fruitful: research with an eye for generalisation and an eye for application does not have to be cross-eyed. It may be too ambitious to say that all design research should try to emulate Pasteur, but the dual striving for knowledge and effect is, in my view, characteristic of tapping the strengths of designers in research and fuelling the motivations of designers for research (and maybe of other researchers for design).

Horváth provides an overview of different types of research with various degrees of design involvement and how they can coexist in a single organisation of knowledge generation and dissemination.[11] In his view, design research takes a middle ground between disciplinary 'basic' research and practical application, and comes in three flavours, channelling the transport of knowledge between the former extremes. These three flavours are research in a design context (employing methods of the basic discipline, applied to the design field), design-inclusive research (employing design methods as a part of generating and applying knowledge), and practice-based design research (applying models, methods and tools from the previous two in realising groundbreaking new products). There may be some similarity between these three flavours and the Bohr, Pasteur and Edison quadrants of Stokes's scheme.

FIG: 02   The linear and four-quadrant models [08]

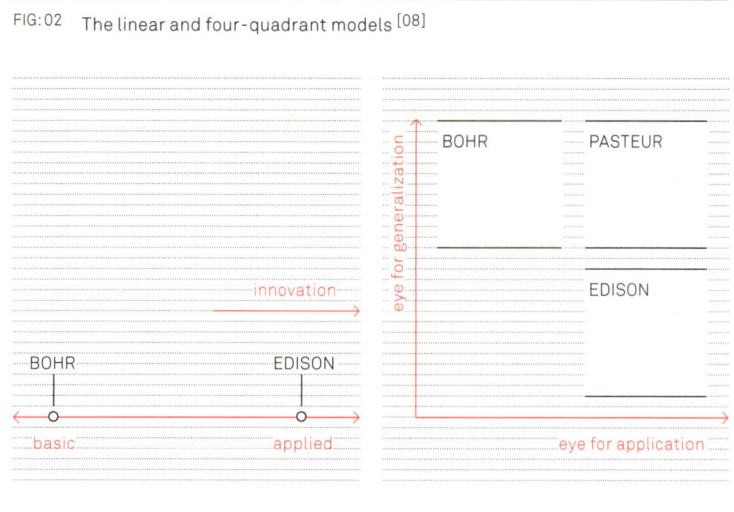

What? The value of explorative studies

The ability to cope with unknowns is typical for explorers, not just the classical maritime explorers who went into *terra incognita* to frame our first understanding of the place, but also for researchers exploring uncharted territory, working at the fringes, or in the overlap of multiple concerns.

Modern product development is increasingly like this. Developing a new mobile phone service requires inputs from technologists, policy makers, infrastructure specialists, business studies, sociologists, psychologists, ethnographers and designers, connecting all this in generating products. The prototypes generated in these projects often incorporate hypotheses in several of these fields, and in the development of these prototypes, these hypotheses are tested. But often the results are not reported back.

How? The value of prototypes

Prototypes and other expressions such as sketches, diagrams and scenarios, are the core means by which the designer builds the connection between fields of knowledge and progresses toward a product. Prototypes serve to instantiate hypotheses from contributing disciplines, and to communicate principles, facts and considerations between disciplines. They speak the language of experience, which unites us in the world. Moreover, by training (and selection), designers can develop ideas and concepts by realising prototypes and evaluating them. In his classic book on general systems thinking, Weinberg stresses the importance of instantiations and examples in establishing successful communication across the boundaries of disciplines, stating as a reason the development that ongoing specialisation in science has brought about a state in which scientists from different disciplines share very few experiences.[12] Prototypes serve as carriers, and realising these shared experiences facilitates communication, as did other typical design tools such as sketches and scenarios.

Therefore, the realisation of working prototypes serves as the core axis that connects the design team or research team: they can form the 'up' arrow in Figure 1. In my view, this is the essence of 'research through design', i.e. that the designing act of creating prototypes is in itself a potential generator of knowledge (if only its insights do not 'disappear' into the prototype, but are fed back into the disciplinary and cross-disciplinary platforms that can fit these insights into the growth of theory.[06, 13]

But much of the value of prototypes as carriers of knowledge can be implicit or hidden. They embody solutions, but the problems they solve may not be recognised. There are two consequences of this:

(i)   efforts should be make to make these explicit and feed this back to the informing disciplines;
(ii) people working on related research topics should be exposed to the prototypes, so that they may learn solutions (gain associations) even if these are not made explicit.

It is in this latter aspect that the design studio is a good approach for furthering the use of insights that spin out of research projects.

Figure 3 shows a sequence of prototypes that were developed at ID-StudioLab. Their core idea was to apply the new media possibilities of computers in realising tools that support designers' visual thinking in the early, conceptual, phases of design projects. This evolution involved half a dozen PhD projects, about a dozen MSc graduation projects and two dozen BSc group research projects. In this mix of projects, we performed contextual inquiries studying existing design practice in the field, explored visionary interactions with new media and developed a range of prototypes.[FIG: 03] We ourselves lived with these prototypes in the studio and tested some of them in educational settings, in the laboratory and – increasingly – with designers in the field.

The research was reported in the academic channels and in personal communications and through the educational programme in Delft. But maybe more importantly, the 'living prototypes' were part of the 'texture' of the StudioLab, influencing and being influenced by dozens of researchers, students and visitors who all brought and took away snippets and insights according to their specific background. This is why design studios are so important for growing knowledge.

FIG: 03   A sequence of prototypes of media-based design tools

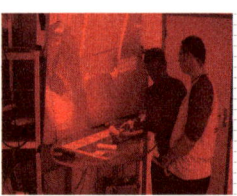   

TRI
A platform for exploring design tools using a sketchy variety of virtual reality techniques [14]

SKETCHBOOK
A digital sketchbook that uses the fluency of real-world sketchbooks [15]

PRODUCTWORLD
An ideation tool that helps designers finding patterns in collections of existing designs by interactive spatial classification [16]

CABINET
An image collection tool that merges virtual and physical images into one seamless collection [17]

PHOTOBOARDING
A technique to capture and retain playacting sessions in a rich and sketchy way and develop them into storyboards [18]

SKIN
A technique to play with and explore colours, patterns and graphics on physical product shapes [19]

INSTANTTEMPLATES
Digital templates of video to support physical drawing of natural two-handed product interactions [18]

IRIS
A shared digital posting board for screenshots, to enhance situation awareness in distributed studios [18]

Where? The value of design studios

Classically, design studios are known for their visual culture. Designers surround themselves with inspiring materials, sketches and prototypes; other designers in the studio absorb these visual sparks as well, and such visual outlets are known to set off unplanned and informal communications, and present people with unexpected inputs, which can serve as part of solutions and lead to serendipitous innovation. In 2001, four research groups from our department started ID-StudioLab, in which staff, PhD students and MSc students on research projects worked in a studio situation to promote contact between different expertises and different projects. Before, most of these groups had had separate laboratories and office spaces and informal connections were limited. In recent years, this ID-StudioLab has provided a base for young design researchers, researching designers, and those who want to be in contact with these groups although they may later pursue a different balance. It promoted the informal contact and sharing of ideas and skills, an undercurrent that can be as important for the dissemination of research findings as the official publication channels.[13, 21] Moreover, it formed a playground in which design researchers could 'live with their prototypes', an important ingredient of 'research through design'. Keller (this volume and [22]) describes how such sequences of prototypes in a studio environment carry many informal crossovers. Saakes discusses the way interventions in practice, in combination with tools development, fits into design research.[19]

Conclusions

The above has been a personal view from a specific vantage point. I have stressed the importance of design skills as a valuable ingredient for research, as opposed to research being an add-on to give a designer academic credibility; of creating prototypes, of fostering design research through studios, and of the need for design research to feed back (publish) its findings to the disciplines from which it feeds. These are the key lessons I drew from my experience.

Not all designers are industrial design engineers. Some are more akin to artists, some are more specialised in generative thought, just as some scientists specialise in evaluative thought. Some are great at concept development, but not at communication. Therefore this argument should not be taken as proposing a general or definitive solution for the field, the logical outcome of how the world must be. But rather, as a design prototype, it demonstrates a way in which designers can work in research and tries to practise what I preached above, to feed the insights from along the way back into the participating professions, not just present the outcome.

References / Bibliography

[01]	Sugiyama K (2003) Results of the Survey of Education in Design Research. *Proceedings of the 3rd Doctoral Education in Design*, Tsukuba, Japan, October 2003
[02]	Chen L (2007) International Journal of Design: A Step forward. *International Journal of Design* 1(1): 1–2
[03]	Frayling C (1993) Research in Art and Design. *Royal College of Art Research Papers* 1(1): 1–5
[04]	Sanders EB-N (2005) Information, Inspiration and Co-creation. Paper presented at the *6th International Conference of the European Academy of Design, 29–31 March 2005,* University of the Arts, Bremen, Germany
[05]	Bos E, Jacobs JJ (2006) *Self-evaluation 2006, Part 2.* Faculty of Industrial Design Engineering, Delft University of Technology
[06]	Stappers PJ (2006) Designing as a Part of Research. In: van der Lugt R, Stappers PJ (eds): *Design and the Growth of Knowledge.* ID-StudioLab Press, Delft, the Netherlands (available from http://studiolab.io.tudelft.nl/static/gems/symposium/zelfprintversie100dpi.pdf)
[07]	Wright O (1988) *How we Invented the Airplane: an Illustrated History.* Courier-Dover, New York
[08]	Stokes D (1997) *Pasteur's Quadrant: Basic Science and Technological Innovation.* Brookings Institution Press, Washington, DC
[09]	Harré R (1981) *Great Scientific Experiments: 20 Experiments that Changed our View of the World.* Phaidon, London
[10]	Feyerabend P (1993) *Against Method.* Verso, London
[11]	Horváth I (2007) Comparison of Three Methodological Approaches of Design Research. *International Conference on Engineering Design, ICED'07, 28–31 August 2007; forthcoming*
[12]	Weinberg G (2001) *An Introduction to General Systems Thinking.* Silver anniversary edition, Dorset House, New York
[13]	Hekkert P, Keyson D, Overbeeke K, Stappers PJ (2001) The ID-StudioLab: Research through and for Design. *Proceedings of the Symposium on Design Research in the Netherlands,* 95–103
[14]	Keller AI, Stappers PJ, Hoeben A (2000) TRI: Inspiration Support for a Design Studio Environment. *Proceedings of the DCNET conference,* University of Sydney
[15]	Hoeben A, Stappers PJ (2001) Ideas: A Vision of a Designer's Sketchingtool. *Proceedings CHI2001: Conference on Human Factors in Computing Systems,* 199–200
[16]	Pasman GJ (2003) *Designing with Precedents.* PhD thesis, Delft University of Technology
[17]	Keller AI (2007) For Inspiration Only: Designer Interaction with Informal Collections of Visual Material. *This volume, p. 119*

[18]   Saakes DP, Keller AI (2005) Beam me down Scotty: To the Virtual and back! In: Wensveen S, Diederiks E, Djajadiningrat T, Guenand A, Klooster S, Stienstra S, Vink P, Overbeeke K (eds): *Proceedings of the Conference Designing Pleasurable Products and Interfaces.* Eindhoven University of Technology, 482–483

[19]   Saakes DP (2006) Exploring Materials: New Media in Design. In: Michel R, Hirt L (eds): *Drawing New Territories.* Swiss Design Network, Zurich, 109–124

[20]   Peeters A, Stappers PJ (2005) Iris: Supporting Workplace Awareness by Triggering Informal Interactions with Visual Material. In: Wensveen S, Diederiks E, Djajadiningrat T, Guenand A, Klooster S, Stienstra S, Vink P, Overbeeke K (eds): *Proceedings of the Conference Designing Pleasurable Products and Interfaces.* Eindhoven University of Technology, 129–148

[21]   Pasman G, Stappers PJ, Hekkert PPM, Keyson, D (2005) The ID-StudioLab 2000–2005. In: Achten HH, Dorst, K, Stappers PJ, de Vries B (eds): *Proceedings of Design Research in the Netherlands, 19–20 May 2005.* Eindhoven University of Technology, 193–204

[22]   Keller AI (2005) *For Inspiration Only.* PhD thesis, Delft University of Technology

Paul Chamberlain
Peter Gardner
Rebecca Lawton

Research

Shape of Things to Come

The investigation of the potential benefits of an identification system employing both visual and tactile cues in the design of a non-interchangeable medical connector

Abstract

Design is often seen as a resource to embellish products towards the end of the research and development process. Designers create artefacts that often encapsulate knowledge emerging from research studies. This case study may help in defining the changing role of design in the increasing trend for multidisciplinary alliances and highlight interdisciplinary human-centred practice-based design research where the creation of artefacts play a central role in enabling the building of new knowledge.

Artefacts in the real world are all too often designed simply by the manipulation of visual cues such as colour and the aesthetics of shape. Human touch (haptic sense) is a powerful way of recognising and discriminating between objects for people with impaired vision or under conditions where the visual sense is impaired by the environmental conditions (e.g. low lighting, restricted line of sight). Additionally, in complex circumstances where similar objects may be confused, the shape and feel of an object can be important in ensuring that the correct object is selected or acted upon. In many medical settings the complications of low lighting, restricted line of sight and complex arrangements of devices will be present.

There has been relatively little empirical work conducted to investigate the haptic sense (active-touch) compared to the visual and auditory modalities and it is therefore less well understood. One situation in which a theoretically grounded, user-centred haptic design approach might be useful is in the design of medical connectors to minimise the occurrence of potentially fatal misconnections. The increasing complexity of medical interventions means that users are required to connect a multiplicity of external tubes to various types of diagnostic and therapeutic devices.

Recent high-profile fatalities have put this safety issue high on the government's agenda. As part of a collaborative research initiative, we are proposing that the ability to distinguish between important medical devices such as medical connectors will be enhanced by the development of objects with distinct haptic cues.

Current drug delivery systems employ a common connector known as the 'luer' irrespective of the drug or route into the body. Our objective is to ensure that the five generic delivery routes (intravenous, intrathecal, respiratory, cardio-vascular and enteral) cannot be connected with one another and are easily distinguishable.

There is now significant pressure for research and development into a system of medical connectors so that misconnection of this kind becomes physically impossible.

The research brings together expertise in general and regional anaesthesia, critical care medicine, human factors and industrial design. The design and testing of the connector system proposed adopts a human-factors design approach; focusing on the needs and characteristics of the user, and rigorous user testing of the human-device interface. This user-centred, iterative approach provides the cultural basis of the work, but has not yet been widely adopted in the design of medical devices.

A series of controlled studies have been undertaken utilising physical and virtual prototype connector designs. These studies informed the design of an easily discriminable set of shapes that have been used in conjunction with a mechanical connection system. The design team have patented a novel engineered solution to enable connection of correctly mating shapes and prevent connection of incorrectly mated shapes. The designers have engineered a mechanical solution to prevent misconnection in combination with shape to speed the process of identification.

From the project has emerged a design solution that may contribute to reducing the potentially fatal misconnection of medical devices, while providing knowledge that may inform the design other safety-critical control situations.

'In theory practice follows theory, in practice theory follows practice'
Anonymous

Design is often seen as a resource to embellish products towards the end of the research and development process. Whilst this may be part of the 'professionals' role' this investigation illuminates the role of the Design Researcher as the lead in a concurrent development across the disciplines of human factors, psychology and critical care medicine. In its broadest sense this approach can be classified as 'action research', which aims not only to understand and report on a given problem, but also to provoke change through action.[01] It is a methodology common to much of the design research conducted within the Art and Design Research Centre at Sheffield Hallam University, where the designers' philosophical approach is based on the old Art School model of learning to make, then making to learn.

This case study may help in defining the role of design in the increasing trend for multi-disciplinary alliances and highlight interdisciplinary human-centred practice-based design research where the creation of artefacts play a central role in building new knowledge.

FIG. 01

The principal lead and designer in this case study has experience of working with sensory and physically impaired users. One outcome of his previous research was the design of the Tac-Tile Sounds System,[FIG. 01] which received two 'millennium product' design awards from the Design Council in 2000. The Tac-Tile Sounds System is a versatile modular vibro-acoustic furniture system, which can be used by people with sensory impairment to explore the world of meaningful sounds through vibration in therapeutic, educational and recreational environments.

Much of the current design methodologies are based on user-centred activities; this project involved a group of end-users who were mostly deaf and blind. Communication in the normal sense was often impossible and the designer/client relationship presented itself in an extreme case. Designers had to be creative in establishing the needs of the user and evaluating the success of the product solutions.

Significantly, the early prototypes that emerged from the project became the communication tools, using touch and vibration as a means to establish user preference and help establish programmes for use, as described by Chamberlain *et al.*[02]

Context

Artefacts in the real world are all too often designed simply by manipulating visual cues such as colour and the aesthetics of shape. Human touch (haptic sense) is a powerful way of recognising and discriminating between objects for people with impaired vision or under conditions where the visual sense is impaired by environmental conditions. Additionally, in complex circumstances where similar objects may be confused, the shape and feel of an object can be important in ensuring that the correct object is selected or acted upon.

There has been relatively little empirical work conducted to investigate the haptic sense (active-touch) compared to the visual and auditory modalities and it is therefore less well understood. However, recent advances in computer-based technologies have generated increased motivation for the development of haptic theory.

One situation in which a theoretically grounded, user-centred haptic design approach might be useful is in the design of medical connectors to minimise the occurrence of potentially fatal misconnections. The increasing complexity of medical interventions means that users are required to connect a multiplicity of external tubes to various types of diagnostic and therapeutic devices, often in low lighting with restricted line of sight.

Recent high-profile fatalities have put this safety issue high on the UK government's agenda. As part of a collaborative research initiative, we are proposing that the ability to distinguish between important medical devices such as medical connectors will be enhanced by the development of objects with distinct haptic cues.

There have been calls for the health service to follow the lead of other high-risk industries in adopting a systems approach to accidents and incidents. In particular, there is an emphasis on the need to redesign medical devices to help avoid errors, following the publication of UK government reports.[03-05] There is now significant pressure for research and development into a system of medical connectors so that misconnection of this kind becomes physically impossible.

The research brings together expertise in general and regional anaesthesia, critical care medicine (Bradford Royal Infirmary), psychology and human factors (Leeds University), and industrial design (Sheffield Hallam University), to develop an engineered design solution supported by a novel means of enhancing the discriminability of a new system of connectors through visual and tactile (haptic) cues. The research team has formalised itself as 're:connect' and was awarded funding to undertake the research by the Department of Health (Health Technology Device Agency) in partnership with a major medical device manufacturer.

One clinical member of the re:connect research team is a member of CEN (The European Committee for Standardization) Technical Board Task Force in Brussels. We presented our study to the committee and informed them of developments so that our work would be disseminated and may inform policy makers.

The design and testing of the connector system proposed adopts a human-factors engineering approach: focusing on the needs and characteristics of the user and rigorous user testing of the human-device interface. This user-centred, iterative approach provides the cultural basis of the work, but has not yet been widely adopted in the design of medical devices.

FIG. 02   Standard 'luer' type connector system

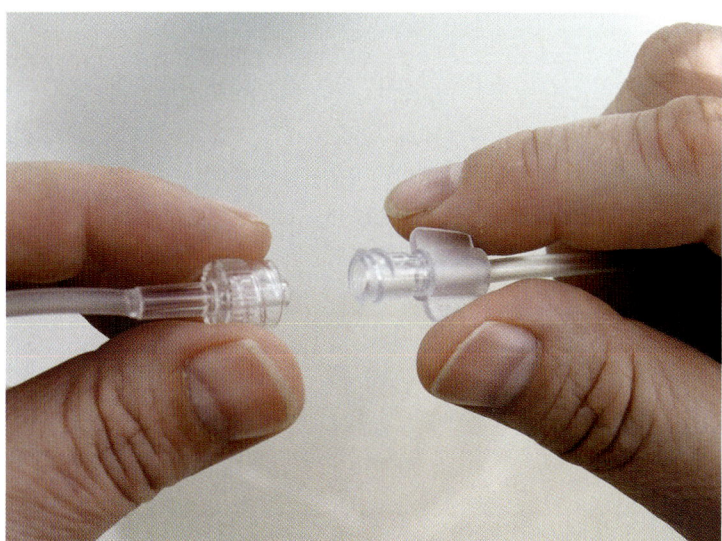

Haptic review

There exist key studies within perceptual psychology discourse that describe the various dimensions of human tactile sensitivity, and the ability to recognise and discriminate between different objects using the sense of touch.[06-08] While useful and relevant, these existing studies are not directly or specifically applicable to the design of products. However, key texts from the field of ergonomics and human factors engineering have provided evidence of the potential benefits of the application of tactile cue, in the design of product interfaces.[09-10]

Norman[11] stresses the importance of designing product controls that 'look and feel different', especially in safety critical applications. He gives an example of a control panel for a nuclear power station where operators have modified similar-looking switches by fitting them with different beer-pump handles to prevent misidentification.

Research carried out by the US Air Force investigated the benefits of shape-coded aircraft controls. In one study, Jenkins found that blindfolded pilots could identify specially shaped control knobs using only the sense of touch.[12] Another set of control knobs proposed by the US Air Force System Command[13] was designed to represent symbolically the intended function of the aircraft controls. These examples indicate the potential benefits of an identification system based on the use of contrasting shapes. However, the control knobs in these studies are much larger than those that would be used for a medical connector, and do not take account of the extensive range of materials, technologies and processes that are available today.

Medical review

Current drug delivery systems employ a common connector known as the 'luer',[FIG. 02] irrespective of the drug or route into the body. The clinical member of our research team, a consultant anaesthetist, conducted a survey that revealed that 23 per cent of possible medical connections could end in death or irreversible injury. Our objective was to ensure that the five generic delivery routes (intravenous, intrathecal, respiratory, cardio-vascular and enteral) cannot be connected with one another and are easily distinguishable.

FIG. 02

Observational research conducted at an intensive care unit at the Bradford Royal Infirmary showed that a 'makeshift' identification system was in use. This involved attaching self-adhesive paper strips onto delivery lines and writing drug codes or names by hand.

Colour could be used as means of discrimination, although there are concerns about relying on such a coding system. It is common practice on intensive care wards to maintain low levels of ambient light, which could make colour identification problematic. Additionally, there are already a huge number of colour-coding systems to contend with in hospitals, which often conflicts with companies corporate brand colours. Therefore, use of colour to

FIG. 03 System approach: The elements of the drug delivery system are linked by mating components with distinctive shapes and texture. They can therefore be matched like for like with other elements in the system.

FIG. 04 3D CAD renderings of 'virtual' prototype components

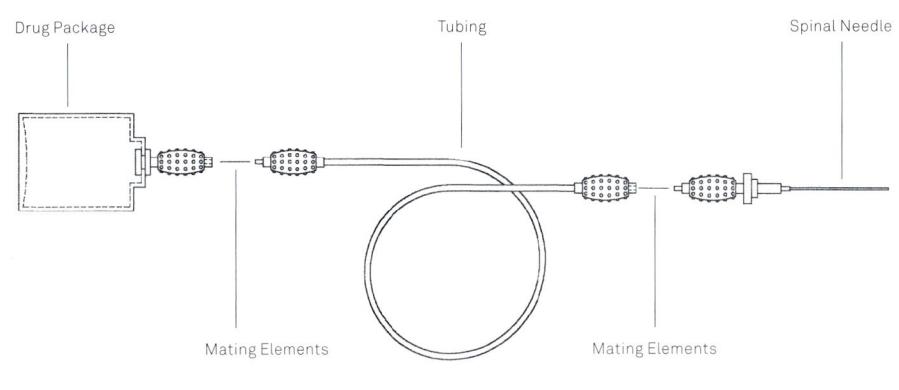

Drug Package

Tubing

Spinal Needle

Mating Elements

Mating Elements

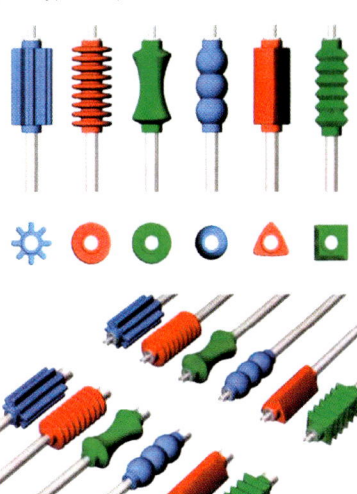

FIG. 05 3D 'real' physical prototype components

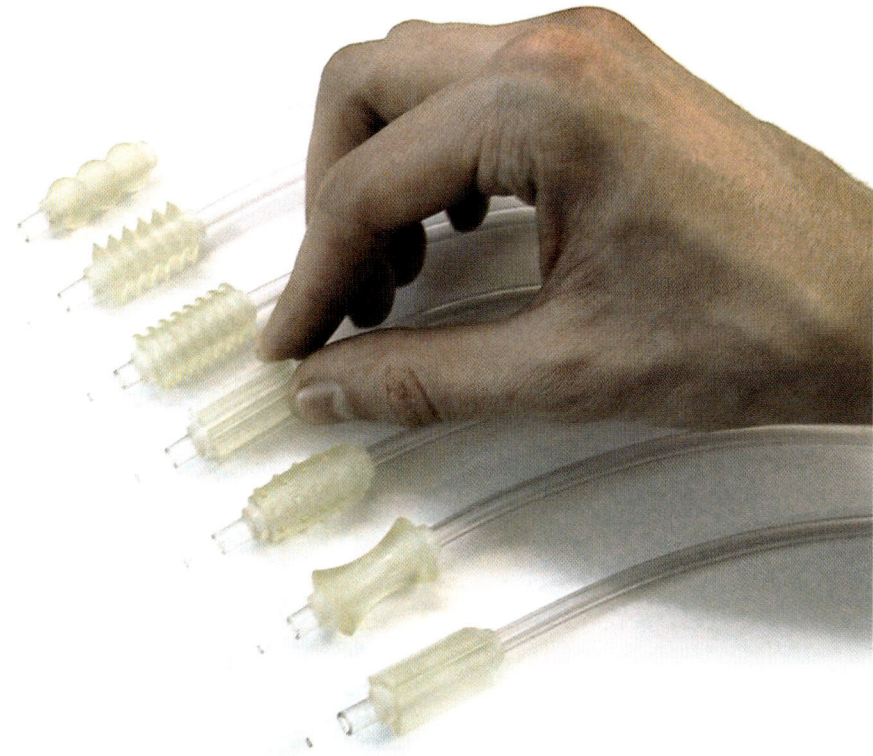

identify connectors may prove problematic; this is supported by NASA guidelines, which warn against applying colour coding to small items.[14]

A system that employs both visual and tactile cues could be particularly useful when clinicians are required to make connections that are often not in their immediate field of vision (clothing or blankets may obscure immediate sight or visual attention is directed to VDU monitors).

A series of controlled studies were undertaken by psychologists at the University of Leeds, utilising physical and virtual prototype connector designs developed by the Design team at Sheffield Hallam University. Studies informed the design of an easily discriminable set of shapes that could be used in conjunction with a non-interchangeable connection system.

Studies

A series of studies was undertaken by the research team to establish the potential benefits of haptic cues in the identification of small connector components.

Can shape help the discrimination and identification of connectors?

The underlying design principle behind the tactile identification system is that one connector with a particular external shape, recognisable using the sense of touch, should be matched with another connector of the same external shape. In other words, connectors should be matched like for like.[FIG. 03]

The design of the prototype connector components was based on combinations of simple, contrasting geometric elements. Some contrasting details may be interpreted as opposites, e.g. concave, convex. The cross section of the components was based on geometric primitives, i.e. square, circle or triangle. Other distinguishing features include the presence or absence of small surface details (texture). Early design concepts were developed through freehand sketches and drawings, leading to 3D CAD drawings [FIG. 04] and physical CAD models.[FIG. 05]

There is clearly scope to explore tactile properties of different materials in combination with shape and texture. However, there are practical limitations to material selection in some medical applications: for example, metal components would not be suitable in MRI scanners. The cost of the component has to be kept to a minimum, and elastomeric (flexible) material could allow a forced fit. For these reasons the team decided at an early stage to limit the material to a rigid plastic.

The testing procedure involved 25 participants who were healthcare professionals working in the intensive care unit at the Anaesthetic Department at Bradford Royal Infirmary. Participants were required to carry out matching tasks using seven prototype connector shapes, with vision and with their hands, and the prototype components hidden from sight behind a screen.[FIG. 06]

FIG. 03

FIG. 04

FIG. 05

FIG. 06

FIG. 07

The time taken to carry out the matching task was recorded using a millisecond stopwatch. Tests were carried out with both gloved and ungloved hands, using standard latex-free surgical gloves. Any identification errors were recorded.

Statistical analysis of the four conditions[FIG. 07] – 1. blind/gloved, 2. blind/ungloved, 3. vision/gloved, 4. vision/ungloved – of the mean identification times revealed an average error rate (connection of non-matching shapes) of 2.73 per cent. The mean identification times for four of the six prototype connectors was between 5 and 6 seconds. Two of the connectors took significantly longer to identify. This was because, at such a small scale, certain tactile features appeared to 'overlap': for example, the spacing of lateral ribs on one connector correlated almost exactly with the spacing of a pattern of bumps on another.

Modifications were made to the design, so that the tactile features no longer overlapped, and a second iteration of prototypes produced. The test procedure was repeated. In the second phase of tests, the mean rate of 'error' dropped from 2.72 per cent to 1.73 per cent.

The study showed the benefits of an identification system based on tactile cues, and highlights the potential for confusion when discriminating shapes without vision. Although the error rate in the second test was low at 1.73 per cent it would be considered unacceptable for safety-critical applications, since the consequences of any error would be very serious. Our recommendation would be to use the tactile identification system in conjunction with a failsafe mechanical system.

While error rate would be a factor in subsequent tests it was noted that, although fatal errors do occur as a result of the current luer type medical connector, the error rate is very small considering the number of medical procedures that take place. It was considered that comparing the findings of further tests and the final design outcome with the luer connector on error rate alone would be impractical due to the number of participant studies that would need to be conducted. It was therefore decided that a comparison would be better made on the basis of usability and 'setup' time to connect a typical system of medical devices. Error of connector identification would always have the safety net of a failsafe mechanical system. The shapes could help identify the correctly mating connectors as quickly as possible.

If the connector system is to have high usability, it is crucial that the connector shapes chosen are easy to tell apart from one another, i.e. they have good discriminability. Another important usability concern is that the shape of the connector must suggest to the user what its mode of connection might be, i.e. it affords the mode of connection. Its operation in use should be intuitive to the user.

At this stage there were a large number of potential connector shapes, which were permutations on four shapes – circle, square, triangle and cross. In order to reduce the number of potential connector shapes before prototyping and physical testing, two experiments were conducted to provide data on the affordances and the visual discriminability of the shapes.

Study 2: Discriminability – Card sort test

Rationale

FIG. 08
Laminated cards were produced with 3D CAD-rendered images of shapes and participants were asked to sort the potential connector shapes into groups based on similarity.[FIG. 08] It was reasoned that shapes seen as similar would be grouped with each other, and therefore these shapes would be difficult to distinguish from one another, but easier to tell apart from shapes in other categories. Shapes named as prototypes of groups should be most easy to distinguish from shapes in other groups.

Study 3: Affordance – computer decision task

Affordances can be defined as the combination of 'perceived and actual properties of the thing – primarily those fundamental properties that determine just how that thing could be used'.[15]

Rationale

FIG. 09
Using the software 'superlab', a study was conducted to determine the 'affordance' of shapes presented on a computer monitor.[FIG. 09] Participants responded to connector shape pairs by pressing either the 'P' key (push) or 'T' key (twist), according to whether their intuitive reaction was to push or twist the shapes together. It was reasoned that if there were high agreement on a certain shape, then that shape would afford the method of connection chosen. Furthermore, response times should indicate how obvious the affordance is for the participant, with fast responses indicating more obvious, stronger affordances.

General discussion and implications for connector system development

The experiments showed that complexity seems to have a bearing on both the discriminability, and the degree of affordance, of a potential connector shape. Where shapes are simple with one clear, distinguishing characteristic, they generally emerge as easily discriminable from other shapes, according to the extent of agreement between participants on how they should be grouped. Simple shapes were also named more often as prototypical of their category. Furthermore, simpler shapes seemed to produce more clear affordances, and generally elicited faster response times.

FIG. 06   User studies testing the tactile components coordinated by human factors team, Psychology Department, University of Leeds

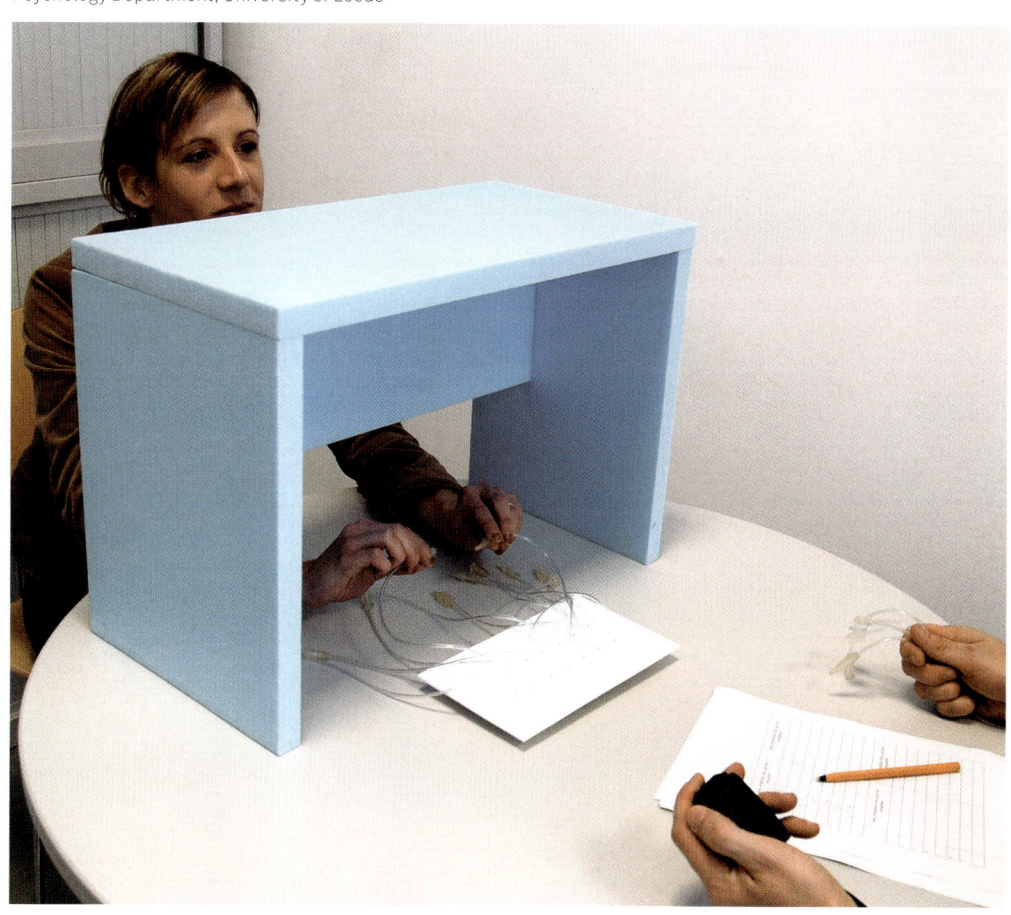

FIG. 07   Connector identification times

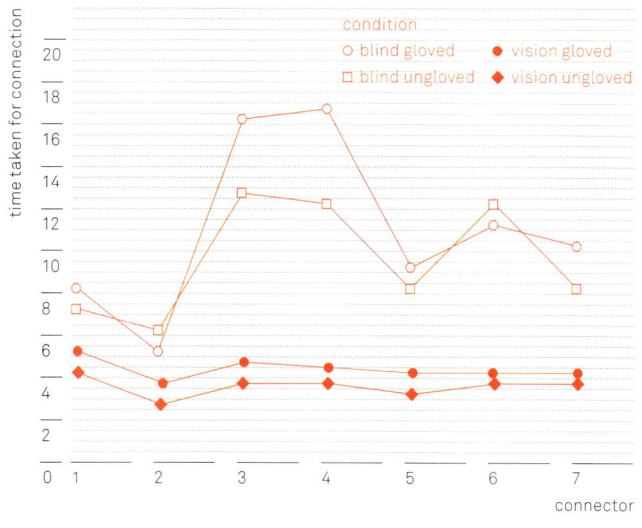

condition
○ blind gloved   ● vision gloved
□ blind ungloved   ◆ vision ungloved

time taken for connection

connector

FIG. 08   Card sort test. Participant sorting shapes into prototypical groups

FIG. 09   Visual affordance test

Participants agreed less on where more complex shapes, comprised of two or more characteristics, should be grouped. These shapes were also less often put forward as prototypes. Furthermore, more complex shapes produced less clear affordances, or affordance choices that were dependent upon the perspective from which the shapes were seen. It also took longer to respond to more complex shapes.

It appears that when shapes are composed of two or more characteristics, there is more capacity for confusion in judging both their discriminability and the mode of connection they afford. It is important that the affordance of the connector is clear from whichever angle it is seen, and so complex shapes, which elicit different affordance choices when viewed from different perspectives, should be avoided.

It is important to remember that the two experiments reported here are only informing us of the influence of visual cues. When participants have an actual connector shape to touch, the affordances of shapes may be different.

Study 4: Physical testing of connector shapes.

Rationale

The aim of the study was to discover if information on affordances and discriminability of connector shapes obtained from previous visual experiments extends to situations in which haptic (touch) cues are available to participants. Four sets of connector shapes[FIG. 10] were selected from the 'best-performing' 36 shapes used in earlier studies, and tested to determine which set contains shapes that are easiest to discriminate from one another, and hence quickest to correctly connect.

FIG. 10

Method

The participants' task was to identify the correct partner for each connector, and then to connect the male and female parts together. Participants wore surgical gloves at all times.

The time it took (in seconds) for participants to identify and join together all six pairs of connectors was recorded, as were the number of 'errors' (i.e. connectors attached to a connector of a different shape) and 'near-misses' (i.e. connectors almost connected to a connector of a different shape) made. These three measures (group connection time, number of errors, and number of near misses) were the dependent variables. Connections took place under two different lighting conditions: normal lighting and low light (to simulate conditions of an ICU at night). Each participant therefore connected eight sets in total (four groups of shapes x 2 light conditions). Figure 11 depicts the mean time taken to connect each group of connectors, in the two lighting conditions. Participants took significantly longer to connect

FIG. 11

FIG. 10   Set of 'physical'
connector shapes

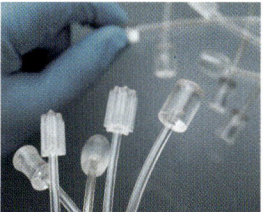

FIG. 12   Developing the connector system through physical prototyping, both enaled and
was informed by quantitative and qualitative data that emerged from the user-studies.

FIG. 11   Time taken to connect each group of connectors

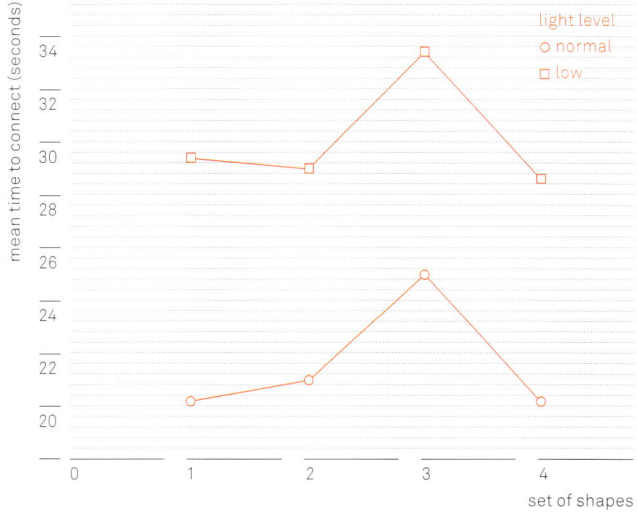

FIG. 12

the shapes in low light than in normal light. It can be seen that mean connection times for Sets 1, 2 and 4 are similar in both light conditions, whereas Set 3 took longer to connect under both light levels.

From these studies, optimum sets of shapes emerged that were most easily discriminable from one another. The outcome would now inform the design of non-interchangeable connector system.

Using the optimum discriminable sets of shapes that did not impede the function of connection by affording their mode of operation, the design team applied the knowledge in designing a connector system. They have created and patented a novel engineered solution as a means to enable connection of correctly mating shapes and prevent connection of incorrectly mated shapes. The design team have engineered a mechanical solution to prevent misconnection in combination with shape to speed the process of identification.FIG. 12

The designers were challenged by the intricate scale of the components and the engineering tolerances required to achieve operational standards, e.g. to provide a secure seal under pressure. The external shape, internal design details and material specification all have consequences as the manufacture and materials selected have had to be economic, medically approved and produced in a controlled environment to maintain engineered consistency.

Findings

Our early studies have demonstrated there is potential confusion of some shapes in the absence of vision, and that tactile cues can play an important role in helping identify and discriminate shapes. Further findings from our studies reveal that visual complexity seems to have a bearing on both discriminability and the degree of affordance of a potential connector shape. Testing of physical sets of shapes showed that some combinations of shapes are more difficult to identify and discriminate. However, while easy identification and discriminability are considered key factors in the design and usability of the proposed connection system, other functional factors described have defined the 'optimum' set of shapes. Importantly physical prototypes have proved to be vital tools in communicating and informing human response to haptic cues, as in the case of the Tac-Tile Sounds modules with deaf users, described above.

Conclusion

Design as an academic subject is still in its infancy compared with more established subjects such as engineering and science. There is much debate that aims to define the role of design research and its relationship with design practice. Designers and academics now face a significant milestone in shaping the role of design research and industrial production in the future global economy.

While this case study could be superficially viewed as design practice, providing a solution to a problem through the design of the a non-interchangeable medical connection system, knowledge and both quantitative and qualitative data have emerged from the project that may inform the use of haptics in other safety-critical situations.

Key to the research has been the designer's role in creating tools to establish this knowledge. As Rust suggests, 'creating artefacts can give us access to tacit knowledge, and can stimulate people to employ their tacit knowledge to form new ideas'.[16]

Fallman presents an interesting model that aims to define why 'Research-oriented design isn't Design-oriented Research'.[17] He suggests there is Design-oriented Research, which he describes as 'true', based on logic and analysis and usually involving our academic peers. He goes on to define Research-Oriented Design as 'real' based on judgment and intuition and normally involving a client.

From our studies we have established a set of 'shapes' that are most discriminable. We could describe our logical analytical approach in our early haptic studies in Fallman's terms as 'true'. However, through judgement, intuition and research-oriented design, the design team has now produced a detailed medical connector, and through addressing issues of manufacturability, cost and usability, have made some compromise in the implementation of the 'optimu' most discriminable shapes. The 'product' that has to satisfy the needs of both the manufacturer and user (clinician/patient) in Fallman's terms has become 'real'.

References / Bibliography

[01]	Foth M, Axup J (2006) Participatory Design and Action Research: Identical Twins or Synergetic Pair? In: Jacucci G, Kensing F, Blomberg J, Wagner I (eds): *Proceedings of the Participatory Design Conference 2006; Expanding Boundaries in Design*. Trento, Italy
[02]	Chamberlain P, Roddis J, Press M (1999) Good Vibrations. *Proceedings of the Third European Academy of Design Conference*. Sheffield Hallam University, UK, Vol. 3, 18–39
[03]	Berwick DM (2001) Not Again! *Br Med J* 322: 247–8
[04]	Toft B (2001) *External Inquiry into the Adverse Incident that Occurred at Queens Medical Centre, Nottingham on 4 January 2001*. UK Department of Health. www.npsa.nhs.uk/site/media/documents/824_toftqueensmedical.pdf (accessed 6 June 2007)
[05]	Woods K (2001) *The Prevention of Intrathecal Medical Errors: A Report to the Chief Medical Officer*. UK Department of Health. www.npsa.nhs.uk/site/media/documents/513_intrathecal.pdf (accessed 6 June 2007)
[06]	Gibson JJ (1962) Observations on Active Touch. *Psychol Rev* 69: 477–491
[07]	Hughes B, Jansson G (1994) Texture Perception via Active Touch. *Human Movement Science* 13: 301–333
[08]	Lederman SJ, Klatzky RL (1998) The Hand as a Perceptual System. In: Connolly K (ed.): *The Psychobiology of the Hand*. Cambridge University Press, Cambridge, 16–35
[09]	Burnett GE, Porter JM (2001) Ubiquitous Computing within Cars: Designing Controls for Non-visual Use. *International Journal of Human Computer Studies* 55: 521–531
[10]	Sanders MS, McCormick E (1993) *Human Factors in Engineering and Design*, 7th edition. McGraw Hill, New York, 184–196 and 334–344
[11]	Norman DA (1988) *The Psychology of Everyday Things*. Basic Books, New York, 95
[12]	Jenkins WO (1947) The Tactual Discrimination of Shapes for Coding Aircraft Type Controls. In: Fitts PM (ed.): *Psychological Research on Equipment Design*, Research Report 19, US Army Air Force, Aviation Psychology Program
[13]	Air Force System Command (1980) *Design Handbook 1–3. Human Factors Engineering*, 3rd edition. US Air Force
[14]	NASA Color Usage Research Lab. *Guidelines for Color Discrimination and Identification*. http://colorusage.arc.nasa.gov/guidelines_discrim_id.php/ (accessed 6 June 2007)
[15]	Gibson (1977) The Theory of Affordances. In: Shaw R, Bransford J (eds): *Perceiving, Acting and Knowing: Towards an Ecological Psychology*. John Wiley, London, 67–82
[16]	Rust C (2004) Design Enquiry: Tacit Knowledge and Invention. *Science Design Issues* 20(4): 76–85
[17]	Fallman D (2005) Why Research-oriented Design isn't Design-oriented Research. In: *Proceedings of Nordes: Nordic Design Research Conference* 29–31 May Copenhagen, Denmark

Research

For Inspiration Only

Designer interaction with informal collections of visual material

Abstract

To find out how designers collect and use visual material, this PhD research project combined working prototypes, theories and methods from different disciplines and contextual observations in a 'research through design' approach.

Initially working prototypes were used to infer knowledge from theory and practice; at the end the working prototypes were used to explore and gain knowledge about theory and practice.

Cabinet, the final prototype from this research, demonstrates how designers can be supported; it was placed in the designer environment to find its effect on collecting behaviour.

Research question

Designers surround themselves with visual material, such as snippets from magazines, photos and advertisements, as a source of inspiration in their work. These source materials are used in the design process in collages and moodboards presenting the vision or direction of a project. Currently designers use computers[01] to make these collages and so digital media and the Internet have been added as an important source for imagery. This shift to the digital comes with a great change in the way visual material is collected, used and organised.

In this research project the main questions were: (1) how do designers currently collect visual material for inspiration and (2) how can new media tools support this.

Background

This project was carried out in a line of research into tools for the conceptual phase of design called the IDEATE project.[02] The research was grounded in previous research on how designers use existing products in their design process [03, 04] and theories of design as an activity of organising and structuring.[05] Before the project, the IDEATE project had researched and developed tools and methods for sketching,[06] 3d-modelling [07] and visual interaction.[08]

In 1999, this research line was integrated into the ID-StudioLab,[09] a user-centred design community in the Faculty of Industrial Design of the Delft University of Technology. The ID-StudioLab aims to perform research from the perspective of a designer, which includes working in a studio environment on different projects, working and communicating visually and stimulating the creation of working prototypes. Because most of the researchers at the ID-StudioLab are designers, and the goal of the research is to build tools for designers, a special emphasis is put on living with the prototypes. This means using the prototypes oneself on a daily basis on one's own initiative: the research equivalent of 'eating your own dog food'.

Methods

The two research questions needed methods that both look at the current situation of the design practice and forecast to the future for the possibility of new media tools.[10] To accomplish these goals a mix of methods was used; it consisted of theoretic exploration, ethnographic observations, interaction design explorations, usability experiments, and action research through working prototypes. The common thread linking these methods is that they are all scientific equivalents of existing design methods: where a designer would use observation techniques to gain a better understanding for design, a design researcher would use ethnographic methods to generate knowledge about a phenomenon, and where a designer would sketch and generate models as a solution for a problem, a design researcher would develop a working prototype as a container, demonstrator and generator of knowledge about a phenomenon. This new approach to design research, and specifically the prototyping part, is the foundation for the 'Research through Design' approach.[11]

The remainder of this chapter will illustrate this method of 'Research through Design' in both methods and results, by explaining how the research project took us from building a theoretical framework FIG. 01 towards setting out a working prototype in practice.FIG. 02

At the outset of the project a theoretical framework was developed by involving research and design experts from different fields, with their own jargon, theories and contexts. Using a creative elicitation technique called Mind Mapping,[12] these experts were asked to make associations with images showing collections of visual material. The keywords and references that came out of these sessions were used as input for a literature search over different disciplines varying from design methodology to computer science and from cognitive psychology to library studies.FIG. 01

The theoretical framework was used as input for an exploration of technology through working prototypes. To find out about the current use of visual material by designers a contextual inquiry was also performed.

At the end of the project, Cabinet, a working prototype of a tool for designers to collect visual material, was put in the designer work practice for three months.FIG. 02 This experiment, set up as an action research, aimed to research the effect of new tools and the new uses they can generate.

Results

Literature on collections of visual material can roughly be divided into two disciplines: (1) the 'categorisation approach' from library studies and media studies, in which collections are seen from the perspective of adding material, and (2) the 'engineering approach' from computer science and computer human interaction, where collections are seen from the perspective of taking material out. Literature on the role of visual material in creativity and design methodologies focus much more on design as an iterative activity, where visual material is a tool for iteration and exploration.[13] These activities require expressive tools that are sensitive to the context in which creative activities take place.[14]

The traditional tools and environment of designers are filled with rich visual material such as sketches, photos, models and collages.FIG. 03 With the advent of new media and powerful graphic computing in the last decade, tool developers have been too focused on the numerous possibilities of these new tools and have become insensitive to the richness of media, social interaction with colleagues, and whole body interaction.FIG. 04

The first prototype developed in this project, the TRI Setup,FIG. 05 was a *context-sensitive technology exploration* in bringing these aspects back into tool development. The TRI Setup (short for Three Ranges of Interaction and 'trying') is a human-scaled interaction

FIG. 01
FIG. 02

FIG. 01

FIG. 02

FIG. 03

FIG. 04
FIG. 05

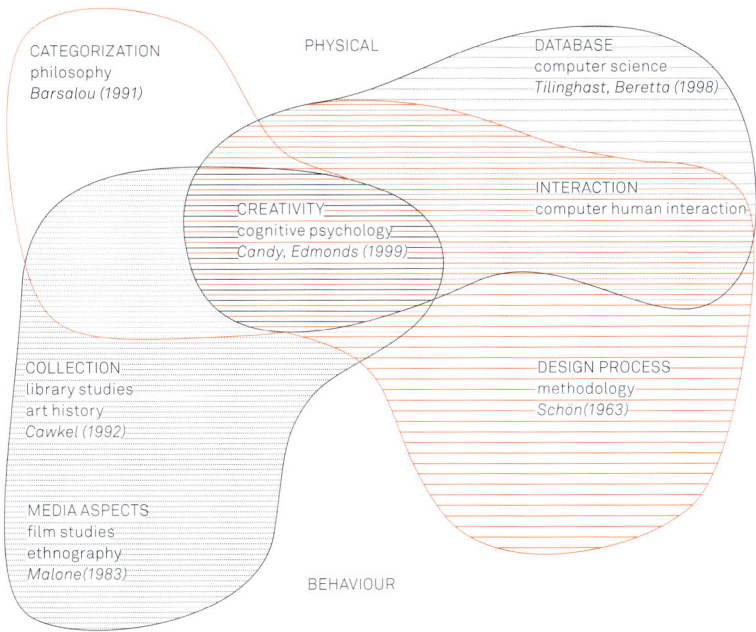

FIG. 02   Cabinet: a working prototype
of designer's tool for collecting visual
material in use by a designer during
field research

FIG. 03   Typical work environment for
a designer: surrounded by collages,
photos, sketches and other visual
material for reference and inspiration
on the walls and table. Note that
the colleague can see the designer's
work right away.

FIG. 04   Typical work environment for
a designer as seen from the perspective of new tool developers: the
computer is the only omnipotent
tool, replacing the rich environment
and social interaction in one multi-
purpose tool with limited input.

platform, in which new media can be easily and expressively mixed with physical media on large projection displays and with novel expressive input devices.[15] The TRI Setup was not a solution in itself, but a platform on which tools and prototypes could be created and, most of all, an experiment in living with prototypes as it was an integrated part of the ID-StudioLab for over five years.

FIG. 06

The contextual inquiry with five designers – consisting of a sensitising cultural probe, an interview at the workplace and a tour of the design agency – provided rich material about how designers currently use visual material. The main observation was that designers really surround themselves with a rich collection of physical visual materials. FIG. 06

FIG. 07
TABLE 01
FIG. 08

However the designers all used the computers to make collages forcing them in a verbal, goal-oriented mode. FIG. 07 Finally the contextual inquiry led to six considerations for a tool to support the collecting behaviour by designers. TABLE 01 These six considerations were the main input for the development of the Cabinet prototype. FIG. 08

TABLE 01   Considerations for a collecting tool derived from contextual inquiry

Active collecting	Designers collect visual material as a part of their way of working, as an ongoing background activity; not as a focused task. Cabinet should always be available to support this activity.
Merger of physical and digital worlds	The separate physical and digital collections of visual material serve the same function: as a source of inspiration. Designers want to use the images together, but a task such as scanning physical material is too large a threshold for a smooth, inspirational
Visual interaction	Designers use digital images only for collages and for presentations to clients. Computer workflows force the designer into a verbal mode: searching on keywords, naming files and placing them in named directories. Cabinet's interactions should support visual thinking.
Serendipitous encounters	Designers personalise their physical environment and surround themselves with rich information sources. They often stumble upon interesting artefacts and they enjoy being surprised or reminded. Cabinet should allow this to happen.
Breaking the rhythm and involving the body	The body plays an important role in creativity: breaks from the computer, and large movements of the body are found to loosen the mind. Cabinet should involve the full body, not just the hand.
Social aspects of visual material	Designers who share a studio know about each other's work through visible physical collections. Cabinet should also bring the collection out in the open.

FIG. 08, 09

Cabinet, the final prototype from this research integrates the results from the research done before. Cabinet FIG. 08, 09 is a tool that helps designers to collect, organise and use visual materials in their daily work.

FIG. 05   TRI Setup in use in a design context: large wall projection shows collages, physical models can be enhanced with projected textures and interfaces on the table projection.

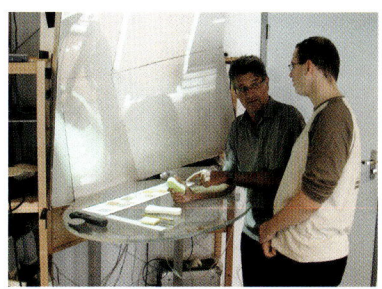

FIG. 06   Observations on work environment: designer surrounded by visual material, which is collected over time, arranged on a large area, but still within reach.

FIG. 07   Observations on computer: collages are made on the computer, with folders and names for each element on the collages, in a goal-oriented and efficient manner.

FIG. 08   The Cabinet prototype (right) in a designer context, placed near the printer, to allow for serendipitous encounters.

FIG. 09

Cabinet consists of a table-sized interaction area with an overhead projection and grabbing system. With Cabinet designers can easily collect both digital and physical material and interact with digital visual material in a physical, expressive way. FIG. 09

The purpose of Cabinet was both to show the possibilities of new media and to gain knowledge of how new media could influence the role of visual material in the design process. Cabinet was therefore set out in the field for three months at three different agencies

FIG. 01, 08

in a *technology supported contextual exploration*. FIG. 01, 08 In this action research-based experiment, designers were asked to use Cabinet in their current design processes and on their own initiative. The six considerations from the contextual inquiry served as hypotheses in the experiment.

Results from the log-files, observations and interviews showed that the line between

FIG. 10

physical and digital visual material really was blurred, FIG. 10 and that collecting visual material became an integral, continuous activity in the designer's work processes.

Although Cabinet itself was not the subject of the experiment, but an instrument in it, the three months in the field did provide us with a lot of feedback on Cabinet as an interface and tool. The interaction with Cabinet was readily accepted by all participants with minimal instructions (a seven-minute instruction movie on a DVD). We received 19 suggestions and features that could improve the interaction with Cabinet, such as allowing multiple croppings, and changes in physical appearance of Cabinet. Most of all, the collections by partici-

FIG. 11

pants were varied and produced unexpected combinations. FIG. 11 Most notably, all the designers integrated their own solutions, in the form of sketches, renderings and illustrations, with the material by others collected for inspiration, blurring the line between collages and concepts. [16]

Discussion

The ambition of this research project was both to gain knowledge of the role of visual material in the design practice and to see how new media tools could support this. The first part is readily supported by the current scientific methods and discourse. The methods and discourse are still in development for the latter part, but it is typically an area where design research should play a role. The design methods and skills are typically adept to approach questions that require integrated knowledge from diverse disciplines and to offer a vista into future possibilities.

This method of generating knowledge through the creation of working prototypes is also very suitable for a researcher with a design background – or a designer doing research. The combination of a quest for fundamental understanding and consideration of use as described in 'Pasteur's Quadrant' [17] can easily be translated from the field of medicine to that of design. Similar to Pasteur in table 2, this research project aimed to achieve fundamental

TABLE 02

understanding, without losing sight of considerations of use. Research inspired by: TABLE 02

FIG. 09   Interaction with Cabinet. Upper row: adding physical material by laying a magazine, book or object on the table. The material is photographed from above and projected in place. Lower row: interacting with thumbnails and grouping thumbnails on stacks

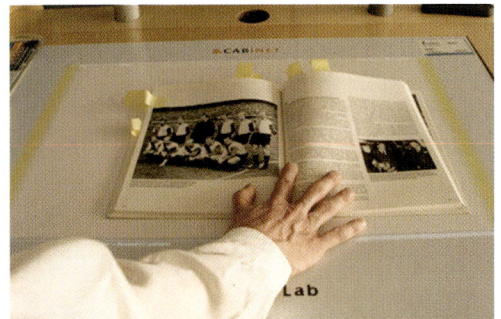

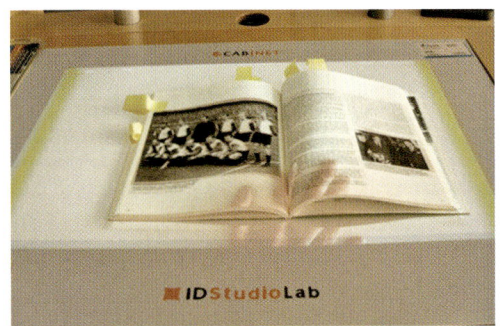

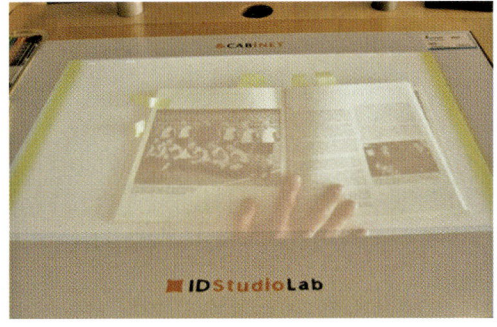

TABLE 02 Pasteur's Quadrant setting out different types of research based on what drives them

		Considerations of use	
		No	Yes
Quest for fundamental understanding	Yes	Pure Basic (Bohr)	Use-inspired (Pasteur)
	No		Pure Applied (Edison)

The knowledge generated has been disseminated both through the regular process of scientific publication, and through the creation of working prototypes.

The prototypes in this project serve the purpose of demonstrating the application of knowledge, but also as the generators of knowledge themselves. By setting out Cabinet in the field, it was possible to observe the designer's behaviour over a longer period of time. The numerous presentations of Cabinet to designers, researchers and other visitors initiated many discussions on visual material and new media tools. Most of the discussions however, entailed new possible applications of such a tool, exemplifying the *research for inspiration* approach.

Acknowledgements

This research would not have been possible without the support of all the members of the ID-StudioLab, especially Aldo Hoeben and Aadjan van der Helm, and the designers who participated in the different field studies.

FIG. 10 Observation of the physical-digital blurring during the experiment: one participant used a physical sticky note on the surface with instructions 'Begin here! [BEGINN HIER!]' (middle) and a digital sticky note scanned in using Cabinet saying 'I mean here! [HIER DUS!]' to instruct her colleagues to stay within a specific stack and keep her own collection untouched.

FIG. 11 Screenshots of three collections by the three participants. A very structured collection of digital material on the left, a combination of illustrations, photos, spreads and interfaces in the middle, and annotated stacks of physical sketches grouped with source material on the right.

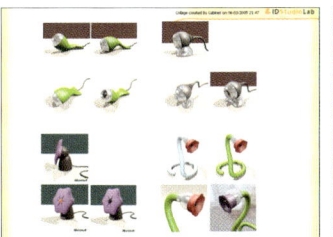

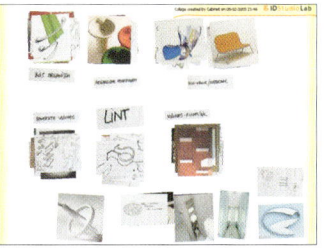

References / Bibliography

_____   _____

[01]   Keller AI, Pasman GJ, Stappers PJ (2006) Collections Designers Keep: Collecting
                Visual Material for Inspiration and References. *Codesign: International Journal of
                CoCreation in Design and the Arts* 2(1): 17–33

[02]   Hennessey JM (1990) The Designer's Toolkit. *Proceedings of the 22nd International
                Seminar on Industrial Design and CIDA Congress, Taipei and Tainan, Taiwan, 2–16*

[03]   Kolli R, Pasman GJ, Hennessey JM (1993) Some Considerations for Designing a User
                Environment for Creative Ideation. *Proceedings of the Interface '93, North Carolina
                State University, Raleigh, NC,* 72–77

[04]   Pasman GJ (2003) *Designing with Precedents.* PhD thesis, Delft University of
                Technology

[05]   Muller W (2001) *Order and Meaning in Design.* Lemma, Utrecht

[06]   Hoeben A, Stappers PJ (2001) Ideas: Concepts for a Designers' Sketching-tool.
                *Proceedings of CHI 2001, Conference on Human Factors in Computing Systems,
                Seattle, WA,* 199–200

[07]   Gribnau MW (1999) *Two-handed Interaction in Computer Supported 3D Conceptual
                Modelling.* PhD thesis, Delft University of Technology

[08]   Stappers PJ, Pasman GJ (1999) Exploring a Database through Interactive Visualised
                Similarity Scaling. *Proceedings of CHI '99, Human Factors in Computer Systems,
                Pittsburgh, PA,* 184–185

[09]   Hekkert PPM, Keyson DV, Overbeeke K, Stappers PJ (2000) The Delft ID-StudioLab:
                Research through and for Design. *Proceedings of Symposium on Research in the
                Netherlands,* Eindhoven University of Technology, the Netherlands

[10]   Sanders EB-N (2004) *Design and the Empowerment of Everyday People.* Lecture given
                at the Delft University of Technology

[11]   Stappers PJ (2005) Designing as a Part of Research. *Proceedings of Design and the
                Growth of Knowledge Symposium, Delft University of Technology,* 10–15

[12]   Buzan T, Buzan B (1994) *The Mind Map Book: How to Use Radiant Thinking to Maximize
                your Brain's Untapped Potential.* BBC Books, London

[13]   Eckert CM, Stacey MK (2000) Sources of Inspiration: A Language of Design. *Design
                Studies* 21(5): 523–538

[14]   Stappers PJ, Keller AI, Hoeben A (2000) Aesthetics, Interaction, and Usability in
                'Sketchy' Design Tools. *Exchange Online Journal* 1(1)

[15]   Keller AI, Stappers PJ, Hoeben A (2000) TRI: Inspiration Support for a Design Studio
                Environment. *International Journal of Design Computing,* University of Sydney

[16]   Keller AI (2005) *For Inspiration Only, Designer Interaction with Informal Collections of
                Visual Material.* PhD thesis, Delft University of Technology

[17]   Stokes, DE (1997). Pasteur's Quadrant: Basic Science and Technological Innovation.
                Washington, DC: Brookings Institution

_____   _____

Research through Design: a Camera Case Study [01]

01 | In this article I report on research that was performed as part of my PhD, emphasising the methodology that was applied. For a complete report I refer the reader to my PhD thesis [01]

Abstract

Information-for-use has become abstracted from human skills during the rise of interactive products. This chapter describes the search for a new interaction paradigm for interactive products, applying a research through design approach. Five conceptual cameras were designed to explore the solution domain for this new paradigm, named rich interaction. One of the proposals was elaborated into a modular, working prototype. The prototype accepts different interface modules to vary the interaction style of the camera from rich to conventional. In an experiment the interaction styles were compared.

FIG. 01

Introduction

This article focuses on highly interactive products. Such products can be seen as having three properties: form, interaction and function.[FIG. 01] Central to this model is the notion that these properties are related to each other. For form invites interaction, and in this interaction functionality is achieved.

When we compare interactive products to more traditional non-interactive products we see that they differ in how they provide information-for-use. During the rise of interactive products, information-for-use gradually became more and more abstract. For example, a person can directly perceive what a drinking glass is for, and how it can be used, from its form. The information-for-use is a natural consequence of form and use, and thus is directly available. In contrast, a person needs to read and interpret the labels on the controls of a digital camera to understand what he or she can do with it. In this case the information-for-use is much more abstract. There is a difference in how people's skills are addressed. Overbeeke *et al.* identify three types of human skills that are relevant in this context: perceptual-motor, emotional and cognitive skills.[02] Where the earlier products address all of people's skills, the new electronic interactive products mainly address people's cognitive skills. The focus of interaction with products has shifted from an action-based paradigm to a cognition-based one.

The reason for this shift is that the design of the form and interaction are explicitly separated. In interactive products, a designer is free to choose which controls to use on their interfaces. The controls on the interfaces are not determined by the functional components, but are coupled to electronic hardware through programming. At the same time, designers of interactive products have virtually complete freedom of form. The functional components of interactive products have become so small that they no longer impose a form. Electronics give designers freedom, not only because they are small but also because a designer is free to choose how to control them. With the advent of electronics the 'real' interface was born and interaction style was now 'designable'. This fact made it possible to design the form of electronic products separately from the interaction.

When we regard state-of-the-art interactive products it is striking to see that form is richly varied but interaction is standardised. In fact, design of interaction is heavily influenced by design principles borrowed from the human-computer interaction (HCI) community.[03] For products to offer information-for-use inspired by function and interaction they need to be opened up for all human skills. I believe that the design process of interactive electronic products needs to be adapted to accomplish this. I propose an integral design process for interactive products, inspired by the traditional design process; one where form, interaction and function are explored and designed concurrently in order to integrate them into dedicated interactive products; a design process where information-for-use is inspired by function, and where human skills are central to interaction. But before considering this further, I first explain my research approach and address my research question.

Approach and research question

In this article I explore new interaction paradigms for interactive consumer products. I choose to do this in a typically designerly manner, by designing interactive products, by conducting research through design.

Research through design

Research through design is similar to Archer's 'research through practice'.[04] Archer recognises research through practice as a form of action research, which he defines as 'Action Research: Systematic investigation through practical action calculated to devise or test new information, ideas, forms or procedures and to produce communicable knowledge',[04] p. 6. He warns that since action research is situation-specific it is 'difficult and dangerous to generalise from Action Research findings',[04] p. 12. What is important in this statement is the word: 'situation-specific'. For me this implies two things. First, the skills of the designer play an important role; it is through the designerly skills that the problem area unfolds. Second, the knowledge gained through a research through practice project is applicable to a specific situation. Or as Hummels states, it leads 'to conditional laws instead of general laws'.[05] In the case of design it is applicable to a specific class of products and its design process. Archer states that a practitioner should position himself in opinion and theory concerning the domain in which the knowledge from his research is applicable.[04]

Knowledge on two levels can be gathered when researching product design. We can research aspects of the products themselves, such as form or interface, but we can also research the process of how these products came into existence. When conducting research through design, both types of knowledge are intertwined. Knowledge of products and knowledge of the process of designing these products are generated. Products are designed to explore the implications of theory in context. The resulting products are subjected to experimentation in real-life situations to understand the complex relationship of humans and designed reality. The assumption underlying the research-through-design approach is that knowledge gained from these products, through experimentation, can be generalised in the form of design specifications for future products and in new theory or frameworks.

Four questions and answers

This article is organised around four questions. First, what will be the basis for this alternative interaction paradigm? Second, what is the solution domain of this new interaction paradigm? Third, how does such a new interaction paradigm compare to the old one? Fourth, how can this new paradigm be characterised? Here these questions are answered in a designerly manner, doing research through design. The first question is answered by taking position in theory, the second by designing, the third through experimentation, and finally, the fourth question is answered in a reflection on the answers to the first three.

Question one: on what will this new interaction paradigm be based?

To answer the first question I position myself in theory.[04] Two areas of research form the background for the new interaction paradigm explored in this research: the area of tangible interaction [06, 07] and the theory of direct perception.[08] Tangible interaction is one of the few HCI interaction styles concerned with the physical. It involves the use of physical objects to interact with computer systems, offers function-specific interfaces, and involves more human skills than only cognitive ones. Tangible interaction offers opportunities for embodied interaction.[09] The theory of direct perception (particularly the notion of affordances) provides deeper insight into how information-for-use can be given.

Rich interaction

Inspired by tangible interaction and the concept of affordances I propose the term 'rich interaction'. This is a new interaction paradigm for interactive consumer products. Tangible interaction inspires the use of 'action-driven' interaction, while the concept of affordances inspires and steers the usage of information-for-use. Respecting and starting from people's skills, rich interaction aims for aesthetic interaction through a unity of form, interaction and function. In more detail this means:

— *Starting from people's skills:* Information-for-use relates directly to all human skills (perceptual-motor, emotional and cognitive skills), instead of abstractly to cognitive skills alone.
— *Aiming for aesthetic interaction:* Several researchers in the area of design-related research pursue something that they have dubbed 'aesthetic interaction' [05, 10, 11, 12, 13]. Opinions differ on what aesthetic interaction is. For now I propose to use the working definition: 'aesthetic interaction is the aesthetic experience that only can be had while interacting.'
— *Integrating form, interaction and function:* In the introduction I mentioned three properties of interactive products; form, interaction and function. In traditional artefacts these properties are strongly and meaningfully related. For example, the form of a hammer invites interaction: we can grab the shaft to swing the hammer. In this interaction with the hammer its functionality is reached: hammering nails into pieces of wood. The form of the hammer not only invites us to hammer, it also expresses the hammer's function. The relations between form, interaction and function carry information-for-use.

In state-of-the-art interactive products there is no technical reason for these meaningful relations to exist. As a result they are eased. A product can have any form, buttons are added for interaction, and functionality is delivered in unified software platforms. However, in line with Wensveen *et al.*, who state that form is not arbitrary,[14] I argue for the restoration of these meaningful relations to accomplish a unity of form, interaction and function. Rich interaction is about inviting us to interact through form, thus achieving functionality. It is about expressing functionality in form and action-possibilities. The designerly skills of product designers are essential for accomplishing this.

FIG. 02

Although product designers are trained in such integration in traditional products I believe that interactive products offer more aspects that need integration. I distinguish six aspects that can be explored in a design process.[FIG. 02]

Of course, the six fields of exploration do not all operate at the same level, and they should not be regarded in isolation. The framework demonstrates the width of the exploration space and provides handles for designing the three properties of interactive products and their relations concurrently. For example, by exploring the interplay between form and interaction (e.g. how does form invite specific interactions, how can different action-possibilities be expressed in form), the relation between the two is explored as well.

———————————————

Question two: what is the solution domain of this new interaction paradigm?

Exploring and demonstrating rich interaction by designing

I explained above what rich interaction is in words. But I believe that what is meant by rich interaction is best explored and demonstrated with product designs. In 'doing design' the knowledge that is implicit in design skills is made explicit. Through the process of designing actual product concepts rich interaction is physically defined. Theory of tangible interaction and affordances is applied to the new concept in a designerly manner. The resulting product concepts are physical hypotheses to test rich interaction, which can be tested in experiments.

FIG. 03

Five digital camera concepts were designed.[FIG. 03] The design explorations were done in an experiential manner, using the framework for exploration introduced above. A combination of sketching, foam-core modelling and cardboard modelling techniques was applied, while user-actions (as part of interaction) were used as a starting point for the designs. Step-by-step combinations of form, interaction and function were researched, put into form and tested, thereby exploring all six fields and evaluating their solution domains.

The design process is an iterative one in which pre-models are built, tested and modified until they meet the requirements set by the designer. Through the cycle of building, testing and changing pre-models, the quality of the combinations was assessed in terms of aesthetics of interaction and information-for-use.

To spark the creative process of designing rich interactive cameras, five sub-themes were defined. The themes were restrictive so as to force design challenges to the surface, a common practice in creativity techniques.[10] There was another reason for creating the themes as well. The themes were defined to cover a broad area of the potential solution domain for interaction paradigms. I tried to find a balance between real-world design problems

FIG. 01   Three properties of interactive products

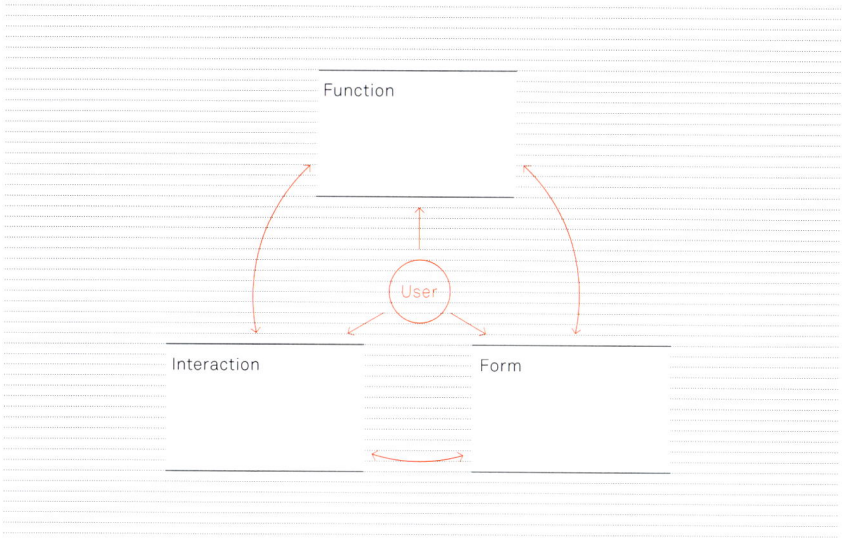

FIG. 02   A framework for exploration

and trends in HCI research. They range from technology driven solutions to human-centred solutions and from the pragmatic to the unusual.

Characteristics of rich interaction

While designing the five concept-cameras, I found that two typical characteristics of rich interaction kept resurfacing as a result of integrating form, interaction and function: mode-relevant action-possibilities, and mode-of-use reflected in physical state.

Mode-relevant action-possibilities (MRAPs)   Mode-relevant action-possibilities are action-possibilities that are only provided when they are relevant for the mode-of-use. They can be characterised as: (1) dedicated to a function, (2) offering meaningful integration of form and function, and (3) expressing functionality in form and interaction. For example the lever to browse saved pictures is accessible only when the 'Labelless Cam' is in view-mode. This contrasts with products with ordinary interfaces that often show all action-possibilities all the time, even if they have no function.[FIG. 04]

FIG. 04

Mode of use reflected in physical state (MURPS)   To reflect the mode-of-use in the physical state means that in each mode-of-use the form of a product is different. MURPS can be characterised as: (1) offering integration of form and function, and (2) offering autonomy (symmetry) in product behaviour in relation to user actions. For example, the 'Control per Function Cam' looks different when in camera mode than when in view-mode. This differs from ordinary interfaces, which commonly do not change shape, but always have the same form.[FIG. 05]

FIG. 05

Explorative user study

FIG. 03

The 'camera without labels on its controls'[FIG. 03] was chosen for use in a first, explorative experiment because it fitted the theoretical background of this research-through-design project best. Moreover, it integrated the two typical characteristics most beautifully. From here on this camera is referred to as the Rich Interactive Camera (RUI camera). It was compared with a more traditional camera in terms of intuitiveness of interaction. For this experiment, two cardboard mock-ups of the digital cameras were used. Two main conclusions were drawn from the experiment.

First, to assess the quality of an interaction style, we need working, interactive prototypes. Interaction is an intangible quality of products, which is present only while interacting. Imagined interaction is not interaction. The consequence of this is obviously that to assess the quality of rich interaction a working, interactive prototype of the camera needs to be built.

Second, people were unable to compare the use of the cameras because the difference in form was an obstacle. The form of the cameras proved to suggest different contexts of use,

FIG. 03   Five digital camera concepts

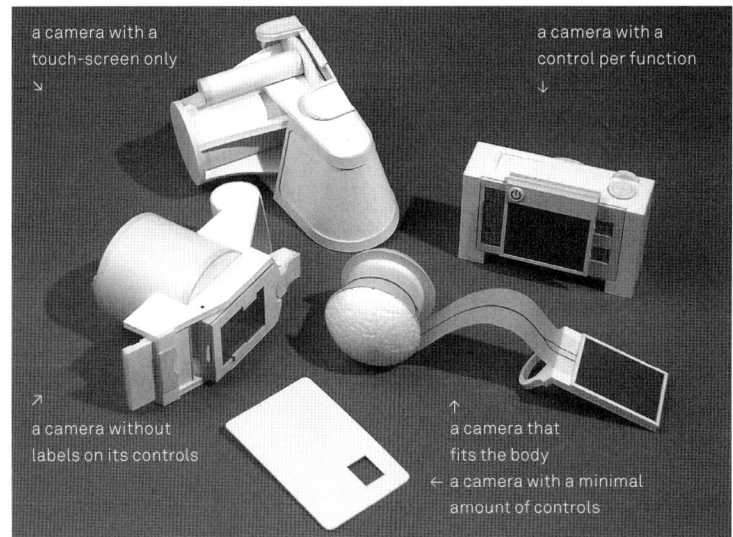

a camera with a
touch-screen only
↙

a camera with a
control per function
↓

↗
a camera without
labels on its controls

↑
a camera that
fits the body
← a camera with a minimal
amount of controls

FIG. 04   Mode-relevant action-possibilities

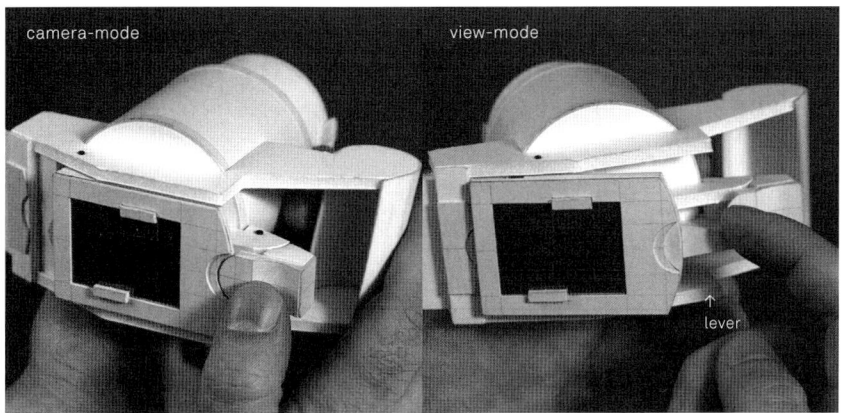

camera-mode

view-mode

lever

all action-possibilities
always visible

FIG. 05   Mode-of-use reflected in physical state

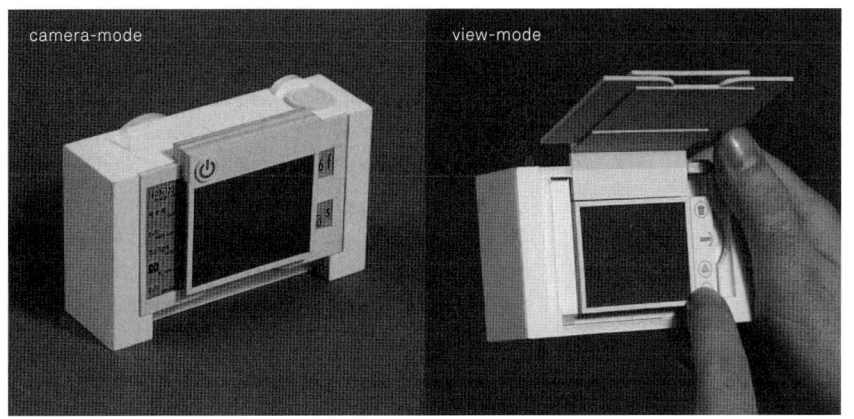

camera-mode

view-mode

same form in each
mode-of-use

and thus to imply different interaction possibilities. To minimise the influence of form it should be the same for each camera compared. That is, the form of the cameras should be as similar as possible, while the interaction style of the cameras is varied.

This means that to compare the rich interaction style with a more conventional interaction style experimentally, we need working prototypes that have the same form as far as possible. To accomplish this I decided to build a modular working prototype of the digital camera, so that it can accept different interface modules, each reflecting different interaction styles.

Working prototype with interface modules

The design of the digital camera was slightly adapted for reasons of modularity and manufacturability. The design was also scaled up 125 per cent to fit the functional parts. The workings of the digital camera are based on a commercially available camera. The body of the camera and the interface modules were machined out of aluminium.[FIG. 06]

FIG. 06

Modules   Above, I identified two typical characteristics of rich interaction that resulted from the integration of form, interaction, and function; 'mode-relevant action-possibilities' (MR APs) and 'mode-of-use reflected in physical state' (MURPS). These two characteristics adequately describe the differences between the rich interactive camera (RUI camera) and a camera with a conventional interface. The RUI camera has both MR APs and MURPS; a conventional camera has neither. Four interface modules were designed. Each module has a different interaction style, systematically varied based on the differences between the original RUI camera and conventional digital cameras. Together, the four interface variations span a range of interaction styles from rich to conventional.[FIG. 07]

FIG. 07

The four interface modules each offer the same basic functionality and have the same three modes-of-use. Pictures can be taken in 'camera-mode', and they can be played back in 'view-mode'. The camera also features a special 'instant-review-mode' in which one can choose to save or discard pictures after they are taken.

The first interface variation is the RUI camera (cell I). It provides controls that express what they are for and how they can be operated. The camera offers only the controls that are relevant for the active mode-of-use; in each of the modes-of-use it offers different action-possibilities. It also expresses its mode-of-use in its form.

The second interface variation has MURPS but not MR APs (cell II). It provides a combination of ordinary buttons and expressive controls. Its form expresses which mode-of-use it is in, but it does not offer mode-relevant controls; instead it offers all controls all of the time.

The third interface variation has MR APs but not MURPS (cell III). Next to an ordinary button and a switch it provides a touch-sensitive surface where buttons can be projected. It offers (projected) controls only when they are relevant for the mode-of-use. Its form does not express its mode-of-use; it does not change form.

The fourth interface variation is an adaptation of a conventional camera (cell IV). It has only ordinary buttons. It offers all controls all of the time and it does not change form.

FIG. 06   Working prototype of the RUI camera

FIG. 06   Working prototype of the RUI camera

FIG. 07   Four interface variations in a grid

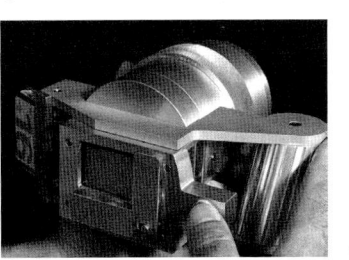

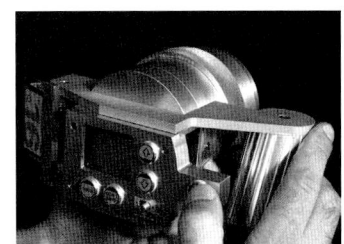

Question three: how does such a new interaction paradigm compare to the old one?

Experiment

An experiment was set up to compare the rich interaction paradigm with the more conventional interaction paradigm. The experiment is expected to provide insight into the concept of aesthetic interaction. The experiment tests the influence of MR APs and MURPS. Finally, the experiment is expected to offer insight into the relevance of HCI usability measures for the domain of interactive consumer products.

Participants   Twenty-four participants, ranging in age from 19 to 29 years old, took part in the experiment. They were all students from the Architecture Department of the Eindhoven University of Technology.

Stimuli   This experiment compared the four interface variations, which were fitted onto a working prototype of a digital camera, resulting in four prototypes of digital cameras with different interaction styles.[FIG. 07] A composition of books and vintage computers was set up to act as a still-life to be photographed in the experiment.[FIG. 08]

FIG. 07
FIG. 08

Setting   The experiment took place in a photographic studio. The still-life was set up on a table and lighted by means of three studio lamps. A white line was marked on the ground 60 cm in front of the table. A table with video equipment, a computer and a turntable was placed in the back of the studio. Two chairs were placed at the table, one for the participant and one for the experimenter. A video camera was set up in the middle of the studio. It could be pointed at the still-life setup or at the table setup.[FIG. 09]

FIG. 09

Procedure   The experiment took about 1.5 to 2 hours per participant. During this time they each observed and used all four cameras and finally compared them. The experiment consisted of three parts.

— Part 1: The camera was observed and the AttracDif 2 questionnaire for assessing product quality was completed.[15]
— Part 2: The participants were shown a training video, after which they used the camera, and completed the AttracDif 2 questionnaire again. They were given the assignment to make three beautiful pictures of the still-life. To ensure that they encountered each of the cameras' three modes-of-use they were told that they were to save only 'beautiful' pictures. Moreover, they were asked to review the pictures after they were done.
— Part 1 and 2 were repeated for each of the four cameras. When the participants were filling out the post-use questionnaire the experimenter exchanged the interface module out of view of the participants.

FIG. 08 Still-life setup

FIG. 09 Setting

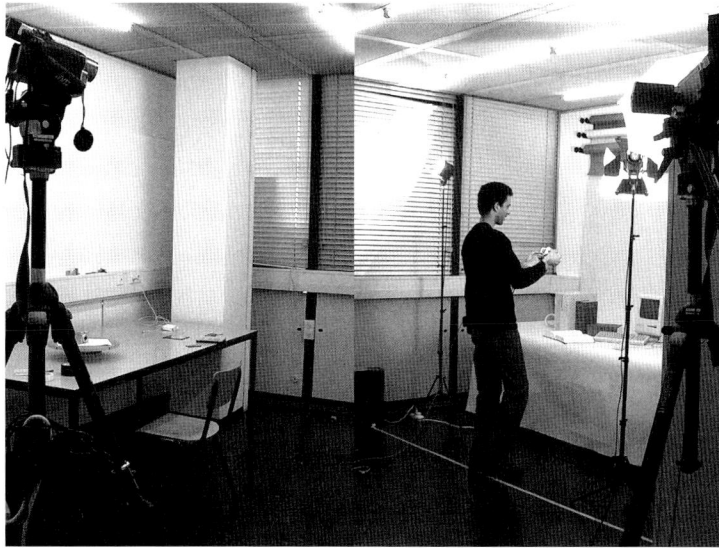

— Part 3: After four successive sessions of observing and using the cameras, the participants were asked to compare the cameras by means of a comparison questionnaire.

The order in which the four cameras were shown and used was counterbalanced. The experiment was videotaped with permission of the participants. The participants were paid €7.50 for their cooperation. Figure 10 gives an overview of the procedure.

FIG. 10

Main findings

The results of the experiment were extensively analysed and reported.[01] They break down into three parts.

Aesthetic interaction   Analysis of the experimental results indicates that aesthetic interaction is present in the RUI camera, the camera that has both MR APs and MURPS. Moreover, it was found that 'perceived beauty' seems to influence the 'perceived goodness' of a camera, regardless of the 'perceived ease of use'. Finally, severe usability problems, hampering the functionality of a product, eliminate the presence of aesthetic interaction. It was concluded that there seemed to be different kinds of 'hard-to-use'; a kind of 'hard-to-use' that renders a product 'inoperable' and one that does not hamper the operation of a product (ineffective vs. effective).

Differentiating factors   The experiment also reveals that MR APs influence the perceived ease of use positively, and that the cameras that employ MR APs are preferred over the other cameras. MURPS, on the other hand, did not seem to influence perceived ease of use or preference, positively or negatively.

Classic usability measures   Finally, the RUI camera is not found to differ in efficiency and effectiveness from the conventional camera. Only one of the cameras is found to differ in these measures, the one that employs MURPS, but not MR APs. This is attributed to a usability problem that is found to be present in that camera.

Summary

In sum, it is possible to find an alternative for the conventional interaction style. The rich interaction style forms a viable alternative, yet it does not imply another standardisation of interaction style. Instead, it offers variation in interaction as a logical consequence of the variation in form and function.

FIG. 10   Procedure of experiment

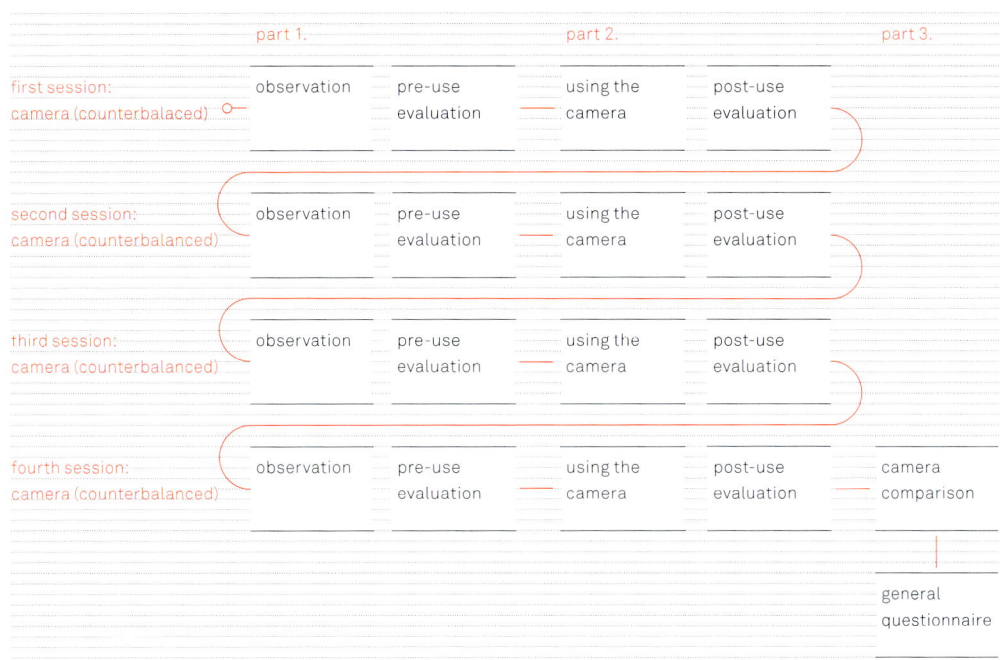

Question four: how can this new interaction paradigm be characterised?

Refined definition of rich interaction

I set out to define, demonstrate and investigate the concept of rich interaction. In the introduction I described how information-for-use became more abstracted from human skills. A lifetime of experience with the physical world[07] and a body that is capable of doing very refined things[16] become obsolete. I therefore argued for providing information-for-use through form, making functionality immediately accessible (i.e. not mediated) for human skills.

I went on to describe rich interaction as 'starting from human skills, aiming for aesthetic interaction, and integrating form, interaction and function'. I also provided a 'framework for exploration' that can be used to design for rich interaction. Consequently I define rich interaction as follows:

— *Rich interaction:* A paradigm for interactive consumer products that results in a unity of form, interaction and function, and taps human skills (perceptual-motor, cognitive and emotional skills) for information-for-use, thereby setting the stage for aesthetic interaction.

This definition emphasises three aspects of rich interaction. I expand on each of these three aspects by reflecting on the work described here.

1. Integrating form, interaction and function Above, a 'framework for exploration' was introduced that indicated six fields of exploration that need to be explored when designing for rich interaction. I want to highlight two consequences of the integration of form, interaction and function.

— *Experiential:* To integrate form, interaction and function it is essential to explore the relations between them. Having decided to design for rich interaction, this needs to be done in an experiential way, as to know the quality of an interaction is to experience it. Consequently, the design process has to be taken from 2D sketching to 3D modelling practice, and from the 2D screen 'interaction simulation' to the 3D hands-on 'experience simulation'.
— *Specific functionality:* Unity of form, interaction and function also implies that rich interactive products are specific in the functionality they offer. This means that rich interactive products express all of their functions and action-possibilities in their form. For example, a rich interactive mobile telephone that is capable of phoning and texting also expresses both of these functions and specific action-possibilities in its form. As a consequence, changing the functionality changes the form and action-possibilities, thus changes the product.

2. Information-for-use inspired by human skills – affordances
Human skills are tapped for information-for-use. Consequently the actions required to operate a rich interactive product need to be on a human scale, i.e. human skills presuppose a certain size, range and diversity. The theory of direct perception with the notion of affordances offers inspiration.

Central to my 'implementation' of the concept of affordances is the question of how to get information-for-use to the user. Herein lies the reason for my consistent use of the term 'action-possibility' instead of 'control' or 'button'. Action-possibilities suggest that they *can* be designed, while controls suggest that they *have* been designed. It is therefore necessary for designers to get out of the mindset of buttons, sliders and switches and get into the mindset of action-possibilities. Only after the action-possibilities are designed to express how to act and what will happen is there room to incorporate off-the-shelf sensors and controls.

3. Aesthetic interaction   From my experience in designing, building and testing rich interactive cameras I see three prerequisites for aesthetic interaction: (1) the absence of user frustration, (2) the presence of rich action-possibilities (i.e. allowing for broad, expressive and diverse actions), and (3) the presence of other kinds of aesthetics (e.g. aesthetics of appearance,[17] aesthetics of context,[05] or aesthetics of narrative [18]). If these prerequisites are met, aesthetic interaction can be present while interacting. I identify aesthetic interaction through how it impresses the senses during interaction. Aesthetic interaction can be found in the 'feel' of rich action-possibilities.

Closing remarks: Research through design

In a research through-design-process, design methodology meets research methodology, and both contribute. Design integrates knowledge from different areas of research into relevant, highly experiential prototypes that can be seen as 'physical hypotheses'. Research offers the methods to conduct experiments and to draw knowledge from these prototypes.

I finish with a plea for design as a generator of knowledge. I have explored and defined the concept of rich interaction through the process of designing and building conceptual products. Only through building these highly experiential prototypes can the quality of interaction be assessed. Only through designing product concepts can the relevance of new ideas be tested. Designers ask different questions: what will be the use, how will it feel, why do we want that. Different questions produce different answers. Answering those questions is only possible through designing.

References / Bibliography

[01] Frens JW (2006) *Designing for Rich Interaction: Integrating Form, Interaction, and Function.* Unpublished doctoral theses, Eindhoven University of Technology, Netherlands

[02] Overbeeke CJ, Djajadiningrat JP, Wensveen SAG, Hummels CCM (1999) Experiential and Respectful. *Proceedings of the International Conference Useful and critical – The position of research in design.* University of Art and Design, Helsinki

[03] Cooper A (1999) *The Inmates Are Running the Asylum.* SAMS McMillan, Indianapolis

[04] Archer B (1995) The Nature of Research. *Co-Design Journal* 2: 6–13

[05] Hummels C (2000) *Gestural Design Tools: Prototypes, Experiments and Scenarios.* Unpublished PhD thesis, Delft University of Technology, the Netherlands

[06] Ishii H, and Ullmer B (1997) Tangible Bits: towards Seamless Interfaces between People, Bits and Atoms. *Proceedings of CHI'97,* 234–241

[07] Ullmer BA (2002) *Tangible Interfaces for Manipulating Aggregates of Digital Information.* Doctoral thesis, MIT, Cambridge, MA

[08] Gibson JJ (1986) *The Ecological Approach to Visual Perception.* Lawrence Erlbaum, Hillsdale, NJ

[09] Dourish P (2004) *Where the Action Is. The Foundations of Embodied Interaction.* MIT Press, Cambridge, MA

[10] Djajadiningrat JP, Gaver WW, Frens JW (2000) Interaction Relabelling and Extreme Characters: Methods for Exploring Aesthetic Interactions. *Proceedings of DIS'00.* New York, 66–71

[11] Overbeeke CJ, Djajadiningrat JP, Hummels CCM, Wensveen SAG (2000) Beauty in Usability: Forget about Ease of Use! In: Green W, Jordan P (eds): *Pleasure with Products, beyond Usability.* Taylor and Francis, London

[12] Graves Petersen M, Iversen OS, Krogh PG, Ludvigsen M (2004) Aesthetic Interaction – a Pragmatist's Aesthetics of Interactive Systems. *Proceedings of DIS2004.* Cambridge, MA, 269–276

[13] Forlizzi J, Batterbee K (2004) Understanding Experience in Interactive Systems. *Proceedings of DIS2004.* Cambridge, MA, 261–268

[14] Wensveen SAG, Overbeeke CJ, Djajadiningrat JP (2002) Push Me, Shove Me and I Show You how You Feel. *Proceedings of DIS'2002.* London, 335–340

[15] Hassenzahl M (2004) The Interplay of Beauty, Goodness, and Usability in Interactive Products. *Human-Computer Interaction* 19: 319–349

[16] Buur J, Jensen MV, Djajadiningrat T (2004) Hands-only Scenarios and Video Action Walls – Novel Methods for Tangible User Interaction Design. *Proceedings of DIS2004.* Cambridge, MA, 185–192

[17] Locher P, Martindale C, Dorfman L, Leontiev D (2005) *New Directions in Aesthetics, Creativity, and the Arts.* Baywood, Amityville, NY

[18] Dunne A, Raby F (2001) *Design Noir: the Secret Life of Electronic Objects.* Birkhäuser, Basel

Ezio Manzini
Anna Meroni 01 |

Research

Emerging User Demands for Sustainable Solutions, EMUDE

01 | Ezio Manzini has written the paragraphs 1, 3, Anna Meroni has written the paragraphs 2, 4, 5

Abstract

This paper reports on EMUDE (2004/06), a Specific Support Action financed by the European Commission Directorate within the 6th FP. The project started by observing a phenomenon of social innovation: the emergence in Europe of groups of active, enterprising people inventing and putting into practice original ways of dealing with everyday problems, ways that can be considered promising in terms of sustainability. Taking these cases as a base, the research outlines a comprehensive map of emerging sustainable user demands and generates a set of qualitative scenarios of how these demands, and the consequent product-service innovation, may co-evolve.

1. Research background and questions

The transition towards sustainability

We have known for a long time that transition towards sustainability requires radical changes in the way we produce and consume and, more generally, in the way we live.[01, 02] In fact, we need to learn how to *live better* (the entire population of the planet) and, at the same time, *reduce our ecological footprint* and *improve the quality of our social fabric*. In this framework the link between the environmental and social dimensions of this problem clearly appears, showing that *radical social innovation* will be needed, in order to move from current, unsustainable models to new, sustainable ones.[03-08]

Given the nature and the dimension of this change, transition towards sustainability (and, in particular, towards sustainable ways of living) is a wide-reaching social learning process in which the most diversified forms of knowledge and organisational capabilities must be mobilised in the most open and flexible way. A particular role will be played by local initiatives. These can be seen as harbingers of new behaviours and new ways of thinking. The discussion on the potential of social innovation must be situated in this more general framework.[09] And, in particular, the one grassroots innovation in everyday life that is the specific theme of the research we are going to present here: EMUDE. *Emerging user demands for sustainable solutions*.

Promising cases

The EMUDE background is the observation of an interesting phenomenon of social innovation: the emergence in Europe and worldwide of groups of active, enterprising people inventing and putting into practice original ways of dealing with everyday problems. For instance: groups of people who re-organise the way they live their home and their neighbourhood (sharing spaces and services or fostering mobility on foot or by bicycle). Communities that conceive and develop collaborative services (to facilitate the young and the elderly living together, or promoting self-organised micro-nurseries). New food networks encouraging producers of organic items and the quality and typical characteristics of their products (such as the Slow Food movement or the emerging solidarity purchasing and fair-trade groups).02

02 |

Given this phenomenon, the EMUDE initial hypothesis was that these cases could be considered *promising examples* of initiatives where, in different ways and for different motivations, some people have re-oriented their behaviour and their expectations in a direction

02 | For more, and more detailed, examples see: http://www.sustainable-everyday. net/cases

that appears to be a positive step towards sustainability. In other words, they have found original ways of solving practical problems in daily life with unprecedented capacities to *bring individual interests into line with social and environmental ones.*

The EMUDE questions

We have seen that, to foster the transition towards sustainability, it is necessary to look beyond mainstream positions, behaviour and opinions and, in the complexity of signals that society sends us, know how to recognise those that are most promising. Signals emitted by certain minorities who have been able to set up on a local scale radical innovations in ways of being and doing things.[10] Once identified, the following step is to foster them and facilitate their diffusion.

Given that, the research questions behind EMUDE are of different kinds:

— To identify and conceptualise into a map the user demand for sustainable solutions in Europe. This demand can be read in different kinds of social innovations produced by groups of creative minorities
— To draw, from this demand, a set of scenarios of product-service-system innovation;
— To translate these scenarios into roadmaps for future research and development activities, to inform and inspire the decision-makers, and to influence the perception and demands of future end-users.

03 | According to the NMP [03] | Priority, 'there will not be sustainable development without the demand from users for sustainable solutions'. EMUDE was started to give visibility to emerging user demands for sustainable solutions in Europe and to the corresponding needs in terms of research in the field of product-service systems innovation.[07]

2. Method

Interdisciplinary programme and strategic design approach

EMUDE was a highly interdisciplinary programme, carried out using a *strategic design approach*: a particular way of looking at *cases of social innovation* to identify what could be done to improve their potential, to maintain and/or renew their qualities, and to reduce their limits.[11] That is, in this specific case: to look at some active minorities,

03 | The research area 'Nanotechnology and nanosciences, knowledge-based multifunctional materials and new production processes and devices' within the 6th Framework Programme

the *Creative Communities,* and to imagine a strategy to reinforce them and to support their evolution towards a mature model called *Diffused Social Enterprise,* while maintaining (most of) the qualities and values that triggered the original ideas.

The interdisciplinarity of the EMUDE Consortium consists in the presence of some of the most experienced institutions in the fields of research concerned, such as the Politecnico di Milano, INDACO Department (as coordinator); the Norwegian National Institute for Consumer Research (Sifo); the Netherlands Organisation for Applied Scientific Research (TNO); Strategic Design Scenarios; Doors of Perception; Philips Design; the Joint Research Centre – Institute for Prospective Technological Studies; the Central European University, Budapest Foundation; Consumers International; the United Nations Environment Programme.

In addition to the Consortium, a network of observers, called 'Antennas', was set up to perform the research. It consisted of eight design schools: the Academy of Fine Arts in Krakow, Poland; ENSCI Les Ateliers, Paris, France; Estonian Academy of Arts, Tallinn, Estonia; Politecnico di Milano, Italy; School of Design, The Glasgow School of Art, UK; School of Design, University of Applied Sciences, Cologne, Germany; Eindhoven University of Technology, the Netherlands; University of Art and Design Helsinki, Finland.

Hypothesis

Underlying EMUDE activities are the hypotheses that, first, the above-mentioned cases of social innovation present promising signals both from the aspect of environmental sustainability and from that of social sustainability;[04] and second, that these signals might usefully point to a new direction for technological and market research and innovation. In other words, Creative Communities, and the *promising cases* they generate, can both *anticipate a possible future* and offer *concrete indications* as to how technological, production and market innovation could be orientated from now on.

For this reason it was thought that *policies* and *tools* of governance should be outlined to support existing cases and foster the development and orientation of analogous and equally promising activities.

The *field study* carried out by EMUDE has verified the validity of these original hypotheses and has shed light on the characteristics of these promising cases, in the framework of contemporary society and the enormous transformations it is experiencing; and on scenarios that outline ways in which it may evolve in future.

Work focused on the situation in Europe in general, but also looked at the specificities of Eastern European countries. In addition, to make a more solid appraisal, the phenomenon was also considered from the point of view of 'the Global South', in order to verify the extent to which this was specific to Europe or if it could have a global value.

04 |

[04] Promising cases: examples of initiatives where, in different ways and for different motivations, some people have re-oriented their behaviour and their expectations in a direction that appears to be coherent with the principles of sustainable development.

Virtuous circle

The basic, long-term objective of EMUDE was to encourage a *virtuous circle* between social and technological innovation, or between society's capacity to emit positive signals (promising cases), its capacity to recognise, reinforce and effectively communicate them, and then its ability to pick up these signals and act on them, putting them to good use. From this perspective, EMUDE was intended to work as a *signal amplifier,* i.e. something that (1) identifies promising signals, (2) reinforces them, and (3) re-emits them into the system in the most suitable ways and forms.[FIG. 01]

In order to start this virtuous circle, the research process passed through the following stages, each conducted along its own methodologies:

1. *Direct observation*: case identification and analysis
2. *Conceptualisation*: case evaluation
3. *Proposals*: technologies, organisational forms, scenarios and Policy Agenda

The specific characteristic of the EMUDE programme was to combine a system for gathering original information on the dynamics of social innovation, with activities that elaborate and communicate the data collected. The aim was not only to build up a new database, but also to activate a set of tools and communication channels that enable its findings to be used optimally.

Another original aspect of EMUDE came from the decision to use teams of research students and undergraduates from design schools as 'Antennas'. The decision arose from the availability of researchers – the young designers – endowed with a special enthusiasm for and sensibility towards a kind of innovation that is both behavioural and technical. Furthermore, as a spin-off, this choice has meant that the issue of social innovation and Creative Communities, with the sustainable solutions they put into action, was concretely introduced into design schools from the beginning.

Consequently, the possibility arose of training a new generation of designers able to recognise such solutions and develop their implications for design projects.

Direct observation

The search for, identification and analysis of Creative Communities was carried out by direct observation or, more precisely, by '*field observation*' that led researchers (students of the network of Antennas) along a structured path into direct contact with the situations analysed. The work, coordinated by the Politecnico di Milano, was distinguished by the fact that each case was the fruit of personal, direct contact between the designer-researcher and the main stakeholders in the case itself. An absorbing encounter on the verge of ethnography.

FIG. 01

FIG. 01   The *virtuous circle*

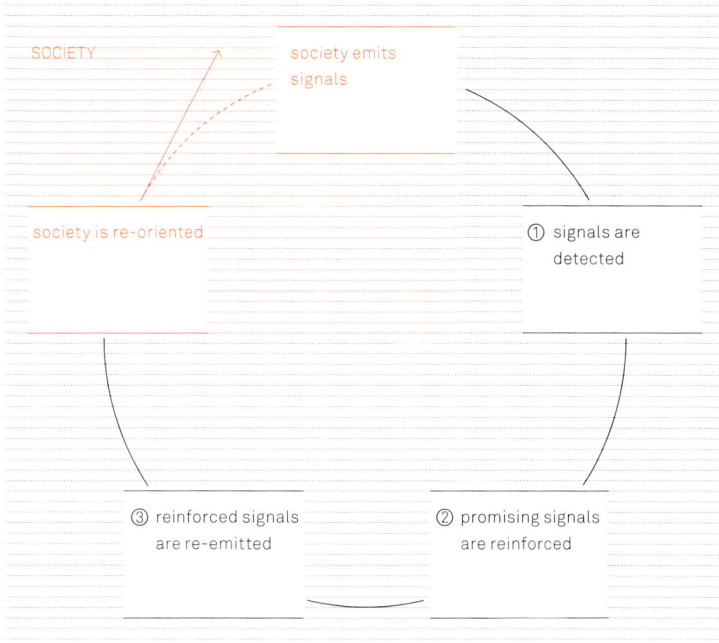

SOCIETY

society emits signals

society is re-oriented

① signals are detected

③ reinforced signals are re-emitted

② promising signals are reinforced

FIG. 02   The web interface of the *Promising Cases Repository* conceived to support the case collection

From the process point of view, case collection was carried out in four main stages using a centralised repository with Internet access.[12] The four operational stages, taking about eight months to complete, were:

1.   Communicating and sharing criteria, aims and research tools;
2.   Gathering an initial cycle of proposals for possible case studies;
3.   Assessing these proposals and selecting cases for analysis;
4.   Further, homogeneous analysis of the selected cases and assembling the collection.

FIG. 02

Stages 1 and 3 were carried out centrally by the research group. The others were carried out locally by the various Antennas, with backup for technical problems and theory issues from a central helpdesk. FIG. 02

In this way more than one hundred cases were gathered, from which 56 particularly significant ones were selected for the subsequent stages of the work.

It emerged from the study that there exists a dynamic new form of creativity: 05 | a *diffused creativity* put cooperatively into action by laypeople, which takes shape as a significant though scarcely studied expression of contemporary society. This diffused creativity is one aspect of the design attitude each one of us must develop if we are to organise our lives in a highly turbulent and therefore unpredictable context.

For all these reasons it would appear legitimate to define these groups of enterprising people as Creative Communities: groups of people who invent sustainable ways of living, innovative citizens organising themselves to solve a problem or to open a new possibility, and doing so as a positive step in the social learning process towards social and environmental sustainability.[12]

FIG. 03 -06

The field observation was carried out using a method that we call '*quasi-ethnographic*' based on direct interviews, taking pictures, collecting evidences and meeting people, guided by specific tools and formats together with a dedicated notebook: the Reporter's Book FIG. 03 -06

This *collection* of significant cases constitutes the basis of the programme's subsequent stages. It is of value as an intermediary result in the research project and also in itself, as a communicative instrument that proposes a vast series of good practices that show how it is already possible to live one's own everyday life in a more sustainable way. To facilitate this function, the cases were presented in a highly communicative format, in several exhibitions and in a dedicated book, *Creative Communities. People inventing sustainable ways of living*, licensed with the Creative Commons rules and freely accessible from different websites.[12]

---

05 | This can be seen in relation to Richard Florida's definitions [13], and to the work of Charles Landry. [14]

Conceptualisation

From the base of knowledge acquired through the activities described above, the EMUDE project developed a series of deeper analyses of Creative Communities, highlighting their special characteristics and impacts on different grounds. Cases were evaluated as reactions to strong societal trends, with regard to their environmental effects, and as situations presenting technological opportunities. They were also considered from the perspective of both Central Eastern Europe and the 'Global South'.[12]

Particular focus was placed on the social and environmental value of these cases and the way they are taking shape as the initial stage in a new generation of social enterprise. A new kind of enterprise that, in its maturity, can be called *Diffused Social Enterprise* (DSE).[06] |

Proposals

The collection of cases can be considered as seeds of potential *new ways for people to organise themselves* to fulfil daily life functions both individually and collectively. To verify this, the cases were clustered in six different '*ways of doing*', i.e. organisational forms that aim to solve day-to-day concerns, which are recognised as potential innovative models toward a more sustainable society. Six such promising ways are:

— Household Micro-entrepreneurship;
— Extended Home;
— Community Housing;
— Elective Communities;
— Service Clubs;
— Producer & Consumer Networks.

A more mature image of these six clusters of promising ways of doing was then developed (considering a 5–10 year time frame), with the aim of projecting these emerging social innovations onto conditions that might enable their common diffusion and *trigger social conversation*. This scenario-building exercise was performed as follows:

1. Exploring the *potential diffusion* of the ways of doing, passing from isolated/emerging niches to practices involving larger groups of users, and generalising the solution idea to other need areas;
2. Building an overall picture of a *scenario* that could emerge if groups of early adopters grew into larger market shares;

06 | Diffused social enterprise: this is diffuse enterprise that auto-produces social quality, where the term 'diffused enterprise' indicates people who, in their everyday life and in a stable way, organise themselves to obtain the results that directly interest them.

FIG. 04 Finland, Helsinki, Happihuone – 'Oxygen Room' cultural greenhouse, By O2 Finland; research by Cindy Kohtala, University of Art and Design Helsinki, Finland

FIG. 07

3. Sketching five related solutions (called *improved solutions*) for each way of doing, illustrating its main characteristics. These solutions, visualised in one picture showing the user/s using it in an appropriate context, were designed into a draft project. They constitute drafts of possible social enterprises to be developed further and implemented.

To enable the reader to project him/herself into these emerging scenarios, five '*personae*' (profiles representing people's needs and motivations as seen in the EMUDE collection) were developed and matched with the solutions, selecting the most characteristic six.[15] FIG. 07

Moving on from these *micro-scenarios,* it was possible to glean some insight into a possible macro environment for EMUDE communities. By looking at how the behaviour of a user might affect the macro areas or be affected by them, it was possible to list some likely characteristics of the *macro-scenario*. After integrating these into one consolidated picture of macro conditions, a set of coherent *storylines* was drawn up that described a possible macro framework emerging along with the social enterprise.

---

3. Results

To summarise, EMUDE has produced five main results.

A collection of cases of Creative Communities

A collection of *promising cases of Creative Communities*, intended as groups of active, enterprising people inventing and putting into practice original ways of dealing with everyday problems.

The demands brought to light by the promising cases and the prospects of *active welfare* 07 | and new forms of *local development* they indicate suggest that these issues may rapidly become very important for private enterprise and, in general, for all economic operators interested in developing products and services for new markets. Indeed, if the forerunners of new ways of being and doing highlighted by EMUDE mature and grow, substantial demands may be revealed that now appear only as potential ones. This means that, depending on the success of the new ideas of welfare and local development they propose, new markets may emerge for a new generation of products and services.

07 |

07 | Active Welfare: a welfare system where people who are directly involved participate directly in defining and achieving the results they intend to reach. Welfare that extends into our everyday lives, responding to the currently emerging, widespread new demand for wellbeing and citizenship. Welfare where the role of public bodies is that of fostering the capacity of individuals to face up to and resolve their problems or to favour the balanced development of citizens' ability to 'be enterprising', and to 'produce sociality'.

FIG. 05-06   Sketches and notes from the *Reporter's Books*

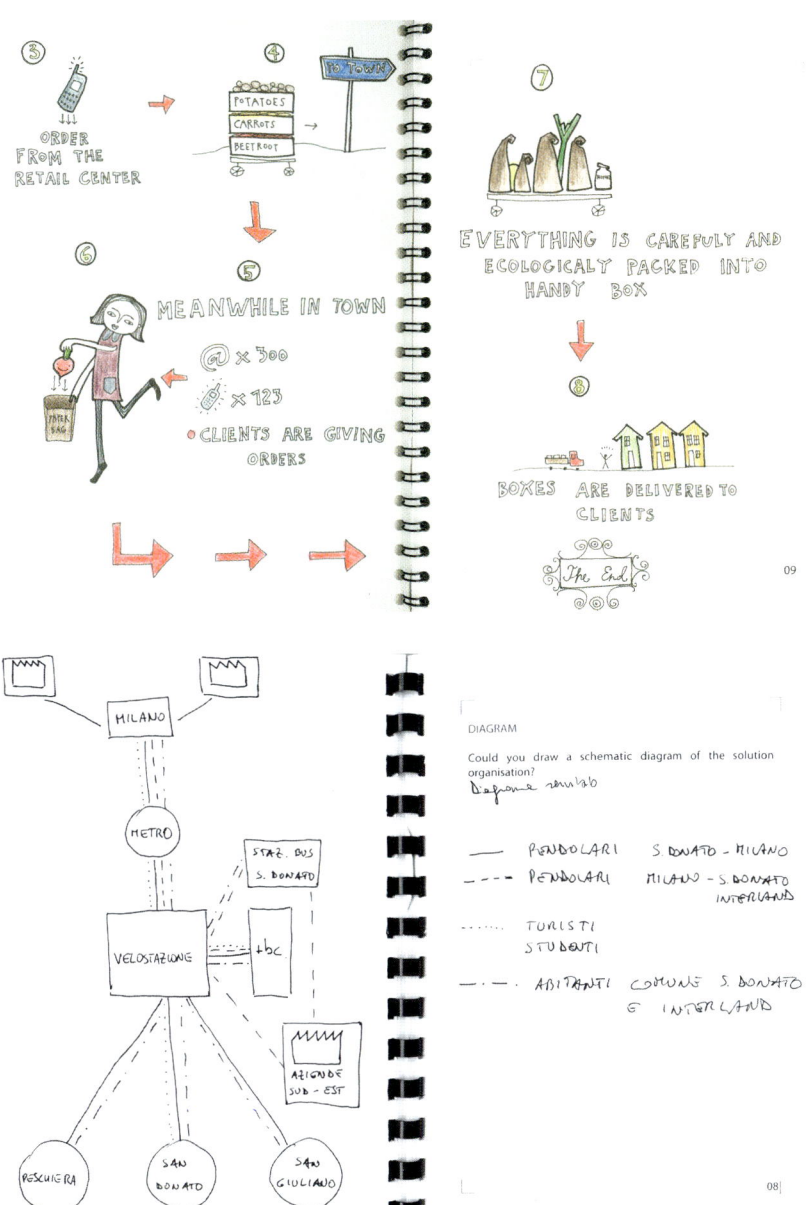

③ ORDER FROM THE RETAIL CENTER

④ POTATOES / CARROTS / BEETROOT

⑤ MEANWHILE IN TOWN
@ x 300
🔋 x 123
• CLIENTS ARE GIVING ORDERS

⑥

⑦ EVERYTHING IS CAREFULY AND ECOLOGICALY PACKED INTO HANDY BOX

⑧ BOXES ARE DELIVERED TO CLIENTS

The End

09

DIAGRAM

Could you draw a schematic diagram of the solution organisation?
Diagramma simulato

MILANO

METRO

STAZ. BUS S. DONATO

VELOSTAZIONE + bc

AZIENDE SUD - EST

PESCHIERA   SAN DONATO   SAN GIULIANO

——— PENDOLARI   S. DONATO - MILANO
– – – PENDOLARI   MILANO - S. DONATO INTERLAND
· · · · · · TURISTI STUDENTI
— · — · ABITANTI COMUNE S. DONATO E INTERLAND

08

The concept of diffused creativity

The discussion of these Creative Communities as positive examples of *diffused creativity*, in the framework of a knowledge-based society and in the perspective of the transition towards sustainability.

What emerged from EMUDE is a society that is also a great *laboratory of ideas and innovations* for everyday life: ways of being and doing that express a capacity to formulate new questions and find new answers by means of initiatives taken by individuals endowed with special design skills, who set themselves specific objectives and find satisfactory tools to attain them.

The concept of Diffused Social Enterprise

The definition of the concept of *Diffused Social Enterprise (DSE)* – Creative Communities evolved into more mature and lasting forms of social organisation – and the discussion of its implication in currently emerging ideas on welfare and local development.

EMUDE has identified this stage in the transition from a nascent heroic state, the true Creative Community, to a more mature state where they take the form of a Diffused Social Enterprise that reaches into the everyday lives of a large number of people organising themselves to achieve the results that interest them and in so doing producing sociality.

Introducing the concept of the DSE allows us to confront important issues in contemporary society in a new way: the promising cases appear as models of a new idea of wellbeing, social justice and citizenship. They bring an interesting contribution to two important issues currently under discussion: welfare after the crisis in the welfare state, and new models of local development.

The scenario of the Diffused Social Enterprise

The proposal of a scenario (the *scenario of the diffused social enterprise*) and of the *enabling platforms* that could enhance it.

EMUDE has enabled us to understand better how Creative Communities actually work and what they require to work better and to become more easily replicable and/or upgradable. This has led to the identification of certain prevalent organisational typologies, and to the explicit or implicit demand for support technology that they voice.

The concrete result of this part of the EMUDE project is a *list of technologies and organisation forms* that, if developed in the direction indicated, could facilitate the application, diffusion and orientation of Diffused Social Enterprise towards social and environmental sustainability.

FIG. 07 solutions matrix
–   30 improved solutions were developed to represent a state of maturation and diffusion
     of the cases of social innovation supported by appropriate technologies and policies
     measures;
–   6 scenarios presenting promising ways of doing towards a more sustainable daily life.
     Each one is presented through 2 introductory visualisations and 5 emblematic solutions;
–   5 personae showing snapshots of their daily life and their motivations as adopters or
     providers of these improved solutions.

6 ways of doing

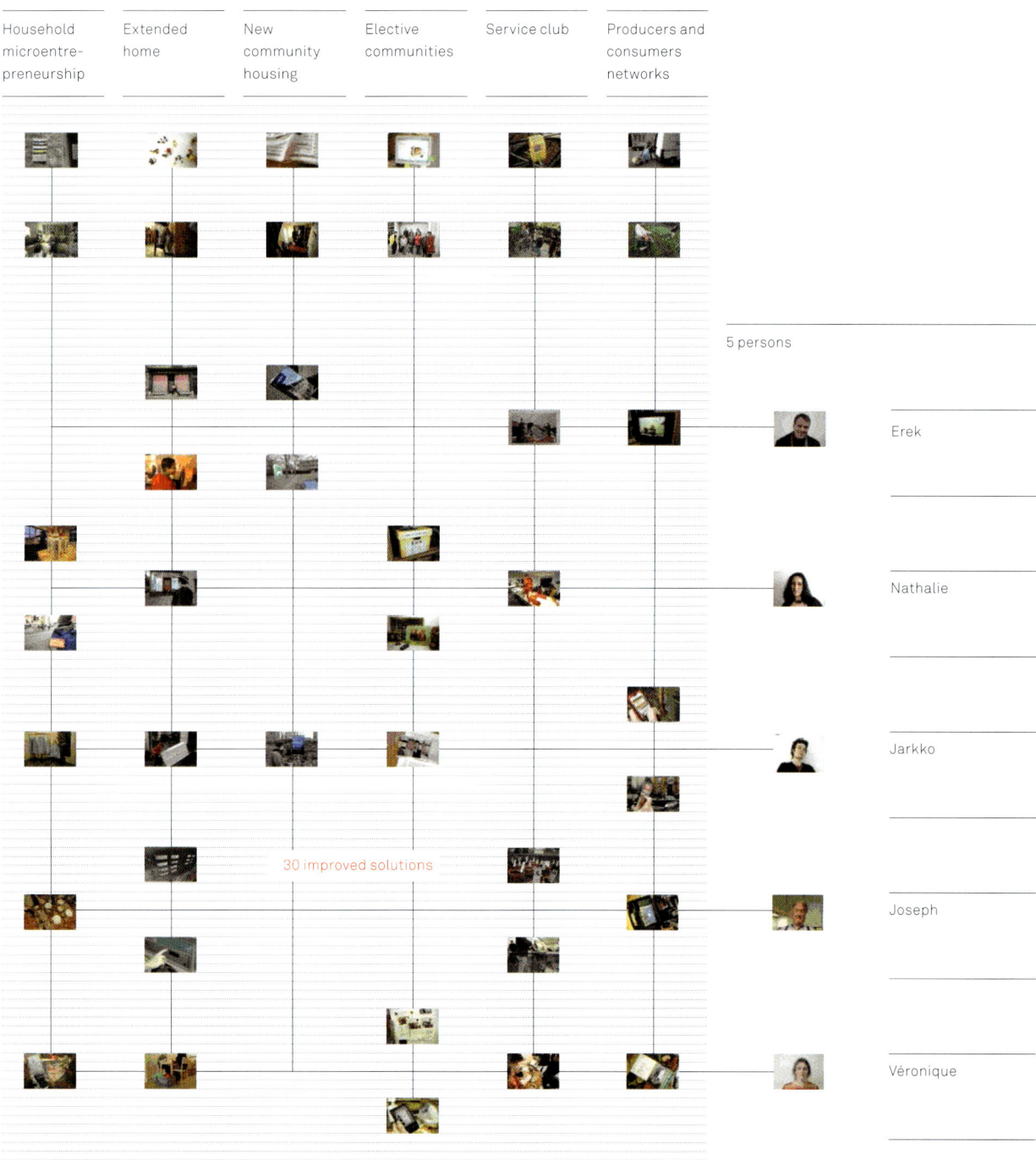

Household microentre-preneurship	Extended home	New community housing	Elective communities	Service club	Producers and consumers networks		
						5 persons	
							Erek
							Nathalie
							Jarkko
		30 improved solutions					Joseph
							Véronique

The *scenario of the diffused social enterprise* is articulated in a series of proposals and experiences (on the part of different hypothetical users) offering an overview of what everyday life could be like in a society where the idea and practice of the DSE is widespread, and where the proposed activities are supported by appropriate *enabling solutions*. [08] |

These *micro-scenarios* were then integrated with a *macro-scenario* that both describes what the general economic, social and political conditions should be like to make the development of the micro scenario more probable and effective, and gives an overall vision of what the wider context might be like in a society where Creative Communities and DSE are widespread.

The last operative concept developed by EMUDE is the one of *enabling platforms*: systems of technologies, infrastructures, legal frameworks, and modes of governance and policy-making.

Considered as a whole, their role is to create a favourable environment for Creative Communities, to facilitate their evolution into diffuse social enterprises and to direct them towards more sustainable social and environmental solutions.[08, 16]

A policy agenda

A *policy agenda* articulated around three main questions: how Creative Communities and Diffused Social Enterprise support the existing European policy agenda? What kind of policy agenda is suitable to support Creative Communities and the DSE? What are the Creative Communities and DSE implications for industrial research funding?

The EMUDE results suggest that Creative Communities and Diffused Social Enterprise can become core elements of an active civil society with a better quality of life and enhanced chances for sustainable economic development. This is particularly true for some policy arenas that form a core part of the European Community policy objectives:

1. *Innovation capability in a knowledge based economy*
    DSE could become a facilitator of transition towards a knowledge-intensive economy by acting as an interface between innovators and users, enabling joint learning and customising of innovation. Furthermore, it could help companies to orient their innovation activities towards future demands and foster the competencies that are considered vital for knowledge workers.
2. *Decoupling of economic growth and environmental impact*
    By functioning as a 'niche of change', DSE initiatives might become strong enablers of socio-technical transition towards decoupling economic growth and environmental impact.

08 | Enabling solution: a system of tangible and intangible elements (such as products, services, communication and procedures) that seeks to support a specific typology of promising cases, and to make them more accessible, effective, replicable.

3.   *Social cohesion and sustainable welfare*
     DSE might become a core element of an 'active welfare society', i.e. a society better suited to address the enormous future challenges to our welfare systems.
4.   *New modes of governance*
     The DSE is part of the social fabric needed for the concept of open governance to succeed.

EMUDE results indicate that if these weak signals are taken up, strengthened, connected and spread, their benefits can be greatly enhanced. The policy measures to support this process could operate on three different levels:

— Direct support to Creative Communities to realise their ideas and become DSE (strengthening the promising signals)
— Measures to enable more people to start Creative Communities and DSE initiatives and to connect them to each other (spreading the promising signals)
— Complementing measures creating framework conditions for transition using the diffused social enterprise as enabler (activating the social enterprise for transition)

These three levels of policy action could create a pathway from the weak signals of Creative Communities towards an active civil society with a wide range of Diffused Social Enterprises, finally leading to a society that incorporates the principle of sustainability in its social, environmental and economic dimension.

---

4. Discussion

Creative Communities as source of motivation
The results of this research cover a wide range of design and social issues: for the purpose of this essay we want now to focus briefly on the topic at the base of the research, the Creative Communities.

The reason for choosing this discussion perspective from among several others lies in the originality of the intuition behind the initial input to the research and on the strength of its conceptualisation. It also underlines the need for a non-conventional research vision at the base of a 'creative' research path.

The case studies of Creative Communities were immediately recognised by the entire research group as sources of motivation, and not only of information. This gave a large store of enthusiasm to everybody to go on with the work, something that does not occur on a regular basis and must be investigated as a powerful knowledge driver in this knowledge-intensive society.

Field research efforts

The direct observation method, which has brought the researchers onto the field, visiting the places, meeting the people and touching the solutions, has been one big stimulus to research commitment.

This kind of research experience does not leave people cold: EMUDE case studies were perceived as interesting because they were not only innovative, but also 'beautiful', meaning that there is something in the way they appear that invoked, and invokes positive emotions in the observer. They express vitality and a spirit of initiative: they are the unthinkable made possible, the alternative getting itself into working order. And they are also 'good': whether intentionally or by coincidence they propose solutions in which individual interests converge with those of society and the environment, creating conditions for a more satisfying use of resources (human, environmental and economic), which restores, or bestows, meaning and value to everyday activities and therefore seems promising as a transition towards sustainability.

This enthusiasm has fuelled the engine of the research. Somehow, EMUDE has become a sort of research about *happiness*.

Heroes' motivations

Another reason for the strong commitment of the research group was the will to understand the motives behind those we call the 'heroes' of the Creative Communities: 'ordinary people' able to make the extraordinary possible, if given the opportunity, '*heroes*' of everyday life.[17] Hearing them talk, these people give no hint of the difficulty of their actions, but seem to do the most unusual things quite normally: their true heroism lies here. What EMUDE has understood about them is that community spirit is the secret that moves them and fuels their actions; community both in terms of the group that supports, shares and recognises the value of what they are doing, and in terms of the sense of togetherness to which they aspire. So, it is in the community, or in community as a goal, that the creative character of these heroes becomes fully apparent.

From outside, the industriousness shown by the Creative Communities exerts an inexplicable attraction, because it appears incredibly demanding, and it often is. However, it was interesting to discover that precisely in what, to others, looks like fatigue, lies a good part of the deeper quality that Creative Communities attribute to their activities. So it is not fatigue, but quality of experience, pleasure in relationship, pleasure in doing, recovery of a sense of togetherness and a source of real satisfaction.

Psychology teaches us that to activate creativity, it is not enough to have a problem to resolve. It is essential that the individual perceive a discordance between his/her own way of acting and interpreting reality and that of the social system of which he/she is part.[18] In other words, he/she must have a vision of how things could go, be sufficiently motivated to follow it, and feel able to do so alone or with the support of others. In short, it is essential to be imaginative, determined and self-confident to change the rules and roles in society.

Social psychology upholds that in rich countries, in spite of materialist pressure, subjective wellbeing is related to a belief in interpersonal relationships:[19] the capacity to bring people together around an idea, to get people moving, to get together to resolve a problem, all of which are characteristics that are clearly expressed by Creative Communities. They are therefore a way of building community values and also of instilling a sense of personal wellbeing.

The heroes of the Creative Communities have gone beyond themselves, creating combustion between intuition and experience and finding that the impossible can be possible, if we start thinking it is. The discovery was that the quality of life lies not only in the results obtained, but in the way of doing things and the richness lies in the unfolding of convivial social relationships expressed in the formation of innovative social, economic and work networks, which correspond to what we call diffused creativity.

Finally, these networking relational strategies have also affected the research group, stimulating an increasing number of new activities moving on from the search for and the observation of cases of Creative Communities.

---

5. Conclusions

New forms of civil society

09 |

The EMUDE results (and those of other research projects working in the same direction 09 |) have shown that Creative Communities are to be considered as new civil society organisations. Considered as a whole they are to be seen as a *diffuse social enterprise* where people organise themselves to achieve results of common interest and, in doing so, produce not only individual benefits, but also sociality. In other words they regenerate the social fabric of which they are a part.

It should be added that, like any invention (if it is really to be an innovation or, as in our case, a social innovation), Creative Community initiatives have to stabilise and consolidate their structure. EMUDE has identified this stage in the transition from a nascent heroic state, the true Creative Community, to a more mature, lasting state, where they take the form of social enterprise. To do this, they have to be supported by other entities in a *complex interplay between bottom-up and top-down initiatives*.

---

09 | We should point out that, in recent years, the EMUDE research results have become an input for several other research and implementation activities (such as the UN international research project CCSL, where European creative communities are compared with similar cases in other contexts – in particular, in China, India and Brazil). However, until now, none of them has specifically focused on the environmental dimension of the creative community initiatives and on the possibility of giving civil society organisations a major role in their promotion and direction.

In conclusion, Creative Communities should be seen as active and mainly informal civil society organisations, *grassroots civil society organisations* whose existence and initiatives regenerate civil society. At the same time, to exist and be effective in the long term, they require different kinds of help from the larger, stronger and more formal organisations: the cases realised by creative communities are in fact as fragile and difficult to repeat as they are promising.

The reasons for this fragility are numerous: some have to do with the wider context (such as the rigidity of the norms or the inadequacy of the infrastructure). Others depend on the lack of specific support tools, able to support all the peculiarities of each case.

To overcome these difficulties an intervention strategy is required to foster both a favourable environment and a new generation of supporting tools. More specifically, it is a question of knowing how to combine the freedom required for creative activities with the implementation of top-down normative actions that create more favourable conditions for developing and steering a new generation of grassroots social innovations and, given what we have said in the previous paragraph, for orienting them towards more sustainable solutions.

References / Bibliography

_____   _____

[01]   Jansen JLA (1993) *Toward a Sustainable Oikos. En Route with Technology!* CLTM

[02]   Braungart M, McDonough A (1998) The Next Industrial Revolution. *Atlantic Monthly* 282(4): 82–92

[03]   Sachs W (1999) *Planets Dialectics.* Zed Books, London

[04]   Brezet H, Hemel C van (1998) *Ecodesign. A Promising Approach to Sustainable Production and Consumption.* UNEP, Paris

[05]   Charter M, Tischner U (eds) (2001) *Sustainable Solutions.* Greenleaf, London

[06]   Pauli G (1997) *Svolte epocali,* orig. title: *Breakthroughs – What Business Can Offer Society,* Baldini & Castoldi, Milan

[07]   Manzini E, Vezzoli C (2002) *Product-service Systems and Sustainability. Opportunities for Sustainable Solutions.* UNEP, Paris

[08]   Manzini E, Jégou F (2003) *Sustainable Everyday. Scenarios of Urban Life.* Edizioni Ambiente, Milan

[09]   Young Foundation (2006) *Social Silicon Valleys. A manifesto for social innovation.* www.discoversocialinnovation.org/Social%20Silicon%Valleys.pdf

[10]   Moscovici S (1979) *Psychologie des minorités actives.* Presses Universitaires de France, Paris

[11]   Burns C, Cottam H, Vanstone C, Winhall J (2006) *Transformation Design.* RED paper 02, Design Council, London

[12]   Meroni A (ed.) (2007) *Creative Communities. People Inventing Sustainable Ways of Living.* Edizioni Polidesign, Milan (also available from www.sustainable-everyday.net with CreatiVe Commons licence)

[13]   Florida R (2002) *The Rise of the Creative Class. And how it's Transforming Work, Leisure, Community and Everyday Life.* Basic Books, New York

[14]   Landry C (2000) *The Creative City. A Toolkit for Urban Innovators.* Earthscan, London

[15]   EMUDE (2006) *Creative Communities and the Diffused Social Enterprise: The Socio-technical Innovation in a Bottom-up Perspective.* EMUDE Executive Summary and Final Results Document (FRD)

[16]   Manzini E, Collina L, Evans E (eds) (2004) *Solution Oriented Partnership, How to Design Industrialized Solutions.* Cranfield University Press, UK

[17]   Ray PH, Anderson SR (2000) *The Cultural Creatives, How 50 Million People Are Changing the World.* Three Rivers Press, New York

[18]   Inghilleri P (2003) *La 'buona vita': Per l'uso creativo degli oggetti nella società dell'abbondanza.* Guerini e Associati, Milan

[19]   Latouche S (2004) *Survivre au développement.* Mille et une nuits, Paris

_____   _____

Wolfgang Jonas

Design Research and its Meaning to the Methodological Development of the Discipline

Title and hypothesis

I will take the title as suggested by the editor and reflect upon the *relation* between *design research* and *the methodological development of the discipline.* Neither concept is sufficiently clarified.

'Design Research ... is systematic enquiry whose goal is knowledge of, or in, the embodiment of configuration, composition, structure, purpose, value and meaning in man-made things and systems'.[01] Cross suggests that: 'design research would therefore fall into three main categories, based on people, process and products:

— Design epistemology – study of designerly ways of knowing
— Design praxiology – study of the practices and processes of design
— Design phenomenology – study of the form and configuration of artefacts.',[02] p. 6

And he emphasises (p. 7): '... that we do not have to turn design into an imitation of science, nor do we have to treat design as a mysterious, ineffable art. (...) we must avoid totally swamping our research with different cultures imported either from science or art. ...'

He calls this 'designerly ways of knowing', claiming that design is a genuine way of knowledge production, different from science and art, which may lead to the 'Sciences of the Artificial'.[03] So, since there is no substantial progress in defining design research, I will follow the concept of *about/for/through*, which – by means of 'through' – offers the semantic category of a designerly mode of knowledge production.

Regarding the *methodological development of the discipline* one might ask: Towards which goal? Towards autonomous designerly ways of knowledge production? This, again, points to the concept of 'research through design' (RTD). Before discussing this concept further, below, I give my hypothesis:

→ RTD provides the epistemological concepts for the development of a genuine design research paradigm, which is a condition for methodological development.

Towards its own paradigm

There can be no doubt that there is progress in research *about* design as well as *for* design. But this does not essentially contribute to the development of design as a knowledge-creating discipline. The challenge lies in the further clarification of RTD. What kind of process model, guiding research *through* design, might be able to provide something like 'foundations'?

Figure 1[04] tells a story of design theory building: frequent disciplinary crises lead to the adoption of short-term design theories/ideologies, which are able to displace the problem for a while by providing meaning and theoretical support for practice. On the other hand, there are long-term theory-building activities that serve the same purpose but show considerable delay before they produce useful practical effects. We all know the big efforts of the 1960s. The immediate effects were rather negative and caused researchers such as Alexander and Jones to retreat completely. Others saw their prejudices confirmed, because they did not want to believe in theory and methodology anyway. Nevertheless there are long-term effects such as this text.

Working on the basis of these short-term ideologies (currently: breathless research activities under mostly foreign standards) has the side effect that proprietary theory-building is neglected. Competencies and academic incentives to follow this path autonomously become stunted under the compulsion of quick payoff. Other than in medicine – another 'science of the artificial' aiming at purposeful action – the necessity of continuous theory work is barely accepted in design. Theory-building (mostly *about* design) is left to those reflecting disciplines as philosophy, cultural studies etc. that are only marginally interested in design's fitness for its essential function: the conception and projection of human conditions of living. Although the descent will be concealed for a while due to its economic relevance, this is a vicious circle, turning design into an appendix of marketing.

If design wants to strengthen its social and academic status, it must *broaden its self-conception* and *claim* an appropriate share of the *definition power* regarding future conditions of living. An extended demand and a clearer concept of design's own role will support theory-building again.

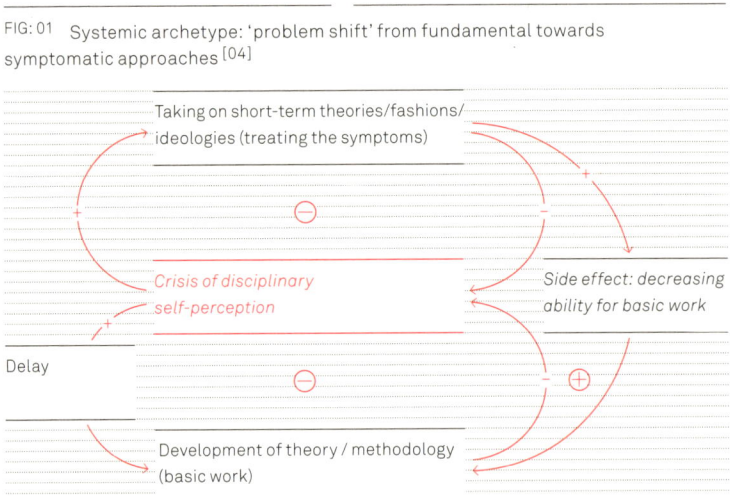

FIG: 01   Systemic archetype: 'problem shift' from fundamental towards symptomatic approaches [04]

Taking on short-term theories/fashions/ideologies (treating the symptoms)

Crisis of disciplinary self-perception

Side effect: decreasing ability for basic work

Delay

Development of theory / methodology (basic work)

So, what are these 'fundamental' approaches that support the construction of design methodology based upon the processual concept of RTD? The question is even more tantalising, since meanwhile we may know that there are no foundations comparable to those in the sciences, but at best a kind of anthropological basis, which can be described as a cybernetic learning mechanism of acting and reflecting.

→ We have to pursue 'the paradox endeavour to design a foundation for a groundless field',[05] aiming at the development of an RTD paradigm.

Motivation and scope

I am not aiming to design a grand new theory, but to clarify inconsistencies, references to developments and some further contributions. The focus, as stated above, is the concept of RTD, and the issue of dynamic / cybernetic 'foundations' of this approach.

Schneider's text 'Design as practice, science and research',[06] a hybrid of a political-strategic and scientific paper, asserts in a full-bodied and slightly simplifying manner, that design is a discipline that 'rests on certain foundations and is thus distinguished by the way it progressively develops its knowledge and practice.' This refers to Friedman,[07] whose comprehension of the foundations is in no way indisputable. For example, he strongly challenges the possibility of research 'by' (through?) design, which Schneider accepts. Despite this ambiguity Schneider proclaims two main categories of design research: *into* and *through* design. This is defensible, of course, but what about research *for* design? I don't want to insist on the third category (maybe the former two provide contributions *for* design and thus implicitly include it), but it should at least be mentioned.

Friedman's article,[07] arguing against RTD, misquotes some references, neglects further clarifications and developments (Findeli, Jonas etc.), and finally returns to a kind of action – reflection approach, which comes close to what RTD could effectively mean. He states:

'Much of this confusion is linked to an ambiguous definition of design research proposed by Frayling in a 1993 paper. Frayling (1993) suggested that there are three models of design research, research into design, research by design, and research for design. Frayling is unclear about what "research by design" actually means and he seems never to have defined the term in an operational way. In a 1997 discussion (UK Council 1997: 21), he notes that it is "distantly derived from Herbert Read's famous teaching through art and teaching to art." This leads to serious conceptual problems.

... In addition to the difficulties this has caused in debates on the notion of the practice-based PhD, it also creates confusion for those who have come to believe that practice is research. The confusion rests, again, on a failure to read.

Beyond this arises the problem of what "research by design" might mean. If such a category did exist – and it may not – the fact of an existing category would tell us nothing of its contents. ...

While the phrase "research by design" has been widely used by many people, it has not been defined. I suspect, in fact, that those who use the phrase have not bothered to read either Frayling's (1993) paper or Read's (1944, 1974) book. Instead, they adopt a misunderstood term for its sound bite quality, linking it to an ill-defined series of notions that equate tacit knowledge with design knowledge, proposing tacit knowledge and design practice as a new form of theorising.

While these problems are relatively inconsequential outside our field, it is important to understand that they exist if we are to develop a foundation for theory construction in design research. This is why I have given them so much thought.'[07]

Frayling is indeed ambiguous, but Friedman increases confusion still further: Frayling did not speak of 'research *by* design', but rather of 'research *through* art and design'.[08] And he considered the category of 'research *for* art and design' to be the most problematic one, as it raises the issue of research being embodied in the artefact. So, which category does Friedman mean: Frayling's 'through' or Frayling's 'for'? And who is to blame for their failures to read?

→ The following is not about Frayling's 'through', but about Findeli's 'through', which is different. And there is progress indeed in clarifying what RTD might be!

Some clarifications

TABLE: 01   Presentation of some 'trinities' of design research concepts:

	INTO / ABOUT	FOR / FOR	THROUGH / BY	REMARKS
Frayling [08]	INTO '...the most straightfor-ward, and ... by far the most common: – Historical research – Aesthetic or perceptual research – Research into a variety of theoretical perspectives on art and design – social, economic, political, ethical, cultural, icono-graphic, technical, material, structural... whatever. ... there are countless models – and archives – from which to derive its rules and procedures.'	FOR 'The thorny one is Re-search for art and design ... Research where the end product is an artefact – where the thinking is, so to speak, embodied in the artefact, where the goal is not primarily com-municable knowledge in the sense of verbal communication, but in the sense of visual or iconic or imagistic communica-tion. ...'	THROUGH '...less straightforward, but still identifiable and visible. – materials research – such as the titanium sputtering or colorisation of metal projects ... – development work – for ex-ample, customising a piece of technology to do something no-one had con-sidered before, and com-municating the results. ... – action research – where a research diary tells ... of a practical experiment in the studios, and the resulting report aims to contextualise it. Both the diary and the report are there to commu-nicate the results, which is what separates research from the gathering of refer-ence materials. ...'	Frayling's categorisation is inconsistent and rather fuzzy: Frayling's 'through' com-prises much of Findeli's 'for'; only action research may relate to 'through / by' with both authors. Frayling's 'for' is something very different from Findeli's 'for'; Findeli would probably not consider it as research at all
Findeli [09]	INTO / ABOUT Separation of design research and design practice (weak theory), 'little or no contribution to a theory of design', see the field of 'design studies'.[10]	FOR Design as applied science (no theory), complex, sophisticated projects (Research and Develop-ment)	BY / THROUGH Conciliation of theory and practice (strong theory) Embedded, implicated, engaged, situated (Sartre, Situationist) theory. 'Such research helps build a genuine theory of design by adopting an epistemo-logical posture more con-sonant with what is speci-fic to design: the project.'	Findeli's categorisation provides an epistemolo-gically and semantically much clearer concept.
Jonas [11]	ABOUT 'Research about design operates from without, thereby keeping its object at a distance. The re-searchers are observers who work scientifically and try, wherever pos-sible, not to change their object. Examples include design philosophy, design history, design criticism...'	FOR 'Research for design also operates from without, supporting the process selectively. The researchers serve designers as "suppliers of knowledge". The know-ledge supplied is valid only for a certain period of time, because it is related to a reality that design aims to change. Examples include market research, user research ... product semantics ...'	THROUGH 'Research through design refers to a research and design process intrinsic to design. Designers / researchers are directly involved in establishing connections and shaping their research object. Examples potentially include every "wicked problem" in Rittel's sense of the term (1992).' [12]	Jonas refers to Findeli's categorisation.

The epistemological status of RTD is still weak. Grounded theory and action theory will probably contribute: *Grounded theory* aims at theory-building, while accepting the modification of its subject matter. *Action research* aiming to modify reality, while observing and processing theoretical modifications. Both approaches admit the involvement of the researcher as well as the emergence of theories from empirical data, in contrast to the traditional concept of theory-building as the verification of previously formulated hypotheses. Findeli argues that:

> ' ... *"project-grounded research" ... is a kind of hybrid between action research and grounded theory research, but at the same time it reaches beyond these methods, in the sense that our researchers in design are valued both for their academic and professional expertise, which is not the case even in the most engaged action research situations.*
> *...although the importance of the design project needs to be recognised in project-grounded research, it should never become the central purpose of the research project, otherwise we fall back into R&D. Therefore, the design project and its output find their place in the annex of the dissertation, since practice is only a support for research (a means, not an end), the main product of which should remain design knowledge.*'[09]

→   The inconsistencies seem to result from the obvious shift of meaning of *for* and *through* between Frayling and Findeli. Again, this is about Findeli's RTD or 'project-grounded research'.

An anthropological assumption

The ability to design and to be conscious of doing so (i.e. to be retrospective and *projective* regarding one's own position in the environment) distinguishes humans from the rest of the living world. The proper construction of this position and ability to act in relation to nature is one of the unresolved challenges of modernity. According to Latour, Boyle's *Invention of the Laboratory* and the Scientific Community as factory for the production of facts concerning nature adds to the transcendence of naturalised nature the immanence (feasibility) of socialised nature.[13] Hobbes's *Invention of Leviathan* as representative of the unpredictable mass of citizens, seduced by their passions, adds to the immanence (mundane chaos) of the social transcendence of a scientifically substantiated, eternal order. It is thus that the three *paradoxical constitutional guarantees of modernity* arise:

1.   Even when we construct nature, it is as if we did not.
2.   Even when we do not construct society, it is as if we did.
3.   Nature and society must remain absolutely separate; the work of purification must therefore remain separate from mediation work.

Design, as *the means*, or the mediation, cannot take part in the scientific endeavour of purification. It has to ignore the modern separation of nature and society. Conceiving and realising *projects* necessarily includes *natural and social* components. Even Simon (p. 139–167), the protagonist of cognitive models, argues that design, seen as a socio-cultural phenomenon, follows evolutionary patterns and has no final goals.[03] The intentional transfer of system states into preferred ones (state 1 à state 2) opens up the hybrid field of the 'Sciences of the Artificial'. Management philosophy has argued that the separation of natural and artificial is insufficient:[14] there are systems, which are the outcomes of human activities, but *not* the results of human purpose. And of all things it is these delicate hybrid systems that are the subjects of management and design interventions.

According to Rittel, these 'wicked problems' can be overcome only by opening up the closed algorithmic problem solving process (1st-generation methods) and initiating a process of *argumentation* and *negotiation* among the stakeholders (2nd-generation methods). In other words, he suggests a change from 1st- to 2nd-order observation: it is not systems being observed, but systems of observing systems.[15] Under these conditions we have to account for the fact that the problem itself is not 'given', but will be designed by the stakeholders, and, in consequence, will change its character in the course of the solution process. No information is available, if there is no idea of a solution, because the questions arising depend on the kind of solution one has in mind. One cannot fully understand and formulate the problem before it is solved. Thus, in the end, the solution is the problem. Rittel therefore argues for the further development and refinement of the argumentative model of the design process and the study of the designers' reasoning, their rules of asking questions, generating information, and arriving at judgements. He concludes, slightly ironically:

> '*All of which implies a certain modesty; while of course on the other side there is a characteristic of the second generation which is not so modest, that of lack of respect for existing situations and an assumption that nothing has to continue to be the way that it is. That might be expressed in the principle of systematic doubt or something like it. The second-generation designer also is a moderate optimist, in that he refuses to believe that planning is impossible, although his knowledge of the dilemmas of rationality and the dilemmas of planning for others should tell him otherwise, perhaps. But he refuses to believe that planning is impossible, otherwise he would go home. He must also be an activist.*',[16] *p. 326*

Jones puts it more generally and metaphorically, while emphasising the necessity of designing the design process itself.[17] A considerable part of the design capacities has to be re-directed from the problem to the process. The designer as 'black box' (the artist), as well as the designer as 'glass box' (the scientist, follower of 1st-generation methods), have to change their attitude towards a self-conception of *designer as 'self-organising system'*, who is observing the evolving artefact plus him- or herself observing the evolving artefact.

→   Design ability is the essential human characteristic. It is *the means* for obtaining knowledge of the world. We cannot overcome our involvement in the process.

─────────────────

Evolutionary feedback patterns

There is no evidence that socio-cultural processes follow a kind of plan or design. The concept of evolution appears to be promising for theoretical support and methodological progress. It relieves us from assuming an Intelligent Artificer at some mysterious point of origin. Utter undesignedness, pure chaos was the starting point, and no further conditions, no foundations are required[18] (p. 69): 'A designed thing, then, is either a living thing or a part of a living thing, or the artefact of a living thing, organised in any case in aid of this battle against disorder.' A good design theory, as a designed artefact, should be able to explain its own emergence. And so far, Darwinian thinking has provided the only descriptive model that satisfies this self-referential requirement. Other explanations would run into vicious circles or infinite regress.

The epistemic nature of design can be considered as a *learning process*, which is biologically grounded in the need of organisms to survive in an environment. The aim cannot be final, 'true' representation of some external reality, but rather a process of *(re-)construction* for the purpose of appropriate *(re-)action*. Evolutionary epistemologists argue that the Kantian transcendental must *a priori* be replaced by the assumption of an *evolutionary fit* between the objects and the subject of recognition.[19] The evolutionary model of knowledge production suggests structural identity from the molecular up to the cognitive and cultural level.[20] It reveals a circle of trial (based upon expectation) and experience (leading to success or failure, confirmation or refutation), or of action and reflection. Starting with passed cases, the circle consists of an inductive / heuristic semi-circle with purposeful learning from experience, leading to hypotheses and theories and prognoses about how the world works, and a deductive / logical semi-circle, leading to actions and interventions, which result in the confirmation or refutation of theories due to new experiences, etc. Internal or external perturbations (called ideas, creativity, or accidents, environmental changes etc.) influence the circle, leading to stabilisations (negative feedback) or amplifications and evolutionary change (positive feedback).

Only very recently this scheme was split into the 'ratiomorphous' (Konrad Lorenz, in [20]) systems of *recognition* and the rational systems of *explanation* / understanding, with its most extreme form: the logical positivist dualism of 'context of discovery' (acting) versus 'context of justification' (thinking). While the ratiomorphous process of recognition has a high potential in dealing with complex, evolving phenomena, it is not always useful for causal explanations, and vice versa. But this 'dilemma' is not inherent in the nature of knowledge production, but rather a consequence of the dualistic concept, which we have imposed on the process. Toulmin traces it back to the mid-17th century and distinguishes rationality from reasonableness, the latter losing authority in the sciences.[21] Language is too much locked in the 'black-and-white' tradition to be able to distinguish or indicate the beautiful transitory shades of 'grey' between the poles of recognition and explanation.

TABLE: 02   Recognition vs. explanation,[20] pp. 53–55

Recognition	Explanation
- networks, many causes	- linear cause-effect relations
- simultaneous (simul hoc)	- sequential (propter hoc)
- 4 Aristotelian causes considered	- only causa efficiens considered
- only local validity, context is crucial	- global validity claimed, context excluded
- allows no experiments, mostly irreversible	- relies on experiments, mostly reversible
- prognosis is projection	- prognosis is forecasting
- correspondence of organism / artefact in a milieu	- coherence of elements inside a system
- reaches into high complexity	- reduces complexity
- fitness, 'truth' means strong design	- 'truth' means correct causal relations
- is labelled 'pre-scientific'	- is labelled 'scientific'

The argument of *naturalised epistemology* appears in various forms. Dewey argues that processes of circular action, driven by intention, are the essential core of knowledge generation.[22] The separation of thinking as pure contemplation and acting as bodily intervention into the world becomes obsolete; quite the reverse: thinking depends on real world situations that have to be met. Thinking activity is initiated by the necessity to choose appropriate means with regard to expected consequences. The active improvement of an unsatisfactory situation is the primary motivation for thinking, designing, and, finally – in a more refined, purified, quantitative manner – for scientific knowledge production. According to Dewey, knowing is a manner of acting and 'truth' is better called 'warranted assertibility'. Schön's epistemology of 'reflective practice'[23] can be regarded as the design-related description of these concepts. It might be this general pattern that Cross characterises as 'designerly ways of knowing'.[24]

The theory of socio-cultural evolution seems to be a useful framework to denote the unpredictability of project outcomes, and thus the limits of causal explanations, in a scientific manner. This is not to deny that designers are able intentionally to design and manufacture a new teapot, a new aircraft, or a new constitution. But these *designs are temporal interventions into evolutionary processes*. Most results disappear, a few are integrated into the further process. Failures as well as successes become part of the socio-cultural archive of humankind.

→   Evolutionary epistemology explains the ongoing production and re-production of both artefacts and knowledge, finally of design and science. There is no need for any specific nature of knowing in design.

FIG. 02

FIG. 03

FIG. 04

Variation – selection – re-stabilisation

Autopoietic systems show a high independence from internal and external perturbations (negative feedback compensates for the irritations). On the other hand, circularity can cause *deterministic chaos.* Minimal differences in initial conditions of the system parameters can produce completely different outcomes, so that predictability of final states is lost (positive feedback amplifies perturbations and triggers evolutionary change). [FIG. 02]

Natural evolutionary patterns of development, with their sequence of stable phases and sudden variations seem to be based on the interplay of negative and positive feedback mechanisms. The evolution of artefacts shows similar patterns. [FIG. 03]

We seem to know where we come from, but we do not know where we are going. At least we know the ancestors of our current artefacts, which means we have some capacity for interpreting design history. Nevertheless, we do not normally know the influences that acted upon the bifurcation situations and resulted in exactly this and no other selection. Representations of design processes reveal these patterns too, which indicates similarity of ontogenetic and phylogenetic processes in designing. [FIG. 04]

FIG. 02   Simple feedback processes, as in the logistic equation $x_n+1 = r\,x_n\,(1-x_n)$, produce bifurcation cascades and deterministic chaos. [25]

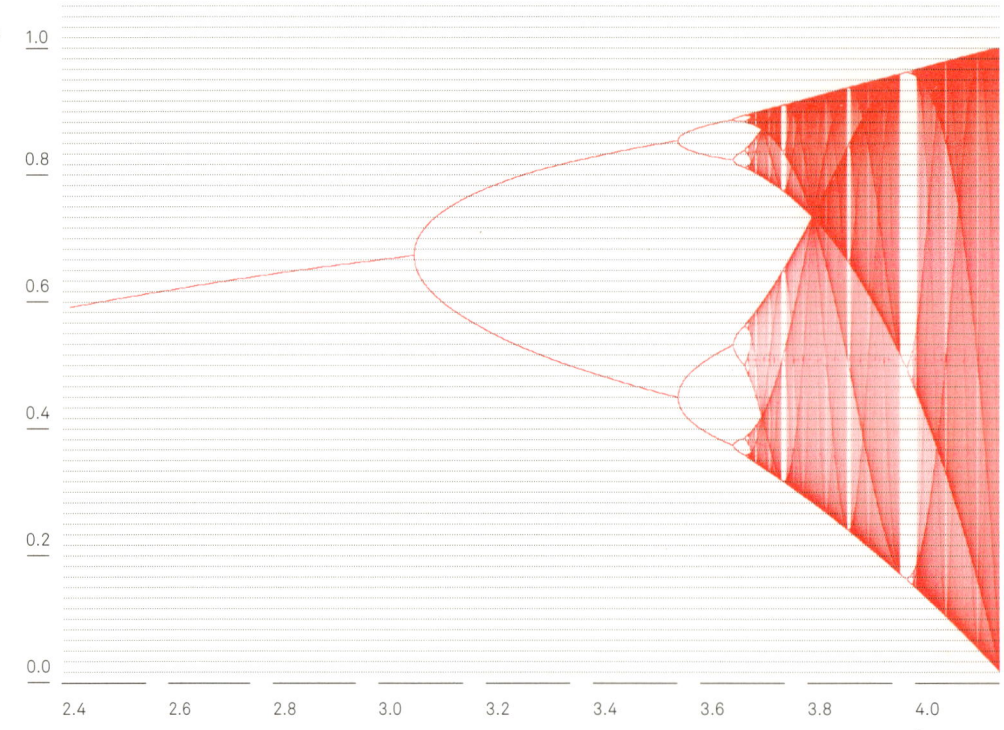

FIG. 03   Bifurcation patterns in the evolution of artefacts [26]

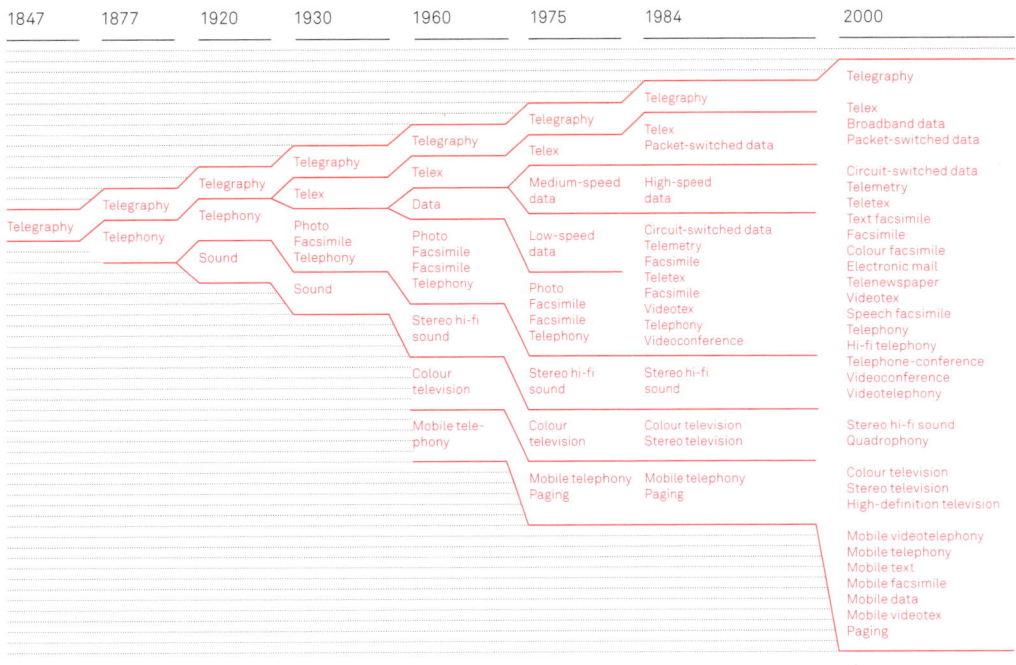

FIG. 03   Bifurcation patterns in the evolution of artefacts [26]

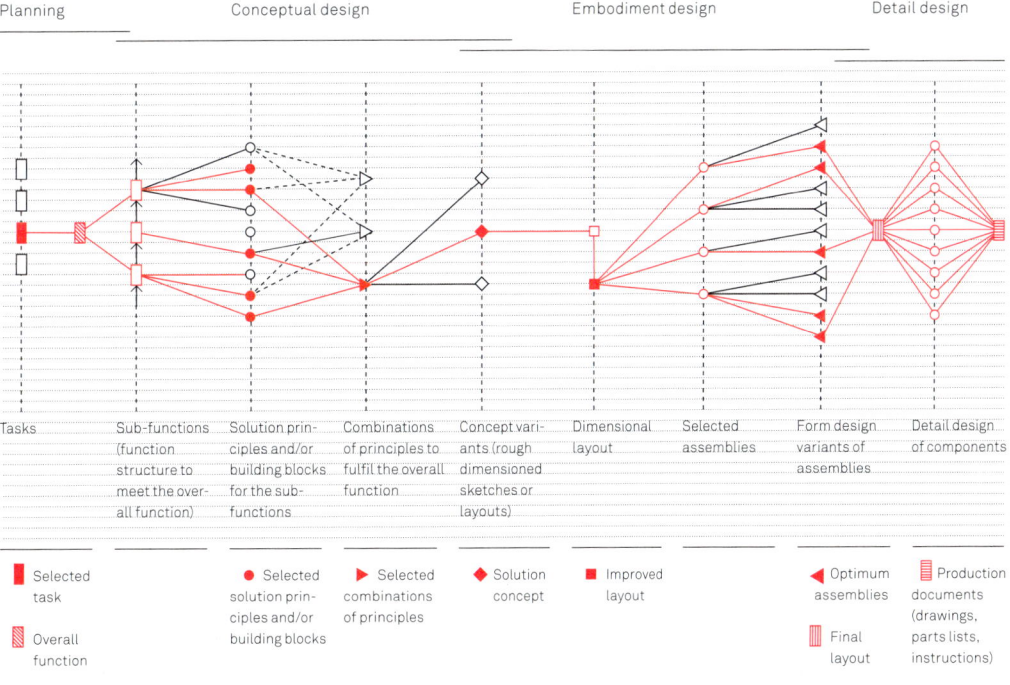

FIG. 04   Bifurcation cascades in the design process [27]

The nicely cut branches after the bifurcations suggest the existence of rational criteria to overcome the indeterminacy, to take a decision, which provides more than a random chance of future viability. Rittel comments on this, laconically:

> *'Constrictions are not "natural conditions" but deliberate restrictions of the variety of solutions, mostly implicit signs of resignation. ...*
> *... In reality there is no opposition / sharp conflict between an ... intuitive approach to solve a problem and ... a controlled, reasonable and rational approach. The more control one wants to exert, the more well-founded one wants to judge, the more intuitive one has to be. The endpoints in the more and more ramifying tree of causal explanations are always spontaneous judgements.'* [28]

These evident analogies in the patterns of natural and artefact evolution confirm the use of evolutionary patterns in design theory. Luhmann's concept of *social evolution* is based upon the *system / environment* distinction;[29] it is this difference that enables evolution. Evolution theory does not distinguish historical epochs, but the circular sequence of *variation*, *selection* and *re-stabilisation*. It explains the emergence of essential forms and substances from the accidental, relieving us from attributing the order of things to a form-giving *telos* or origin. It simply turns the terminological framework of world description upside-down. Evolution theory is not a theory of progress, and it does not deliver projections or interpretations of the future. Adaptation is a condition, not the goal or outcome of evolution: on the basis of being adapted it is possible to produce more and more risky ways of non-adaptation – as long as the continuation of autopoiesis is guaranteed.

The three processual components of evolution can be related to the constituent components of society, conceived as a communicative system:

— *Variation* varies the *elements* of the systems, i.e. *communications*. Variation means deviating, unexpected, surprising communication. It may simply be questioning or rejecting expectations of meaning. Variation produces raw material and provides further communicative connections with wider varieties of meaning than before. In design this means new artefacts, conceived as materialised communication.
— *Selection* relates to the *structures* of the system. Structures determine the creation and use of *expectations* that determine communication processes. Positive selection means the choice of meaningful relations that promise a value for building or stabilising structures. Selections serve as filters to control the diffusion of variations. Religion has been one such filter. Truth, money, power, as symbolically generalised media serve as filters in modern societies. In design they may be phenomena such as fashion or taste.
— *Re-stabilisation* refers to the state of the evolving *system* after a positive / negative selection. It has to take care of the *system-compatibility* of the selection. Even negative selections have to be re-stabilised, because they remain in the system's memory /

archive. In design this is the long-term viability of an artefact, in a functional as well as a semantic sense.

This can be related to Langrish's memetic concept of recipemes / selectemes / explanemes as information units.[30] And, more pragmatically, to Sanders, who refers to the concept of usable / desirable / useful as success criteria.[31] She argues that we are quite good at designing usability, at making progress in designing desirability, but are still weak in designing usefulness. I agree with her diagnosis, but – against the evolutionary backdrop – I am highly sceptical as to substantial progress regarding desirability or even usefulness.

→   If we are aiming for new descriptions and tools for the design process, we have to identify those patterns of natural evolution that can be transferred to the evolution of artefacts: variation – selection – re-stabilisation.

A generic design process model

Design, as a sometimes highly rational endeavour, is embedded in overall trial-and-error processes. *It covers only the variation phase of socio-cultural evolution.*

FIG. 05   The conscious design / learning process as part of the evolutionary trial and error process

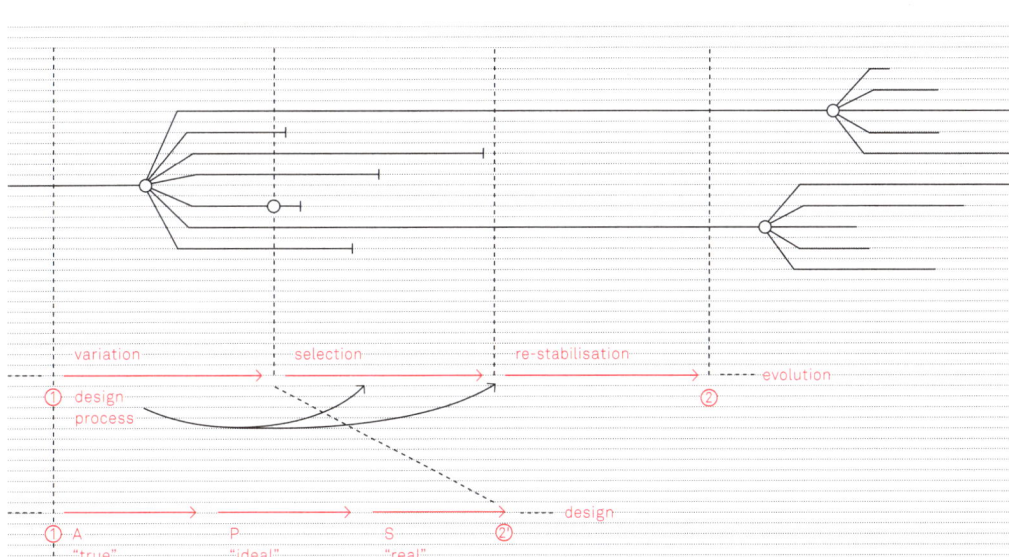

Although design activities – by means of methods – desperately try to consider selection and re-stabilisation, they are necessarily de-coupled from these phases. There is no causal link between variation – selection – re-stabilisation. Bringing a man to the moon may turn out to be the first step into the universe, or just a singular historical event. So state 2 should better be labelled 2', leaving 2 for the actual future state, which cannot be determined. Design is about what is NOT (yet), which expresses the main epistemological problem the discipline has to face. The issue has been addressed by Nelson and Stolterman, who argue that design is an inquiry into three domains of knowing: the true, the ideal and the real, with incompatible ways of reasoning.[32] The process model of ANALYSIS – PROJECTION – SYNTHESIS can be considered as a more pragmatic and operationalised version of the true / the ideal / the real.[04]

The well-known circular design process models, with the one of the Institute of Design Chicago (research – analysis – synthesis – realisation) as a prototype, are adaptations of Kolb's 'learning cycles'.[33] The latter, in turn, seems to relate to the USAF's basic cybernetic OODA model.[34] They all neglect the long-term projective claim of design.

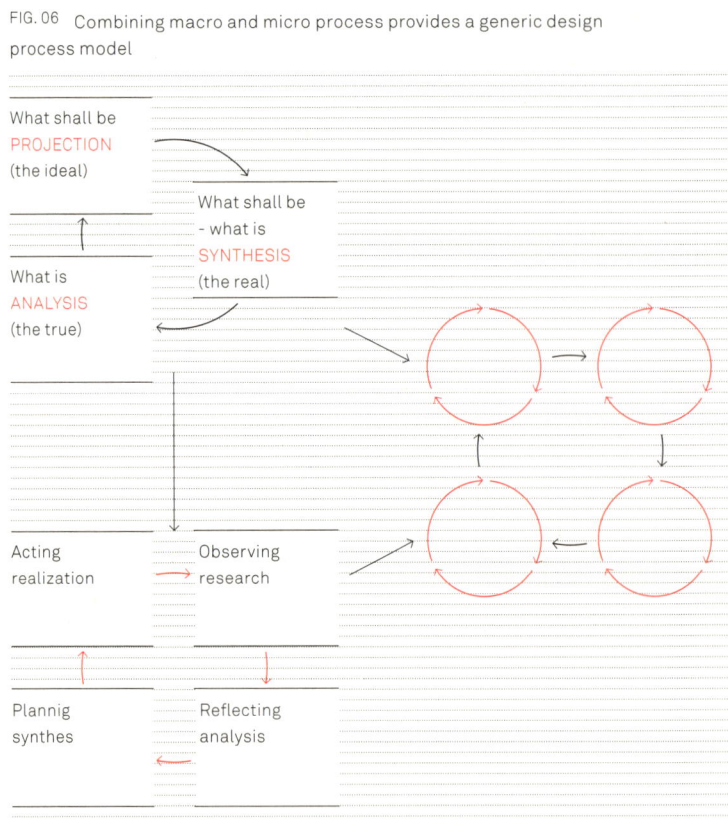

FIG. 06   Combining macro and micro process provides a generic design process model

What shall be
PROJECTION
(the ideal)

What shall be
- what is
SYNTHESIS
(the real)

What is
ANALYSIS
(the true)

Acting
realization

Observing
research

Plannig
synthes

Reflecting
analysis

A combination of the *macro model* of ANALYSIS à PROJECTION à SYNTHESIS (domains of knowing) and the *micro model* of research à analysis à synthesis à realisation (learning phases) provides a hypercyclic *generic design process model*.[35] Hypercycles are basic process patterns at the transitory stage between chemical and biological evolution; in other words: explanations of the origin of life.[36] The design argument becomes highly metaphorical here: hypercyclic processes produce autopoietic closure. Feedback cycles describe prototypical learning processes of autopoietic systems. They produce patterns of deterministic chaos and evolutionary development. Natural and artificial evolution follow comparable processes. All this supports the concept of conscious design as being necessarily embedded in evolutionary processes. Only the variation phase of artificial evolution is fully conscious and controllable. That means most of the time the 'watchmaker' is actually blind.[37] He experiences some rare enlightened moments in an eternity of blindness.

If we switch from metaphor to operation, we can interpret the hypercyclic scheme of the design process as a toolbox of three rows and four columns. Each of the 12 compartments that represent the complete process contains methods and tools for the respective process steps. If we assume 10 methods per compartment and 12 process steps, we arrive at 10^{12} different paths / processes. Each path is a legitimate roadmap of the design process, transferring state 1 à state 2'. The scheme is open for various 'flavours' of design research: technological, cultural, user-centred, semantic, systemic etc., and it is just one possible model of a process, the validity of which will have to be debated elsewhere.

The distinction between design and research becomes fuzzy. The more one limits the inquiry to single domains of knowledge or even to single process steps, the more it becomes possible and important to match the standards of scientific research. On the other hand, processes covering several boxes or even the whole process necessarily have to creatively deal with knowledge gaps.[13]

→ The formulation of a genuine design research paradigm requires a generic design process model, which serves as a framework for RTD. It has to account for the (impossible but necessary) projective character of the project.

Re-contextualising the scientific paradigm

Successful design depends on the variation phase of the evolutionary process. The subsequent phases (selection, re-stabilisation) are causally de-coupled. Scientific contributions may possibly improve the probability of successful design. The field of HCI is facing similar problems. Fallman tries to clarify the role of design in HCI research and argues that 'it makes more sense to regard HCI as a *design discipline* rather than as a more traditional academic research discipline.'[38] This is remarkable, since the design discipline is on the same road, but heading in the opposite direction, towards scientific research. Fallman distinguishes design and research in HCI as two poles of a continuum and coins the terms of 'research-oriented design' and 'design-oriented research', which can immediately be related to the present concepts of 'research through design' and 'design through research'.^{TABLE: 03} TABLE: 03

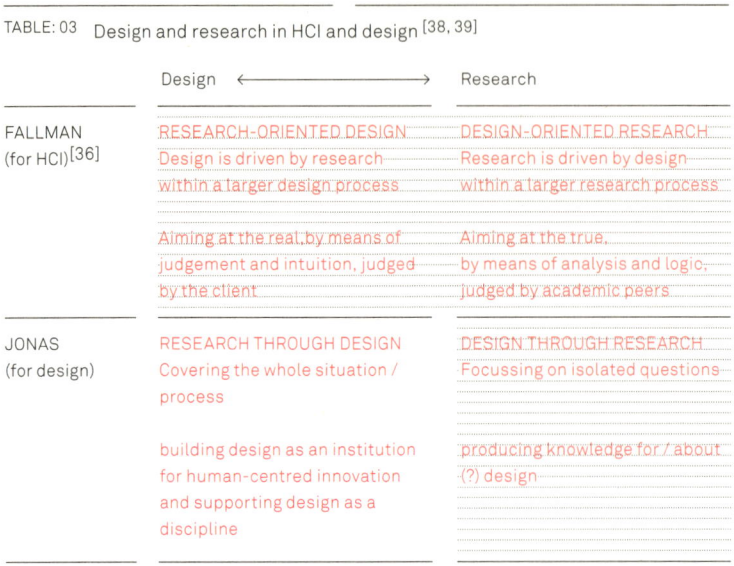

TABLE: 03   Design and research in HCI and design [38, 39]

	Design ⟷	Research
FALLMAN (for HCI)[36]	RESEARCH-ORIENTED DESIGN Design is driven by research within a larger design process	DESIGN-ORIENTED RESEARCH Research is driven by design within a larger research process
	Aiming at the real, by means of judgement and intuition, judged by the client	Aiming at the true, by means of analysis and logic, judged by academic peers
JONAS (for design)	RESEARCH THROUGH DESIGN Covering the whole situation / process	DESIGN THROUGH RESEARCH Focussing on isolated questions
	building design as an institution for human-centred innovation and supporting design as a discipline	producing knowledge for / about (?) design

'Design through research' assumes that the 'swampy lowlands' of uncertainty[23] will be subsequently replaced by well-grounded knowledge. But exclusively scientific research is unable fully to recognise the implications of acting in a space of imagination and projection. The 'knowledge base position' needs to be complemented by the 'un-knowledge base position'[40] or by the competencies to deal with not-knowing.[41] It is not science as a method, but science as a guiding paradigm for design, which is being called into question. Furthermore, the hierarchical separation of basic / applied / clinical research does not make sense in this conception of design. Basic research for real needs has to be closely related to real-world situations, i.e. basic research, in order to be basic, has to be embedded / applied in clinical situations.

The idea of RTD is based upon a concept of domains of knowing and a generic structure of learning / designing, which has been derived from practice. Design process logic, according to the argument in this text, is a cybernetic logic of creating the objects of the world. Relevant design knowledge is not *knowledge of* the objects, but *knowledge for* the creation of the objects.[42] Every design process (more or less) follows this generic structure, making use of the various (scientific) methods provided for each of the steps. The inherent fuzziness of the process model is able to bridge the causality gaps occurring between the different, often incompatible, scientific contributions. One might even go further, following Glanville,[43] and argue that RTD is the generic pattern for scientific research (aiming at purified, de-contextualised, generalisable etc. knowledge) as well as for artistic practice (aiming at undisciplined, subjective, singular etc. knowledge).

The hypothesis was: RTD provides the epistemological means for the development of a genuine design research paradigm. Now we have to do research *about* RTD, in order to understand the process of RTD better, research *for* RTD, in order to improve the process of RTD, and research *through* RTD, in order to establish and stabilise the disciplinary paradigm…

→   The Scientific Paradigm has to be embedded into the Design Paradigm:
       — Research is guided through design process logic, and
       — Design is supported/driven by phases of scientific research and inquiry.

→   Only design research conducted under the designerly paradigm can contribute to design's methodological development and its disciplinary stability/autonomy. Both depend on each other in a circular manner.

References / Bibliography

[01]   Archer B (1981) A View of the Nature of Design Research. In: Jacques R, Powell J
         (eds): *Design: Science: Method*. Westbury House, Guildford

[02]   Cross N (1999) Design Research: A Disciplined Conversation. *Design Issues* 15(2): 5–10

[03]   Simon HA (1996) *The Sciences of the Artificial*. MIT Press, Cambridge, MA

[04]   Jonas W (1996) Design als systemische Intervention – für ein neues (altes)
         'postheroisches' Designverständnis. *17. designwissenschaftliches Kolloquium Objekt
         und Prozess*, 28–30.11.1996, Burg Giebichenstein, Halle / Saale

[05]   Jonas W (2000) The Paradox Endeavour to Design a Foundation for a Groundless
         Field. *Proceedings of the International Conference on Design Education*, 12/2000,
         Curtin University, Perth, Australia

[06]   Schneider B (2006) Design als Wissenschaft und Forschung. *Presentation at DGTF
         Conference*, Berlin, May 2006

[07]   Friedman K (2002) Theory Construction in Design Research. Criteria, Approaches,
         and Methods. *Common Ground, Proceedings of the DRS International Conference*,
         Brunel University, 5–7 September 2002

[08]   Frayling C (1993) Research in Art and Design. *Royal College of Art Research Papers*
         1(1): 1–5

[09]   Findeli A (1998) A Quest for Credibility: Doctoral Education and Research in Design at
         the University of Montreal. *Doctoral Education in Design*, Ohio, 8–11 October 1998

[10]   Margolin V (1991) The Need for Design Studies. *Design at the Crossroads: A Conference
         Report*, CIRA Working papers Series 3

[11]   Jonas W (2004) Research through Design. In: Findeli A (ed.): *Reader des Ersten Design
         Forschungssymposiums des Swiss Design Network, 13–14 May 2004*

[12]   Rittel HWJ (1992) *Planen, Entwerfen, Design*. ed. by Reuter WD, Verlag
         W. Kohlhammer, Stuttgart, Berlin

[13]   Latour B (1998) *Wir sind nie modern gewesen. Versuch einer symmetrischen
         Anthropologie*. Fischer, Frankfurt [French original 1991]

[14]   Hayek FA von (1967) The Results of Human Action but not of Human Design. In: Hayek,
         Studies in Philosophy, Politics and Economics. University of Chicago Press, Chicago

[15]   Foerster H von (1981) *Observing Systems*. Intersystems Publications, Seaside, CA

[16]   Cross N (ed.) (1984) *Developments in Design Methodology*. Wiley, Chichester

[17]   Jones JC (1970) *Design Methods. Seeds of Human Futures*. Wiley, London; 2nd edition,
         Van Nostrand Reinhold, New York 1992

[18]   Dennett DC (1995) *Darwin's Dangerous idea. evolution and the meanings of life*.
         Penguin Books, London

[19]   Campbell DT (1960) Blind Variation and Selective Retention in Creative Thought as in Other Knowledge Processes. *Psychol Rev* 67:380–400

[20]   Riedl R (2000) *Strukturen der Komplexität. Eine Morphologie des Erkennens und Erklärens.* Springer, Berlin, Heidelberg New York

[21]   Toulmin S (2001) *Return to Reason.* Harvard University Press, Cambridge, MA

[22]   Dewey J (1986) *Logic: the Theory of Inquiry.* Southern Illinois University Press, Carbondale, IL

[23]   Schön DA (1983) *The Reflective Practitioner. How Professionals Think in Action.* Basic Books, New York

[24]   Cross N (2001) Designerly Ways of Knowing: Design Discipline Versus Design Science. *Design Issues* 17(3): 49–55

[25]   Logistic equation: http://en.wikipedia.org/wiki/Logistic_function (accessed 6 June 2007)

[26]   Graham S, Marvin S (1996) *Telecommunications and the City. Electronic Spaces, Urban Places.* Routledge, London

[27]   Roozenburg NFM, Eekels J (1995) *Product Design: Fundamentals and Methods.* Wiley, Chichester

[28]   Rittel HWJ (1972) Second-generation Design Methods. In: Cross N (ed.): *Developments in Design Methodology.* Wiley, Chichester, 317–327

[29]   Luhmann N (1997) *Die Gesellschaft der Gesellschaft.* Suhrkamp, Frankfurt

[30]   Langrish JZ (2004) Darwinian Design: The Memetic Evolution of Design Ideas. *Design Issues* 20(4): 4–19

[31]   Sanders E (2006) Design Research in 2006. *Design Research Quarterly* VI(1): 1–8

[32]   Nelson HG, Stolterman E (2003) *The Design Way. Intentional Change in an Unpredictable World.* Educational Technology Publications, Englewood Cliffs, NJ

[33]   Kolb DA (1984) *Experiential Learning: Experience as the Source of Learning and Development.* Prentice-Hall, New York

[34]   OODA Loop: http://en.wikipedia.org/wiki/OODA_Loop (accessed 6 June 2007)

[35]   Hugentobler HK, Jonas W, Rahe D (2004) Designing a Methods Platform for Design and Design Research. *Futureground, DRS International Conference*, Melbourne, November 2004

[36]   Eigen M, Schuster P (1979) *The Hypercycle. A Principle of Natural Self-organization.* Springer-Verlag, Berlin, Heidelberg, New York

[37]   Dawkins R (1986) *The Blind Watchmaker.* Norton, New York

[38]   Fallman D (2005) Why Research-oriented Design isn't Design-oriented Research. *Proceedings of Nordes: Nordic Design Research Conference*, 29–31 May 2005, Copenhagen

[39]   Jonas W (2006) Research through DESIGN through Research – a Problem Statement
         and a Conceptual Sketch. *Proceedings of wonderground, DRS international confe-
         rence*, November 2006, Lisbon

[40]   Jonas W, Chow R, Verhaag N (2005) *Proceedings of EAD06*. http://ead06.hfk-bremen.de
         (accessed 6 June 2007)

[41]   Willke H (2002) *Dystopia. Studien zur Krisis des Wissens in der modernen Gesellschaft.*
         Suhrkamp, Frankfurt

[42]   Glanville R (2006) Construction and Design. *Constructivist Foundations* I(3): 103-110

[43]   Glanville R (1980) Why Design Research? In: Jacques R, Powell A (eds): *Design:
         Science:Method*. Westbury House, Guildford

Design as Practice, Science and Research

I. Design as Practice

One aspect of design

Design has become a fashionable term that is applied to almost everything. It triggers associations with trendy products, beautiful forms, aesthetic lifestyles, the comforts (and drugs) of civilisation etc. Design, at one time a luxury and the prerogative of the upper classes, has been an article of consumption for the general public since the 1980s. It is now the mass markets' favourite word.

Design exerts a powerful fascination on people and is seen by many as the art form of our time. Design objects enjoy cult status. The old functionalist principle 'form follows function' (an object's use determines its aesthetic appearance) has long since given way to the post-modernist slogan 'form follows fun and emotion' (an object's form ought to be a source of enjoyment and address the emotions).

Design is a mass-cultural phenomenon that shapes human perception and thus has a powerful influence on general judgements of taste. Products such as baseball caps, blue jeans, Coca-Cola, Disney, Hollywood, Nokia and Nike, as well as the various styled images of both sports events and their protagonists, have an enduring impact on collective taste the world over. With its design, the Microsoft computer company, for example, defines the digital-aesthetic perspective of the majority of users.

In addition to advertising products, applying design as a means of differentiating them is one of the most important ways of promoting sales. Product design is, not least, the result of an economic logic by which the world of commodities must remain in a constant state of revolution and where product innovation arises from a 'compulsive desire for eternally novel things' that has meanwhile become a basic cultural pattern. In a recently published book, *The Economics of Innocent Fraud*, economist Kenneth Galbraith writes:

> *'Product innovation and modification is a major economic function, and no significant manufacturer introduces a new product without cultivating the consumer demand for it. Or forgoes efforts to influence and sustain the demand for an existing product. Here enters the world of advertising and salesmanship, of television, of consumer manipulation. Thus an impairment of consumer and market sovereignty.*
> *In the real world, manufacturers and industry in general go far to set prices and establish demand, employing to this end monopoly, oligopoly, product design and differentiation, advertising, other sales and trade promotion.'*[01]

Beautifying everyday life by means of design – in other words, aestheticising most of the objects and images that surround us – has become an important economic factor. For quite some time now, the individualisation of lifestyles and the satisfaction – with sensually modified surfaces – of emotions, wishes and desires have served market expansion. Company profits are now virtually the sole measure of a design's success.

Considered from a critical perspective, design as a sales-promoting stimulant – i.e. as styling – is generally nothing more than the expression of a calculation of the particular interests by those who are ignorant. After all, shouldn't most designed objects be categorised as superfluous? Doesn't stylish design amount to a kind of marketing trick used to flood the world with absurd offers that nobody really needs? Design produces luxury toys for a consumer world that is becoming increasingly meaningless. The obsessive attitude of a society addicted to beauty transforms objects of consumption into fetishes and creates a 'beauty shield' that masks the ugliness of real poverty and environmental destruction. In the process, the cultural standards of the industrial empires are exported as a matter of course into 'underdeveloped' societies. As a result, Third World countries find themselves swamped by a world of goods and images that largely disregards and ignores needs that are articulated and exist locally in a specific world of products and communication. Design is produced primarily by (white) men who view women primarily as consumers and advertising media.

Designers – male and female – are actively involved in this business of creating 'rapidly obsolete products, formally aesthetic trivial games, and the boutiquisation of the world of objects'. In a lecture given at the award of an honorary doctorate at the Universidad Tecnológica Metropolitana in Santiago de Chile, Gui Bonsiepe, a doyen of the international university design scene, said: 'From time to time, one has the impression that a designer who speculates with the idea of two minutes of fame, feels obliged to invent a new label that will serve as a brand distinguishing it from all the other designs in the market.'[02] The future of design, considered from an economic and socio-political point of view, is not hard to predict: for despite fashions in style – such as the innovations of postmodernist new design, new objectivity, the retro-look, high-tech etc. – design will continue to perform its traditional role. Critical debate about this role is, however, almost non-existent. Bonsiepe is worried by the fact that the activity of designers is not called into question at all. Instead, unchallenged concepts such as branding, competitiveness, globalisation, comparative advantage, differentiation, lifestyle design, emotional design, event design, experience design, smart design etc., are now the order of the day.[02]

The other aspect of design

Design involves a lot more than simply creating an attractive world of objects, and far greater attention ought to be given to this fact in the future. Design shapes communication and creates identity. It is a conscious act that aims to create meaningful order, and is thus an essential part of our culture. Ever since it appeared in the early

19th century, design has been ideologically committed to transforming the world for the benefit of human beings and to helping to find intelligent solutions to problems.

How could this look in practice? Design could, for instance, help to make our increasingly complex world more transparent and intelligible in a delightful way. This ambition places design in the normative tradition of the Enlightenment, which sought to alphabetise and democratise knowledge, discoveries and findings. Thus practised, design becomes a discipline that not only provides orientation, but also simplifies and renders comprehensible complex and bewildering masses of data, information structures, processes and objects. Design simplifies the world, making it easier to understand. Initially, at least, design seems to be quite successful at this. It structures information in a way that promotes communication and activity or, in other words, mass visual communication. Hence, design is eminently political and could become a leading discipline within information society.

The fields of activity and the problems of future-oriented design activity as understood in this essay include product and interface design as well as visual communication (graphic design). Below, I name a few of these areas without claiming to provide an exhaustive or representative list.

— *First: designing space.* How – and by whom – is public space designed, and how can it be visually enhanced? How can the boundary between public and private domains, which is being eroded by the new media (among other things), be rendered visible? How would a traffic-guidance system look that integrated motorised, public and parked traffic with the appropriate visual means? In a digitised environment and in public and private spaces, it is not only elderly people who need visual orientation aids and a product world geared to their needs and abilities.
— *Second: visual communication in society (social design).* Visual communication between society's diverse stakeholders is still a largely untouched and unexplored field. What role could the visual level, for example, play in the argument for sustainability in the ecological – and hence also economic – domains? How can communication (which largely takes place via images these days) in the 'patients-doctors-medical technology' triangle be structured in the interest of health and patients? And what tasks will visual communication have to perform in order to integrate sections of the population that speak foreign languages?
— *Third: scientific-technological and didactic communication (information design, knowledge visualisation).* Visual design plays a vital role in the democratisation of knowledge. Designers are therefore urgently called upon to help to make orientation in information networks transparent. The goal must be to transform rapidly proliferating information into communication. How do we render knowledge visible and make scientific discoveries understandable? What significance should be attached to visual knowledge (alongside traditional knowledge imparted via spoken language)? What role can it play in the acquisition of knowledge and in fostering communication between holders of knowledge?

— *Fourth: cultural communication.* With the trend towards a globalised, standardised cultural mishmash, people have an ever-greater need to communicate their own regional cultural identity (for example) to others. What part can visual communication play in this process? How can international communication between different cultures be structured in a way that primarily employs images rather than words? And how does non-paternalistic visual imagery in local development work look at the level of development cooperation?

— *Fifth: political communication (governmental design).* Orientation aids are essential for dealing with the increasingly complicated and bewildering political processes in a democratic society. Designing such aids is a great challenge. How does one present state institutions (government, courts, administration) so that citizens feel that they are being taken seriously and not merely regarded as 'clients'. What role does non-verbal communication play in a state's communication with citizens belonging to foreign-language minorities?

Being of such high technological and social complexity, such tasks can only be solved in cooperation with other disciplines working within the spheres of the cultural, social, natural and engineering sciences. Hence, to ensure that their interdisciplinary activities really are carried out on the basis of equality, designers will have to exercise discipline at the theoretical level if they are to achieve conceptual precision and methodological stringency. In the past, designers had very little reason to concern themselves with such questions. In the next two chapters I show the path taken by design on its way to becoming a science and a research discipline.

Summary: The ambivalence of design turns out to be a contradiction within which designers operate. Alongside design as a market instrument, there also is the demand that design, in future, become a democratic and thus, to a certain extent, an emancipatory discipline that provides orientation. Design's credibility as a discipline that provides orientation will be judged by its comprehensibility, its social commitment and, of course, the functionality of the forms through which it communicates.

II. Design as a science

Right up to the 1980s, design did not have to define itself and reflect as a science; it viewed itself first and foremost as a craft/technical and/or artistic practice. Even so, even in the late 1950s, people were still giving much thought to the nature of design as a discipline, or rather, to the design process itself and the methods employed by designers. The Hochschule für Gestaltung in Ulm played a pioneering role in this regard. During the 1960s, a great deal of work was done in Great Britain, especially at the Royal College of Art in London, to clarify theoretically the concept of design research. [03]

In the 1980s and 1990s, there were various attempts (coinciding with an unprecedented boom in design) at European universities and colleges to establish design as a scientific and research discipline. As a result, scientific communities came into being in Scandinavia (especially in Finland), in Great Britain and the Netherlands, as well as in the USA, Canada, Switzerland and Italy. At the University of Art and Design in Helsinki (UIAH) the first research theses were completed in PhD courses from 1983 on. The Royal College of Art in London awarded its first academic degrees in 1967[01]. At the universities of Delft and Eindhoven, the design faculties offered their first PhDs in the 1990s and 2005, respectively. The Massachusetts Institute of Technology (MIT) devoted attention to theory and research as early as the 1960s. For quite some time, however, the Institute of Design at Illinois Institute of Technology (IIT) in Chicago was the only college in the United States to offer PhDs. They are now being offered at a number of colleges in the USA. The design faculty at the University of Montreal has been running PhDs for quite some time. In the late 1990s in Switzerland, the seven newly founded design colleges were legally obliged to provide research and development. In 2003, these colleges founded the Swiss Design Network (SDN) as a national research expertise network[02]. In Italy, where design research activities were restricted to the design faculty at Milan Politecnico, the first PhD courses were launched in the 1990s.

In the 1980s and 1990s, a number of design research societies were founded, such as the Design Research Society (DRS)[03] with its seat in the UK. They are now networked in the International Association of the Societies of Design Research (IASDR).

A variety of design research magazines have also been published, including *Design Issues*, published by the Massachusetts Institute of Technology, MIT Press[04]; *Innovation*, another US research magazine, published by the IDSA (Industrial Designers Society of America)[05]; *Design Studies, The International Journal for Design Research in Engineering, Architecture, Products and System'*, published in cooperation with the Design Research Society (DRS)[06], and the *Information Design Journal* (idj), which appears in Amsterdam.[07]

01   www.rca.ac.uk/pages/study/history (accessed 10 April 2006)

02   SDN organised its first, second and third Design Research Symposia in Basel (2004), Zurich (2005) and Geneva (2006) respectively. (See the symposium reader at: www.swiss-design.org)

03   www.designresearchsociety.org

04   www.mitpressjournals.org/loi/desi

05   www.innovationjournal.org

06   Published by Elsevier: www.elsevier.com

07   Published by John Benjamins Publishing Company: www.benjamins.com

What constitutes a scientific discipline? It is the totality of basic assumptions, concepts, theories, methods and tools that a specific group of scientists and researchers – the Scientific Community – employs in its work. The essential characteristic of a scientific discipline is its progressive development, or rather the progress it makes in its research and practical activities.[04] When a discipline is young, most of these preconditions seem to be self-evident and require no further consideration. The moment they become the object of reflection, however, the discipline develops its own self-conception. The basic characteristics of a discipline include intersubjective communication, within the research community concerned, about the way it defines its goals and about its subject and methods. The latter are formulated in binding standards.

Thus, for example, the general criteria of the Swiss National Science Foundation (SNF), which apply to the diverse disciplinary research communities for assessing (application-oriented) research projects are: scientific quality; originality and relevance; the state of the relevant research; the suitability of the methodological approach; interest and commitment on the part of the project partner; specialist and managerial competence with respect to the project on the part of the applicants; the applicants' experience in the research field in question; the project's feasibility; fostering a new generation of researchers; the pluri-, inter- and transdisciplinary character of the project; and last but not least, cooperation with other research institutions.

A profession becomes a scientific discipline through a historical process. The discipline is embodied in a scientific community that has grown over time, and whose self-conception and standards have evolved gradually in a discursive process. The canon of that which is deemed knowledge by scientific standards is subject to historical change, thus demonstrating that scientific discipline is not an eternally valid absolute, but a historical category. Many disciplines (such as medicine, sociology and the engineering sciences) enter the canon of sciences in a very specific socio-historical context. Medicine has been classed as a science for some time now, although it was originally considered primarily as a practical discipline that applied science. Sociology became an independent scientific discipline only in the 20th century, when it became evident that there was an urgent need and demand within society for sociological analysis. The same applies to the technical disciplines, which acquired the status of engineering sciences at a very specific, complex stage of the technological development of industrial society.

The question as to whether design, with its specific mode of knowledge and its publication formats, will be able to establish itself in the context of college and university courses cannot therefore be answered in a theoretically abstract manner on the basis of design's nature, but only in historically evolving practical activity. The primary condition for such a process is, however, that design is a discipline; in other words: that design rests on certain foundations and is thus distinguished by the way it progressively develops its knowledge and practice. This condition has certainly been fulfilled.[04] The second condition is that design must be able to impart its ideas intersubjectively and meet the prevailing standards for conducting research as shared by the various scientific communities. This condition has also been fulfilled in the practice of today's scientific design communities. The objective historical conditions for design to a scientific canon are now favourable even in those European countries where a scientific community does not yet exist.

— For some time now, people in Europe have been demanding that design define and prove itself as a discipline within the context of university and college educational policy. This is related to the 'Bologna process', which forces colleges of design to adopt a more scientific approach as European university and college courses become increasingly subject to formal standardisation.

— The demands on design also have economic causes. The fact that design must now position itself as a scientific discipline is linked to its growing importance as an economic and cultural factor. At a time when many products are technically quite sophisticated, quality differences in certain market segments have more or less ceased to exist in fact. Furthermore, with wage and material costs being more or less equal there is hardly any room for flexibility in price formation, making design the last and most important decisive factor in companies' competitive struggle with their rivals. The latest research on the economic value added created by cultural activities in Switzerland impressively demonstrates the economic importance of design and, above all, of communication design.[05]

— However, the demands on design have causes that are primarily immanent to design itself. And these, in turn, lie in the increasingly complex nature of the design profession, or rather in the growing importance of the conceptual aspect of design strategies. The amount of information designers need in order to solve design problems has grown dramatically over the past two decades, with the result that, on their own, designers are no longer in a position to collect all this information, let alone assimilate and process it. Not only has the number of design problems increased rapidly, the nature of these problems is changing faster than ever before, making it increasingly difficult for designers to fall back on years of reliable experience.

— This is certainly true for the technological complexity of the 'craft' side of design. The revolution in information and computer technology (ICT) has changed the profession to such an extent that the designer of yesteryear is now simultaneously a typesetter, copywriter, editor, retoucher, filmmaker, videographer and even sonographer. This is not intended as a plea for author's design or for all-round geniuses – quite the contrary! The (now defunct) notion of the designer as the creative genius who synthesises all the different aspects with inspiration and sheer ability may still be upheld and cultivated at some of our universities and colleges, but these qualities no longer suffice to deal competently with the conceptual demands or with the ever-greater surges of information waiting to be processed. At the same time, reflection, dialogue and multilayered media discourse are indispensable aspects of the design process. (This by no means obviates the need for fundamental exercises in design in the traditional sense.)

The complexity of design is also grounded in its interdisciplinary and transdisciplinary state. A wide range of scientific disciplines from the fields of the human, social and engineering sciences on the one hand, and industry, administration and culture on the other, are called upon to work with designers to solve their design tasks in their full complexity.

Interdisciplinary cooperation not only requires communication but also demands that design develop its own forms of discipline with regard to conceptual acuity and methodological stringency.

'Given the current state of our information and knowledge society and the increasing permeation of everyday life by science, renouncing the instrument of "scientific theory" no longer makes any sense, for the resources of science and research have long since become an integral part of our cultural capital (...) It is no longer possible to conceive of a world without science, and almost impossible to conceive of design without scientific theory.'[06]

Design research has a vital role to play along design's path to becoming a scientific discipline.

III. Design as research

Two essential categories can be made out in design research, both of which have a right to claim to be research disciplines. They are turning design research into an international discipline capable of linking up to a range of other disciplines.

Research into design

This form of design research does research into the discipline of design.

— It is known as research into design[07] (in French, 'recherche sur le design'[08]).
— In this context, design research is conceived as being one among many scientific disciplines. Research areas include, for example, the history of design as well as the fields of aesthetics and design theory, which reflects on the nature of design.
— By analysing design activity, research into design arrives at universally verifiable findings.
— Research into design 'operates from the outside, keeping its subject at a distance. Researchers are scientific observers who avoid changing their subject wherever possible.'[09]
— The disciplines engaged in research into design include aesthetics, rhetoric, semiotics, cultural science, and the social and historical sciences.

Research through design

> In this form of design research, the core competence of design, the act of designing, plays a central role.

— It is known as research through design[10, 07] (in French, 'recherche par le design'[08]).
— Research through design proceeds from the identification of a research question specific to design.
— Research through design adopts a different perspective from research into design. It approaches the world of its (research) objects primarily from the perspective of designability (and changeability) and thus arrives at new ideas. Research into design, on the other hand, observes its object primarily from the perspective of recognisability and generates new knowledge on this basis. (In the research perspective, the recognisability of the subject changes to a certain degree (depending on the approach taken, or on the experimental facility), so that elements of the design also flow into the research.)
— Research through design generally involves three phases: research, design and publication.
— During the research and analysis phase, researchers apply the social sciences (cognitive psychology, political science etc.), cultural sciences, engineering sciences and ergonomics etc. wherever necessary. Generally speaking, this type of design research is, therefore, an interdisciplinary activity.
— This phase of design research is also distinguished by its use of qualitative research methods[08] (such as observation, participatory research, qualitative Interviews, diary entries and video recordings, experimental sampling etc.).[09]
— During the design phase (design, realisation, validation), the various practical methods of design are employed.
— Research through design thus belongs to the category of 'research through practice'[14] or action research.[07] In the UK, the Royal College of Art has launched the field of action research: the 'PhD by project'. This research doctorate, in contrast to 'PhD by thesis', mainly involves practical research.[15]
— Action research involves systematic research through practical activities – in design research this means the design of artefacts – which result in the generation and/or checking of new information, forms, processes, concepts etc., and publishing new

08 |

09 |

---

08 | David Hamilton says: 'Qualitative research methods are key to understanding the issues surrounding design' [11] p. 63. Susan Roth notes: 'Qualitative research employs multiple methods, many of which rely on the complex context in which events take place and on a more intimate or engaged involvement with the subject / participant.' [12] p. 23

09 | A description of these methods in design research can be found in [13], pp. 18–21

communicable knowledge.[14] In German-speaking regions, the term 'angewandte Gestaltungsforschung' appears in the debate on image science.[10]

— Research through design distinguishes itself from the normal design process by the fact that the design is not inspired by the concrete needs of users but by a research question specifically related to research.[17] Under certain circumstances, the research question may be identical with a specific question posed by a user.

— Research through design is reflected design activity.

— Research through design generates knowledge by designing innovative artefacts, models, prototypes, products, concepts etc., and evaluates them (validation process) by conducting various experiments (tests, perception experiments etc.) in order to answer the research question.[11] Evaluation differs from the simple testing of a prototype in that the applicability of the knowledge gained is not restricted to the product on which research is being conducted.

— Research through design also entails experimentally improving design methods, finding novel ways of controlling the design process, and standardising representation methods.

— During the publication phase, research through design has to meet the research standards shared by the various research communities.

— The research result generally comprises two integral parts: [12] a published text or report, [13] and a designed artefact (product, model, various kinds of visual representations, exhibitions etc.). The research procedure is recorded in a verifiable manner and made available to a broader public.

— In order to make the knowledge that research through design generates during the design process transferable, negotiable and communicable, the designed artefact – along with a published text in traditional format – is included as an integral part of

10 | Martin Scholz points out that: 'Applied design research investigates new image phenomena in their practical application' It focuses an 'exploratory use of the medium of the image. ... Exploratory use of the medium of the image means exploring, improving and generalising knowledge arrived at subjectively. The method is initially determined by the designer alone who then aims, with the aid of mass screening, to arrive at generalisable and transferable results.' [16] p. 336

11 | Sandra Kemp, Royal College of Art: ''Knowledge can be generated, and questions answered, through analytic scholarship, iterative experiments and innovative examples of artefact and designs.' [18]

12 | Royal College of Art website: 'The two aspects of the work must be visibly interdependent.' www.rca.ac.uk/pages/research/types_of_research_degree_3159.html (accessed 10 April 2006)

13 | Christopher Frayling: 'Both the diary and the report are there to communicate the results which is what separates research from gathering of reference materials.' [07], p. 5

the argumentation. [14] |Hence there are two lines of argument here: the discursive and the visual. Integral research reports, which comprise two parts, have become the scientific standard in advanced design scientific communities. The examples of Finland, the Netherlands and Great Britain show that art and design artefacts have become accepted as scientific research standards within the university scientific community for defending a design research project (in the form of a PhD thesis).

14 | In the discussion on image science Martin Scholz writes that: 'The results are (…) in turn, available as images (…) To make sure that the characteristic features of language (and their partly linear linguistic logic) do not impermissibly push their way into the foreground, a visual discussion must also be conducted with visual means.' [16], p. 347

References / Bibliography

[01]   Galbraith JK (2004) *The Economics of Innocent Fraud*. Houghton Mifflin, Boston, p. 7

[02]   Bonsiepe G (2005) *Demokratie und Gestaltung*. Unpublished manuscript of the lecture given in Santiago de Chile June 2005, pp. 4 and 3

[03]   Glanville R (1999) Researching Design and Designing Research. *Design Issues* 15(2): p. 80

[04]   Friedman K (2003) Problem and Paradox in Foundations of Design. http://home.snafu.de/jonasw/PARADOXFriedmanE.html (accessed 7 April 2006), p. 2

[05]   Weckerle C et al. (2003) Kultur-Wirtschaft-Schweiz. Ein Forschungsprojekt der HGKZ. www.kulturwirtschaft.ch/files/hgkz_kulturwirtschaft_deutsch.pdf

[06]   Meier C (ed.) (2003) *Designtheorie. Beiträge zu einer Disziplin*. Anabas, Frankfurt, p.15

[07]   Frayling C (1993/94) Research in Art and Design. *Royal College of Art Research Papers* 1(1): pp. 1–5

[08]   Findeli A (2004) *Reader des Ersten Design Forschungssymposiums des Swiss Design Network, 13–14 May 2004*: p. 50

[09]   Jonas W (2004) Research through Design. In: Findeli A (ed.): *Reader des Ersten Design Forschungssymposiums des Swiss Design Network, 13–14 May 2004*: p. 29

[10]   Archer B (1981) A View of the Nature of Design Research. In: Jacques R, Powell JA (eds): *Design, Science, Method: Proceedings of the 1980 Design Research Society Conference*. IPC Science and Technology Press, Portsmouth

[11]   Hamilton D (1994) Traditions, Preferences and Postures in Applied Qualitative Research. In: Denzin N, Lincoln Y (eds): *Handbook of Qualitative Research*: p. 63

[12]   Roth S (1999) The State of Design Research. *Design Issues* 15(2): p. 23

[13]   Robinson R, Nims J (1996) Insight into What Really Matters. *Innovation* Summer 1996: pp. 8–21

[14]   Archer B (1995) The Nature of Research. *Co-Design Journal* 2: p. 6

[15]   Seago A, Dunne A (1999) New Methodologies in Art and Design Research: The Object as Discourse. *Design Issues* 15(2): pp. 11f.

[16]   Scholz M (2005) Kommunikationsdesign. In: Sachs-Hombach K (ed.): *Bildwissenschaft. Disziplinen, Themen, Methoden*. Suhrkamp, Frankfurt: pp. 336 and 347

[17]   Frens J (2006) *Designing for Rich Interaction: Integrating Form, Interaction and Function*. PhD thesis, Eindhoven University of Technology, p. 29

[18]   Royal College of Art website: www.rca.ac.uk/pages/research/research_handbook__3063.html (accessed 10 April 2006)

Susann Vihma

Essay

Design Semiotics – Institutional Experiences and an Initiative for a Semiotic Theory of Form

Design research in its initial academic phase

01 |

When design research activities started at the University of Art and Design Helsinki in the early 1980s, [01] | a common doubt was whether designers were able to carry out research at all. Some critics called attention to the fact that designers lacked academic traditions and education in writing and conceptualising. Designers were generally considered to be poor at verbalising their ideas, although there have always been brilliant exceptions. This is one of the arguments that has proved to be wrong, because many designers who seek training in writing become skilled in this craft, and it does not at all interfere with their performing design tasks. Rather, by improving their verbal skills, they strengthen their argumentations in design practice, which is one of the main reasons for design research.

02 |

In the beginning, in the 1980s, designers were ridiculed in public, as were, for example, intellectually oriented musicians, who also wanted to dig deeper into and better understand problems connected with their performances and interpretations. [02] | Nonetheless, design research at this early stage was supported by some representatives of established academic disciplines, who optimistically challenged design research with the

03 |

attitude 'let's see what they will do'. [03] | In 1981, the University of Art and Design was allowed to organise doctoral education and grant Doctor of Arts degrees.

At that time, many practising designers from various fields showed their interest in attaining a doctoral degree and educating themselves further. A small detail from the series of events that followed illustrates this new situation, however. Of about 50 persons (designers) who participated in a basic course in philosophy, only five passed. Two of them later earned their doctorates; the other three have been successful in their own fields in design practice, ergonomics and administration. The example illustrates the situation at that time: there was great enthusiasm, but many unrealistic expectations.

---

01 | See, for example, *Designforschung Design Research*, an international seminar in 1984 [01]

02 | The situation can be exemplified by a headline in the main newspaper in Finland, 'Singing a Doctoral Thesis'

03 | Whereas, according to my personal experience, in some other countries, scholars' disbelief in such a new initiative has hampered advancement in research for many years.

There were also some designers at that time who thought that successful practice per se would be enough for a Doctor of Arts degree. Craft-based tradition in design education had normally contained no reading and little argumentation. Accordingly, many designers remained alien to writing and criticism. Suspicion towards doctoral-level education flowed from both within and without. Even later, after the first theses had been published, colleagues came down hard on the poor researchers. One strict demand, among others, was that they write in Finnish, not in English, since they were supposed to contribute to the advancement of a design discourse at the national level and would thus promote design nationally. Those who wrote in English were traitors who aimed only to build their own career and thus ignored national educational needs. There was very little discussion of the theses' topics in the early 1990s, and therefore researchers looked for an international audience. They started to participate in international conferences, not only design conferences, in order to strengthen the design research community.

04 | The first thesis at the University of Art and Design Helsinki reported developments concerning advertising in Finland.[02] 04 | Thus far, over 50 theses have been published from various fields within the educational scope of the University. Of these, about 20 come from design studies. [03]

One of the main strategies of the University's research policy has been to cooperate with other universities. Therefore, actual collaboration takes place with scholars from different disciplines at various stages of education and within research projects. Tutoring and examination has often been carried out by researchers outside the University. They have been more than willing to take on this kind of extra work, which is often extra to their normal commitments but without adequate payment. The contribution of these many specialists has helped design research to develop more than hitherto recognised. Their curiosity and critical comments have assisted design researchers in gaining deeper knowledge and creating new kinds of methodological approaches to design-specific problems. The strategy has deliberately avoided the founding of a design research ghetto.

05 | As part of the strategy, a specific mode of research has been developed for the University, that of a specific art and design university. 05 | In other words, a work of art or a design product can be included in a thesis. How can such a 'combination' of two divergent subject matters, art or design work and research (a scholarly written text) fit together? The idea (not easily understood by all) is to conceive the activities as differing from one another and respect their particular characteristics, but 1 + 1 is not the result (= the thesis). The thesis must form a coherent whole, for which the text is in dialogical relation to the (most often visual) design or artwork. One contributes in its own right to the other, and one cannot emerge without the other. Consequently, the design work brings some aspect or

04 | The author Päivi Hovi has a background in art history.

05 | Of course also a more traditional form of written thesis, monograph or articles, can be accepted.

knowledge to the topic in question in a way that text alone would be unable to accomplish. The design (or artwork), in turn, shows and demonstrates rather than merely illustrating a text. By mounting an exhibition or designing an actual product, a design researcher is producing an (visual) argument or result that contributes to the discussion in the scholarly text. The design or artwork brings new questions to the fore.

Some critics have speculated about the double work required, because a student is asked to write a scholarly text and to design or produce artworks as well. This is, however, a misconception. Designers and artists have shown that there is not necessarily double work or double identities at work. Rather, reading and writing will make a statement about the artistic production, and vice versa.

Design research proper?

The claim that design research should be about looking closer at the design process has been a topic of discussion for some time. The Design Methods Movement in the 1960s emphasised systematic approaches to design. Sometimes even scientific methods were introduced to the design process, and the question of whether design was a science or not was posed. Recently, this branch of design research has merged many times with research on user-centred design. The focus of the latter is, namely, on how a designer could better benefit from users' experiences when aiming at new solutions. Design researchers have developed methods, mock-ups and probes, and have applied techniques from ethnological and sociological studies. [04-06]

It seems that sociology, especially consumer studies and material culture studies, has introduced new methodologies that help designers proceed in their research on user requirements, behaviour and needs. It has also contributed important knowledge about use cultures. Nowadays, it is commonly agreed that designers should be well aware of who is going to use the product, be it a concrete thing or a service. Market research is not enough. However, by going deeper into users' needs, a designer cannot be sure that the new solution for a product will be launched. For example, as part of her doctoral study, Helena Leppänen designed new tableware for elderly people with difficulties in seeing and handling dishes. [07] In spite of several well-received ideas and tested prototypes, her design was not accepted for production because of the high economic risk stated by the company. The research produced new knowledge for future purposes nevertheless.

Another study, which used ethnographic methods, was carried out by the Estonian jewellery designer Kärt Summatavet. [08] She looked at cultural legacy as not simply a user-centred inquiry. Her task was to collect information about how women in a local Estonian culture used and conceived their necklaces, rings and ornaments. She interviewed two women in order to understand the cycle of women's lives in that culture better. Along with the process of familiarising herself with a specific cultural tradition, she designed jewellery for a modern woman, and was inspired by the narratives and visual ideas she had come to know. The new designs were not merely copies, applications, transformations or changes, but interpretations.

Of course, then, design research has benefited from other disciplines. Art history should perhaps be mentioned, in addition to social sciences and philosophy.[06] Recently, Anna Valtonen, whose background is in design and art history, completed her thesis on the recent changes that challenge design.[09] Significantly, of the four professors in the field of design research at the University of Art and Design Helsinki, one comes from sociology, the second from art history (both from the University of Helsinki), and the remaining two have a background at this university, their *alma mater*, a textile artist and an industrial designer.

06 |

Design semantics research

In spite of its promising advancements, user-centred design research does not reach out to some of the most vital design questions. It does not explicitly deal with the problems of appearance of the outcome. The question of form is certainly prevalent, but form is conceived as a practical and functional concern. It is a form from the point of view of the users' ability to function with the design outcome (a product or service). Sometimes the form is conceived as pleasurable, and then it seems to enhance usability and customisation. Enjoyable products encourage users in their activities.[10, 11] Usability studies have expanded from strictly ergonomic problems to research on emotional responses in use context.[12] Nevertheless, the focus still remains, literally, on practical use.

Interest towards user-centred research has been shown by companies, as well as by researchers in consumer behaviour studies, including marketing and sociological aspects of consumption. This trend is understandable because of the many technological innovations on the market, innovations that have caused trouble for customers. New electronic equipment has proved to be inconvenient for many people, who fail to use the products properly or become stressed by their complicated interface.

New products with advanced technology have changed everyday living in the Western world. Design reacted to the change, and in the early 1980s design semantics became a hot topic. Two or three different approaches to design semantics were presented in journals and seminars internationally at that time. They all pointed out that there appeared

---

06 | Art history departments still do design research in Finland, as in many other countries, although often as a branch growing out of art history proper. Collaboration between design researchers and researchers at the Helsinki and Tampere Universities of Technology, the Helsinki School of Economics, and the like has been well established since the mid 1990s. A network of Finnish design researchers (economic history, art history, Finnish history, cultural studies) calls itself 'Researchers of Goods' and organises multidisciplinary seminars concerning the dilemmas of the product environment in which we all live.

to be a problem with communication between the designer (designer's and company's view) and the user (the buyer or consumer). The problem could be solved by taking a closer look at the user's conception and action and at the product's functioning in that context. Professor Klaus Krippendorff acted as one of the key representatives for this branch of design semantics, which he called Products Semantics. Up to this point, design semantics remained close to usability studies. The form of the outcome of design (a product or a service) still stayed practical and technically functional. However, form was also conceived as acquiring other dimensions when it is seen in the context of use because this context is culturally defined.

In his recent book on semantics, Krippendorff summarises the advancements of his approach, which started with the publishing of a thematic issue of *innovation* in the spring of 1984.[13] Notably, in that issue, the German design pedagogue Jochen Gros also published an article.[14] His view on semantics in design differs on many points from the one represented by Krippendorff. Their basic theoretical assumptions vary. Krippendorff stands for a constructivist view with reference to Ludwig Wittgenstein and Martin Heidegger, among many others. Gros leans on Susan K. Langer in particular. Both nonetheless make use of language as a metaphor for design. Krippendorff claimed that products have become 'language-like' and that is how they carry symbolic meanings. Gros calls his approach the *Theory of Product Language.* 07 | With respect to this metaphorical idea, both approaches can be criticised, although they also unquestionably contribute to design thinking, which has suffered from a lack of intellectual debate throughout its history.

When a product, a practical tool, has been designed with an emphasis on something other than only its practical functioning, like a gadget or a showpiece, it is said to have acquired language-like properties. The theoretical idea is that, when a concrete product is looked at from a non-practical or non-technical point of view, it becomes language-like. Its symbolic qualities seem equal to those of the verbal language. However, such a metaphorical transformation may be unnecessary or even misleading, although it is rarely questioned by proponents of this conception. How can a concrete, material thing suddenly be transformed into a word-like and sentence-like system? Is the metaphorical proposal truthful or confusing?

At least one exception should be mentioned in the consideration of design research history, especially its theoretical elaboration, namely, the initiatives at the Hochschule für Gestaltung (HfG) Ulm during the 1960s. HfG Ulm can be seen as having formed some of the theoretical roots still prevalent today. Notably, Krippendorff was a student at HfG Ulm. As is well documented nowadays, pedagogy at HfG Ulm stressed rational argumentation and favoured scientifically motivated results.[16-18] Hence, several new disciplines were introduced to the curriculum. Semiotics was among them.

07 | See also [15]

Design semiotics

Semiotics can nowadays be conceived as a wide field of research including many diverging theoretical approaches. Therefore, not only one semiotic theory exists, but many. Its studies, nevertheless, most often centre on problems of signification and communication in cultural contexts. [08] Conversely, Krippendorff, for example, according to his theoretical choices, rejects all kinds of semiotics. His arguments concerning semiotic theories are brief and contain some mistakes. Gros's approach, in turn, comes close to semiotics and whether to include it in semiotics or not is perhaps more a question of taste or theoretical insight. Nevertheless, not all research dealing with signification has to be called semiotics, although the problem field is semiotic by definition.

Another topic of interest, when the differences or points in common of various design semantics approaches are analysed, is the use of information theory (i.e. the application of the mathematical model by Claude Shannon). Krippendorff modified this basic composition of a sender (of messages) and a receiver. Rune Monö, the late grand old man of Swedish industrial design, also applied Shannon's model and combined it with Karl Bühler's linguistic (semiotic) model from 1936 in his much-used textbook. [19]

Semiotics owes many debts to linguistics, from which many of its classics stem. In addition, for example, studies in literature have benefited from theories formed by semiotics. Promising ideas concerning signification and meaning derived in these disciplines can easily enter other fields of research, including design studies. Therefore, design can easily be treated as a sort of symbolic system likened to verbal narrative and storytelling. Moreover, many concepts from them lend themselves in a straightforward manner to other uses in other contexts. Many semiotic insights have spread to everyday thinking and statements in mass media. Ordinary design discourse is packed with statements such as, 'a product *tells* its story', 'a form *speaks* about cultural identity', and so on. Furthermore, in usability studies and consumption research, users are encouraged to tell the story of their daily activities with useful products, and this approach may support the idea of products functioning as units within a language system.

In the discussion below, a design semiotics approach is proposed that avoids the trap of the linguistic metaphor and of abstraction from the material base of design products, which easily follows from the metaphor. Product Semantics, for example in Krippendorff's view, divides design into two entities. On the one hand, there is the concrete functioning product, and on the other, there is the culturally constructed language-like symbol. The theory fails to conceive design (and the design outcome) as an integrated whole. There would be two obstacles to overcome, the language metaphor (design products as language-like symbols) and the separation of materiality from the symbolic.

08 | Interesting results from so-called Zoo-semiotics and Bio-semiotics should also be mentioned here.

Instead, it would be fruitful to conceive of material artefacts as carrying symbolic content as concrete forms in their own right. To conceive material products as *visual* metaphors can be more beneficial for design theory. Why associate (visual) forms with verbal speech and verbal communication in the first place? It is worthwhile discussing this question because, as can be seen, the answer has consequences with respect to design discourse. Speaking and writing about form become different. Instead of saying 'a product *tells* its story', the statement is made that 'a product *expresses (represents, refers to, displays, exhibits, shows, or embodies)*' a quality for someone. Consequently, it also becomes evident that a form in its material and visual presence always expresses (something to somebody). Signification can be regarded as a relation and interaction between the form and the person who perceives it. [09]

09 |

All design semantics theories aim at looking closer at symbolic qualities. They try to produce new knowledge about how design functions in modern societies and in its economic organisations. The *symbol* is a concept they share even though they assign it diverse meanings, because the basic theoretical assumptions behind design semantics studies vary. It is important to examine the assumptions behind the various types of semantics because otherwise it seems impossible to understand the conclusions arrived at and to understand the applicability proposed in the design context. All theories can be traced to some basic philosophical assumptions, even in our postmodern times, in which theories seem to be eclectic and researchers mix ideas from various sources.

Form also embraces characteristics other than those called language-like (if there are language-like qualities at all in the first place). Before proceeding to these qualities, I would like to point out that most design semantic theories seem to reduce form analyses in this respect.

The basic question arises about what (visual) form signifies. Or, more precisely, how does (visual) form signify? The second question follows from the first. What would be the best way to answer this question?

A glimpse at design history can be helpful. And, in addition to design history proper, even a look into cultural history studies may help. When, as seen from a cultural viewpoint, interest towards modern design products in the Western world arose, the first analyses were not made by design researchers. A well-known representative of an early interest in things and their cultural relevance is the French scholar Roland Barthes, who, in the late 1950s, wrote about design and related phenomena. He called one essay *Semantics of the object*.[21] In his brilliantly written texts, many new ideas, which could and still can inspire design studies, were formulated for the first time in a context easily apprehensible to designers. With the help of concrete examples, Barthes showed how a cultural context

---

09 | This is how the semiotic sign can be conceived. Peirce CS: *The Sign*, probably composed early in 1894, was originally the first chapter of a book entitled *The Art of Reasoning*, but was then turned into the second chapter of Peirce's multivolume *Grand Logic*. [20]

for analyses of everyday products can be divided into *paradigmatic* and *syntagmatic* aspects. Let us look at, for example, a table and chairs when they are composed as a set on the paradigmatic axis. They can be associated with dining (in a dining room context), children, office work and so on, on the basis of their form. The syntagmatic axis, in turn, shows the spatial arrangement and relationships between the components of the set (i.e. the table, chairs, lighting fixtures, and other details of the product environment). It shows that forms of tables and chairs go together and affect one another on the basis of contiguity. Only much later were these texts by Barthes recognised in design theory. But they are not very widely known today. 10 | Interestingly, Barthes bases his semiotic analyses on the (language-derived) ideas of the Swiss linguist Ferdinand de Saussure.[22]

10 |

There are other examples from design research history that should be discussed, such as the one already mentioned: the intellectual activity at HfG Ulm with contributions to design theory by, for example, Thomás Maldonado,[23] Gui Bonsiepe,[24] and Abraham Moles.[25] Studies into the symbolic and cultural signification of design at HfG Ulm remained formal and abstract, mostly due to the German philosopher Max Bense's modification of semiotics for design purposes at that time.[26] His teaching at HfG Ulm is fairly well documented, partly by himself and in recent surveys of the history of this institution. These examples, Barthes and HfG Ulm (Bense, Maldonado and Bonsiepe) illustrate the main traditions of semiotics in design studies. Much more research has been done, however, in a field called *visual semiotics*, which still needs to be explored by design researchers. Semiotic studies within architectural theory have been carried out since at least the 1960s, with the Italian scholar Umberto Eco at the forefront. Applied analyses are also available, by, for example, the British architectural theorist Geoffrey Broadbent.[27] The close context of design to architecture, as well as to fine art, may diffuse the fact that all of these fields differ from each other in important ways. For that reason, it seems wise first to limit semantic analyses to topics relevant to design and thereafter possibly try to compare the results with analyses in architecture and fine art. Earlier semiotic studies in architecture have proved to be rather formal according to a structuralistic tradition, according to which elements of a building have been categorised into systems and subsystems, all contributing to the overall signification of the building in question. A famous example of such an analysis is Eco's study of the statue at Trafalgar Square in London that symbolises Lord Nelson's achievements.[28] The analysis becomes reductive because the interpretation seems to be abstracted from the material foundation and construction. Barthes would agree that the interpretation is always affected anyway by the cultural context. Without previous knowledge of the culture (Lord Nelson's achievement), the symbol would remain incomprehensible. Now, the key question of design semantics still remains open, namely, *how* the artefact expresses, represents, refers to and embodies the symbolic content.

10 | This is an interesting small detail concerning design theory when compared with photography theory, in which Barthes' texts, such as the book *Camera Lucida*, are considered classics and are much debated. Could that be a sign of photography being more theoretically elaborated and deepened as compared with design?

If the aforementioned shortcomings and reductions are to be overcome, a design semiotics of a different kind must be introduced. This theoretical approach is based on the thoughts of the American philosopher Charles Sanders Peirce, more familiar perhaps to a wide community as a logician, and, according to encyclopaedias, the founding father of American pragmatism. Yet for decades his semeiotic conceptions have also been discussed by many, and they have been modified for various purposes in different ways, some of which have been developed into strict formal systems and others benefit from them as basic theoretical assumptions, which inspire argumentation. Peirce's philosophy does not stem from linguistics and is, therefore, not easily caught up in traps from of verbal metaphors. One of his most useful concepts for design theory seems to be the *sign*, when research explicitly demonstrates how the sign enriches the analysis at hand. The relation between a perceivable thing and an interpreting subject can be called a sign. As an initial introductory text to the conception of the sign, an early essay *The Sign* can be recommended. [11]

The conception of the sign opens up possibilities for interpreting a product (an image, an environment etc.) as signifying in different ways rather than only as a symbol, as most of the earlier mentioned theories have suggested. In addition, according to this theoretical approach, the symbol becomes a concept constituted on specific grounds (i.e. upon agreements). A symbol refers to a content that is agreed upon in some cultural context and must be known for meaningful interpretation. Consequently, a form cannot 'tell' its content or signifying character as a visual appearance only. A person interpreting the symbolic form (embodied by a replica) must learn about (ask for) its subject matter. In this respect, of course, a (visual) symbolic form comes close to the verbal language system. Other humanmade cultural systems, such as traffic signs, include a combination of visual and verbal symbols, which distance themselves from language because visual (re)presentation enters the picture.

There is still more to be said about signification. In addition to symbol, also other modes of signification exist. A symbolic form does not function unrelated to these other possible sorts of meaning construction. Signification can also be seen as constituted by likeness. [12] A third mode of signification is grounded on the actual connection of the signifying form to its material cause, because a form also shows traces and other causal features dependent on its material conditions. All of these three modes contribute to the interpretation of a signifying form, one sometimes dominating over the others, but still affecting the interpretation and, *nota bene*, the practical use.

Design practice can benefit from such theoretical investigation. With the help of the various modes of signification, a design product can be analysed in its complexity and the form transformed by the designer in a chosen direction. The theory becomes applicable in

---

11   See also previous note in this paper

12   In Peirce's philosophy this is called *iconic*.

practical design work by its capacity to reason about the signifying form at hand at various phases of the design process, starting from the very first ideas drawn on paper or the computer screen. The theoretical approach based on Peircean philosophy presents a more versatile and flexible approach than many others. It seems to be particularly suitable (as a theoretical analysis) for design purposes because it considers the outcome of the design process as a *continuum*, from the first ideas to the realised outcome. It does not limit its scope to analyses of the prototype or end product, be it a concrete product on the market or some plan for organising activities.

The semiotic approach has been applied in design education at the University of Art and Design Helsinki since the beginning of the 1990s. It has introduced the students to aspects that engage in the core questions of design, namely, shaping, visualising and organising signifying forms. The approach has helped designers deal with problems concerning interpretation and evaluation with respect to the semantic aspects of their work. In autumn 2006, a network study module (MA, 5 ECTS) on design semiotics was opened for students at any Finnish university.

Benefits and applications

Designers need conceptual tools to examine their undertaking from aspects other than usability or technology alone, which omit the signifying side of the design proposal. Recently, Turkka Keinonen, professor of industrial design research and also a distinguished expert on user-centred design, was invited to lecture on the relationship between user-centred design and design semantics approaches. He presented them as two diametrically opposing approaches, the first as a bottom-top approach and the second as a theory-led approach. Both could probably meet at some point. Other user-centred studies (also research on, for example, the domestication of design objects) focus especially on methodological issues and practices of design and aim at finding new ways to include users in the planning process, or better ways to understand users' conceptions. [13] Only in passing is the question of how people attach meanings to products posed. These views demonstrate that semantics is still hard to deal with, since it is easier to convince, for example, a product development team through the use of numerical or factual grounds than by interpreting more fuzzy aspects of form. Semantic considerations are omitted, or more precisely they are left unexpressed (*nota bene*, the *tacit knowledge* concept, which seems to be a cherished issue among many designers).

[13] The approaches 'combine ethnographic methods, observation techniques, user self-documentation and participatory design into product development oriented design tools that support and utilise information technology.' [29]

This situation calls for appropriate means with which to recognise problems concerning form signification and interpretation. The design semiotics approach should not, however, be conceived as opposing user-centred studies or as alien to technological problem solving. The various facets of design activity can be seen as interlinked. Actually, they benefit from one another's advancements. User studies require time-consuming material collection about (also from and by) users and contexts of use, which serve the purpose of semiotic analyses as well, because interpretation relies on knowledge about use and the many aspects of other design-related facts. The foundation for a valid interpretation is constructed with knowledge about usability, technology, cultural history and so on. But interpretation is not merely a subjective view of the form, although it always includes subjective preferences.[14]

More precisely, a semiotic interpretation of form aims for intersubjective (interpersonal) dialogue and understanding, not at one fixed objective view, or for a consensus.[15] Several versions of interpretation may appear of the one and same form, and the following question could then be asked: 'Which is the correct one?' Which of the alternatives is best and should be chosen for further development? The answer cannot be authorised by one person, a specialist. Instead, from a semiotic point of view, interpersonal negotiation becomes the key issue for designers. Likewise, instead of stressing everyone's own right for individual choice, the design team may look at qualities that seem to connect interpretations and, in particular, look at the foundations of the possibly diverging interpretations. The foundations, which support an interpretation, actually become the most important issue with respect to design, and not, for example, efficient functioning or low costs, which also have to be taken into consideration. In summary, design semiotic analyses need comprehensive knowledge about usability and technology, knowledge that supports the interpretative act of the signifying form (of a product, environment or organisation) as (visual) expression, display, reference, representation, trace, embodiment, and so on.[16]

Semiotic analyses can back up the choices users make regarding design alternatives; preferences can be explicated and inspired. Such analyses also help users and producers to avoid mistakes that stem from unawareness vis-à-vis the signifying aspects of form, and thus they contribute to the planning of a product environment in which people want to live.

[14] Therefore, the position of the interpreter(s) should be explicated. The researcher with a God's eye view is not plausible.

[15] Therefore, clarification of the position of the one who interprets becomes important when semiotic analyses are carried out.

[16] Design can include planning of sound and tactile qualities in using a product. The signifying form reaches out to analyses of auditory and tangible references, representations, traces etc.

FIG. 01

Aesthetic experience

Before bringing this article to a close, I would like to present one vital point in relation to design semiotics. It concerns the aesthetic aspect of the signifying form. The complex field of design can be illustrated with a diagram.^{FIG. 01} [FIG. 01]

FIG. 01   Design as a complex whole approached from five viewpoints

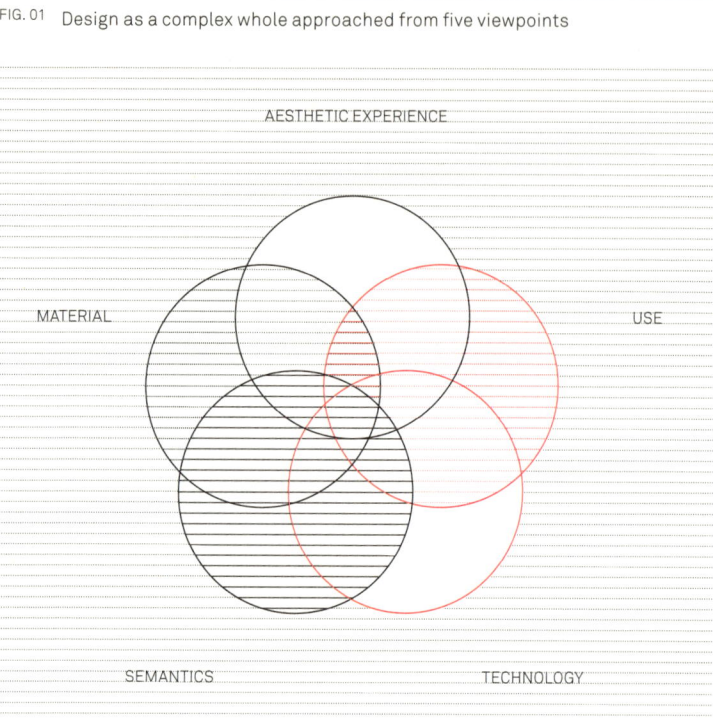

AESTHETIC EXPERIENCE

MATERIAL

USE

SEMANTICS

TECHNOLOGY

This subject matter has been studied comparatively little within design research and has, for example, been omitted from user-centred and many historical studies. However, design is still often conceived as professional expertise, which introduces aesthetic quality to the product environment. A much-celebrated part of the design field even benefits from this conception of design, such as furniture fairs, design museum exhibitions, design-promoting galleries, design magazines, and shops.

In figure 1, five major aspects have been combined to show design in its complexity. Emphasis can be placed on one or several of these areas (circles). Notably, aesthetics is not subsumed by signification (the semantic), but is seen as a dimension of design in its own right and specificity. Aesthetic appreciation and aesthetic value can and should be analysed differently, and aesthetics brings another characteristic to signification. What a form may signify affects the aesthetic experience. From the point of view of design analysis, it seems beneficial to keep these two areas separated, even though, in everyday experience, they merge.

References / Bibliography

[01]   *Designforschung Design Research Symposium 8–11.5.1984 Helsinki.* Publication Series of the University of Industrial Arts in Helsinki A1

[02]   Hovi P (1990) *Mainoskuva Suomessa. Kehitys ja vaikutteet 1890-luvulta 1930-luvun alkuun.* [Development of Finnish advertising art from the 1890s to the 1930s]. Doctoral thesis, Publication Series of the University of Art and Design Helsinki A8

[03]   Hovi-Wasastjerna P (ed.) (2006) *25 Years of Postgraduate Education and Research at the University of Art and Design Helsinki.* University of Art and Design, Helsinki

[04]   Säde S (2001) *Cardboard Mock-ups and Conversations. Studies on User-centered Product Design.* Doctoral thesis, Publication Series of the University of Art and Design Helsinki A34

[05]   Battarbee K (2004) *Co-experience: Understanding User Experiences in Social Inter-action.* Doctoral thesis, Publication Series of the University of Art and Design Helsinki A51, Helsinki

[06]   Mattelmäki T (2006) *Design Probes.* Doctoral thesis, Publication Series of the University of Art and Design Helsinki A69

[07]   Leppänen H (2006) *Muotoilija ja toinen. Astiasuunnittelua vanhuuden kontekstissa.* (Designer and the other). Doctoral thesis, Publication Series of the University of Art and Design Helsinki A72

[08]   Summatavet K (2005) *Folk Tradition and Artistic Inspiration. A Woman's Life in Traditional Estonian Jewelry and Crafts as Told by Anne and Roosi.* Doctoral thesis, Publication Series of the University of Art and Design Helsinki A61

[09]   Valtonen A (2007) *Redefining Industrial Design. Changes in Design Practice in Finland.* Doctoral thesis, Publication Series of the University of Art and Design Helsinki A74

[10]   Tahkokallio P, Vihma S (eds) (1994) *Design – Pleasure or Responsibility?* Publication Series of the University of Art and Design B43

[11]   *Designing Pleasurable Products and Interfaces Conference 22–25.8.2007.* University of Art and Design Helsinki. http://designresearch.uiah.fi/dppi07/index.php (accessed 9 March 2007)

[12]   Design and Emotion Society website: http://www.designandemotion.org/ (accessed 9 March 2007)

[13]   Krippendorff K (2006) *The Semantic Turn: a New Foundation for Design.* Taylor & Francis, Boca Raton, London, New York

[14]   Gros J (1984) Reporting Progress through Product Language. *Innovation. The Journal of the Industrial Designers Society of America* Spring 1984: 10–11

[15]   Steffen D (2000) *Design als Produktsprache. Der Offenbacher Ansatz in Theorie und Praxis.* verlag form, Frankfurt

[16]   Petruschat J (ed.) (2003) hfg ulm. *form+zweck 20*

[17]   Rinker D, Quijano M, Reinhardt B (eds) (2003) *ulmer modelle – modelle nach ulm / hochschule für gestaltung 1953–1968*. Hatje Cantz Verlag, Ostfildern-Ruit

[18]   Lindinger H (ed.) (1987) *Hochschule für Gestaltung Ulm: die Moral der Gegenstände.* Ernst & Sohn, Berlin

[19]   Monö R (1997) *Design for Product Understanding.* Liber, Stockholm

[20]   Peirce CS (1894) *Grand Logic, The Art of Reasoning. Chapter II: What is a Sign?* MS 404, CP 2.281, 285, 297–302

[21]   Barthes R (1964) Semantics of the Object. In (1988): *The Semiotic Challenge.* Basil Blackwell, Oxford, 179–190.

[22]   Barthes R (1967) *Elements of Semiology.* Cape Editions, London

[23]   Maldonado T (1961) Notes on Communication. Non-semantic and Semantic Orientation. *uppercase* 5: 5–10

[24]   Bonsiepe G (1961) Persuasive Communication: Towards a Visual Rhetoric. *Uppercase* 5: 19–34.

[25]   Moles AA (1971) *Information Theory and Esthetic Perception.* University of Illinois Press, Chicago

[26]   Bense M (1971) *Zeichen und Design.* Agis Verlag, Baden-Baden

[27]   Broadbent G (1977) A Plain Man's Guide to the Theory of Signs in Architecture. *Architectural Design* 47: 7–8

[28]   Eco U (1972) A Componential Analysis of the Architectural Sign /Column/. 1972. In (1980): Broadbent GR, Jencks C (eds): *Signs, Symbols and Architecture.* Wiley, Chichester, 213–232.

[29]   Luotain project website: http://tm.uiah.fi/tutpor/index.html. See also: http://designresearch.uiah.fi/index.html?lang=1

Design Research for Sustainable Social Innovation

Over the past hundred years, even when driven by the most positive intentions, designers have been active promoters of the ideas of wellbeing and ways of living that we have recently and dramatically discovered to be unsustainable. That is, designers have mainly been part of the (social and economical) problem that we now have to face. Moving from here to become part of the solution, to become active agents in the transition towards sustainable ways of living, designers must make a profound change in their culture and praxis. New conceptual and methodological tools need to be developed. New ideas, solutions and general visions need to be conceived. And an effort must be made to play a positive role in the social discourse on how to imagine and build a sustainable future.

Given the urgency, dimension and complexity of the problem to be faced, we must conceive an articulated research programme: a worldwide collaborative research programme into design for sustainability, targeted to catalyse and focus all the available design energies. But unfortunately, looking around, I do not see anything like that: on one side, I see the majority of designers (and design researchers) happily continuing to work in a business-as-usual mode, oiling the wheels of a catastrophic consumption machine. On the other side, I can recognise a minority who are trying to do something for the good, moving in different directions, but often wasting their energy and enthusiasm in projects that do not bring real contributions to the creation of useful common knowledge.

There are probably several reasons for this worrying situation, but in my view, one of the major ones is the lack of shared visions. In other words, there is a lack of common ideas on what possible, sustainable ways of living could be like.

For this reason, to give my modest contribution to redressing the lack of social imagination, this paper will start by proposing a general vision, the scenario of the multi-local society, and will continue by indicating some promising research directions.[01] However, before doing so, I will make a short parenthesis to introduce the kind of scenario I will propose and its construction process.

01 |

---

01 | The background to this paper is a series of research projects carried out by the Faculty of DIS-Indaco, at the Politecnico di Milano, in collaboration with other European Universities and research centres. In particular:
– HiCS, Highly Customerised Solutions, within the Growth Programme of the European Community (2001–2004)
– EMUDE, Emerging User Demands, within the VI Framework Programme of the European Community (2004–2006)
– Lola, Looking for likely alternatives, within the framework of the EU CCN, Consumer Citizens Network (2005 – 2006) →

Design orienting scenarios

The notion of scenarios refers to communicative artefacts targeted to different goals. Our interest here will be focused on a family of scenarios called 'Design Orienting Scenarios' (DOS) to stress that they are conceived as tools to be used in design processes.[01] In the case we are proposing here, the scenario-building process is based on some concrete, real cases that, because they meet a set of general criteria, can be considered as positive steps towards sustainability. The questions, of course, are: do these cases exist? How can we be sure they really are positive steps in the direction of sustainability?

In order to answer these questions, our starting point is the observation that, in contemporary society, cases of social innovation are continuously emerging in the form of new behaviours, new organisation models, and new ways of living. Some of these cases are even more unsustainable than the previous ones, but others appear to be interesting moves toward more sustainable ways of living: promising cases where, in different ways and with different motivations, some people have re-oriented their behaviour and their expectations in a direction that appears to be coherent with the criteria for social and environmental sustainability.

Although these promising cases are currently the expression of social minorities, they are crucial for promoting and orienting the transition towards sustainability. They are in fact the social experiments through which different ways of living are invented and tested. And they are also – or could be – the 'raw materials' for building scenarios of possible, sustainable ways of living.

Scenario

Today, we know that the present mainstream idea of wellbeing, the one based on western standards of living – product-based wellbeing – has to change. This is clear when we consider that its promise of individual freedom and democracy of consumption has not only not been fulfilled, but it can never be fulfilled, either now or in the future, because this product-based wellbeing, extended to a worldwide scale, is proving to be intrinsically unsustainable: the planet would not be able to support the weight of 6–8 billion people approaching western standards of consumption. 02 |

02 |

– CCSL, Creative Communities for Sustainable Lifestyles, a project promoted by the Task Force on Sustainable Lifestyles, within the United Nations 10 Year Framework of Programmes on Sustainable Consumption and Production – usually called the Marrakech Process (2006–2007).

02 |

Today, 20 per cent of the population, living near to western standards, is consuming 80 per cent of available resources. If this situation changes and the other 80 per cent succeed in approaching the same standards of living, we face the prospect of an ecological disaster. If, however, they do not succeed, the perspective is one of →

The result is that we now also know that transition towards sustainability requires radical changes in the way we produce, and generally, in the way we live. In fact, we (the entire population of the planet) need to learn how to live better, while reducing our ecological footprint and improving the quality of our social fabric. In this perspective, the link between the environmental and social dimensions of sustainability appears clearly, showing that radical social innovations [03] will be needed, in order to move from current, unsustainable models to new, sustainable ones.

Given the nature and the dimension of this change, we have to see transition towards sustainability (and, in particular, towards sustainable ways of living) as a wide-reaching social learning process in which the most diversified forms of knowledge and organisational capabilities must be valorised in the most open and flexible way. Among these, a particular role will be played by local initiatives that, for several reasons, can be seen as promising cases of new behaviour and new ways of thinking. Below, I consider three main clusters: cosmopolitan localisations, creative communities and collaborative networks.

Cosmopolitan localisations

Contrary to what was thought in the past, the joint phenomena of globalisation and networking have brought us back to the local dimension. Here, the expression 'local' means something far removed from what was meant in the past (i.e. the valley, the agricultural village, the small provincial town, all isolated and relatively closed within their own culture and economy). Indeed, it combines the specific features of places and their communities with the new phenomena generated and supported worldwide by globalisation and by cultural, socio-economic interconnection. Unfortunately, these phenomena are characterised today by extremely negative dominant tendencies. For one thing, there are those that swing between traditionalist stances, supporting local interests, and reactionary stances (all the different forms of fundamentalism hidden behind the

social disaster because a highly interconnected and globalised society cannot for long support a situation where 20 per cent, or less, of the population has access to the promised wellbeing, while the remaining 80 per cent is forced to look on with no real chance of taking part. A further catastrophic prospect, halfway between the first two, exists: a world in a state of both environmental and social crisis, where the number of 'high impact' consumers increases at the same time as the number of those excluded. As we can all see, this third perspective seems dramatically to be the nearest to the present reality.

[03] According to the Young Foundation: 'Social innovation refers to new ideas that work in meeting social goals'.[02] Another definition could be: 'Social innovation refers to changes in the way individuals or communities act to obtain results (i.e. to solve a problem or to generate new opportunities). These innovations are driven by behavioural changes (more than by technology or market changes), which typically emerge from bottom-up processes (more than from top-down ones). If the way to achieve a result is totally new (or if it is the result that is totally new), we may refer to it as a radical social innovation.' [03]

protecting veil of traditions and identity). For another, there are those inclined towards turning what remains of traditions and landscapes into a show for tourist purposes (the tourist-related 'supermarket type' of localisation, which is just another side of the standardising aspect of globalisation, from which there is a desire to break away).

Luckily, however, on closer inspection, more interesting and promising cases can be observed: local communities that invent unprecedented cultural activities, forms of organisation and economic models. We can refer to these initiatives, as a whole, as cosmopolitan localisation.[04 - 06] The most commonly known and quoted examples are quality wine and some niche food products, such as those promoted by Slow Food. Other examples, are the essential oils of the Provence region, Murano glassware, Casentino wool etc., all products that carry with them the spirit and history of a place and a community to the end user. In other words, they are all examples of handicraft products, famous all over the world, which are linked to the identity of their place of origin and to the cultural and social values that characterise crafts.

It is easy to recognise that cosmopolitan localism is the result of the balance between being rooted (in a place and in the community related to that place) and being open (open to global flows of ideas, information, people, things and money.[07] This is quite a delicate balance as, at any time, one of the two sides may prevail over the other, leading to an anti-historical closure or, on the contrary, to a destructive, indiscriminate opening of the local social fabric and its peculiar features.

Based on this unstable balance, the cosmopolitan localisation that we are discussing here generates a new sense of place and culture: a place and local community that are no longer (almost) isolated entities, but junctions in a network, points of connection in both short networks, which generate and regenerate the local social and production fabric, and long networks, which connect that particular place and that particular community with the rest of the world.

What are these cases telling us? They tell us that it is possible to conceive economic models that cluster different activities and actors in an original way, and more importantly, in a way that permits optimum use of existing resources and reinforces and/or regenerates social networks. This is exactly what the main guidelines for sustainability are telling us should be done.

Before making any other comments on them, let us change our point of view and consider, more generally, how people are facing growing difficulties in everyday life.

Creative communities

Observing society as a whole and in general, what we see is rather discouraging. However, if we look at it carefully and selectively, we can also see something different: people and communities who act outside the dominant thought and behaviour patterns. Groups of people who re-organise the way they live their home (as in the co-housing movement) and their neighbourhood (bringing it to life, creating the conditions for children to go to school on foot; fostering mobility on foot or by bicycle). Communities that set up new participatory social services for elderly people and for parents (the young and the elderly living together and micro-nurseries set up and managed by enterprising mothers), or that set up new food networks supporting producers of organic items, and the quality and typical characteristics of their products (as in the solidarity purchasing and fair-trade groups). The list could continue.04

What do these promising cases of social innovation tell us? They tell us that, already today, it is possible to do things differently and consider one's own work, one's own time and one's own system of social relationships in a different light, searching for a form of wellbeing that is less product-intensive and more dependent on common goods (i.e. on social and environmental qualities). They tell us that there are groups of people – the creative communities 05 – who have been able to think in a new way, developing a form of collaborative creativity thanks to which they have managed to put very innovative forms of organisation into action.

Collaborative networks

Of course, as we said, both these phenomena (cosmopolitan localisations and creative communities) may be seen as minority and marginal, but, in my view, this is a mistaken perception. On the contrary, I think that they are the most promising aspects of great, on-going, social and cultural changes. In fact, they are based on, and motivated by, profound supporting trends such as demographic changes, the growing evidence of environmental limits, and the on-going evolution towards a knowledge-based network society.[09-13] With particular reference to this last trend, they can be linked to what is happening in terms of organisation in a network society, or in other words, to the way people participate in collaborative projects.

The starting point of this phenomenon is the organisational model emerging from the Open Source movement.06 Over the last decade the principles behind this highly

04 | A large number of promising cases have been collected in the framework of several different studies (see footnote 1). Many of them can be found on the website http://www.sustainable-everyday.net/cases and in [06, 08].

05 | Creative community: a group of people who cooperatively invent, enhance and manage innovative solutions for new ways of living. This concept was a focus of the EMUDE research.

06 | The best-known open-source collaborative experience is Linux software, originally developed by the Finnish graduate student Linus Torvald. Anyone can use Linux for free as long as any changes or new features are shared with others at no cost. Simple rules, shared goals and clear yardsticks for judging performance, allows this global community to share ideas and, as a result, to improve the software, which is a shared, public good.

collaborative approach have increasingly been applied to areas beyond the coding of software.[14,15] Now we can observe that these principles have been highly successful in proposing collaborative and effective organisational models in several other application fields.[16] Notable examples of this are: the building of new common knowledge, as in the case of Wikipedia, the encyclopaedia that has become the largest in the world in the course of just a few years; new forms of social organisation such as Meet-Up, SmartMobs and BBC Action network: 'platforms for actions' that bring together people interested in doing the same thing (from renting a bus for a journey, to cleaning a river bank) and, once the critical mass has been reached, support them in doing it; the peer-to-peer approach to health care activities, as in the case of Open welfare, a project led by the British Design Council.

The innovative character of these new models must be stressed. All these examples of collaborative networks are characterised by motivations and ways of doing that were unimaginable until a few years ago. Now they appear to be possible and capable of catalysing large numbers of interested people, of organising them in peer-to-peer mode, of building a common vision and a common direction. They are able to develop even very complex projects on a global scale (as in Wikipedia) or on a local one (as in Meet-Up, Smart-Mobs and the BBC Action network). Quoting the British Design Council, which refers to them as Open models, they are new forms of organisation that do not rely 'on mass participation in the creation of the service. The boundary is blurred between the users and producers of a service. It is effectively often impossible to differentiate between those who are creating the service and those who are the consumers or users of the output'.[17]

Multi-local society

Until now, cosmopolitan localisations, creative communities and collaborative networks, have been rather separate phenomena. Except for some minor overlapping, they have been generated by different people with different motivations. Nevertheless, I think that, in the near future, they will converge and become a single, complex social innovation process. In doing so, they will strongly reinforce each other: cosmopolitan localisations and creative communities will bring the lively richness of people involved in real, daily problems to collaborative networks and the new opportunities that have been opened by their brand-new forms of organisation.

On the other hand, the possibility of this convergence has also given rise and consistence to the vision of a possible, sustainable society: the multi-local society. A society where, contrary to dominant trends, the 'global' appears as a network of 'local systems', which is at the same time both local and cosmopolitan, based as it would be on communities and places that are strong in their own identity, embedded in a physical place, but open to (i.e. connected with) other places/communities. A society that rediscovers its capacity for local adaptation, using to best advantage whatever is locally available and exchanging within the network whatever cannot be locally produced.

It must be stressed that the local dimension of this multi-local society does not in the least propose a nostalgic view of the past: it does not refer to little, local autarchic entities, but to places, communities and systems that are, as we said, highly interconnected. As a matter of fact, in the multi-local society, as in every network-based system, the ideas of 'global' and 'local', and of 'large' and 'small', are challenged. In fact, in a highly connected system the small is not small, but it is (or can be) a knot in a network (the real dimension of which is given by the number of links with other elements of the system). Similarly, and for the same reasons, in the multi-local society the local is not geographically local, but it is (or it can be) a locally based, cosmopolitan community.[07]

Today, the vision of a multi-local society is still far from mainstream, but it indicates a direction that, for several reasons, can be successfully followed. In fact, not only is it locally practicable, given that it is based on real cases of social innovation (cosmopolitan localisations, creative communities and collaborative networks), but it is also coherent with such a strong driver of change as the rise of the network society.

Design research

Fostering the vision of a multi-local society is a question of establishing a 'virtuous circle' encompassing social innovation (which we have recognised here in the forms of cosmopolitan localisations, creative communities and collaborative networks) and technological and institutional innovation (which can be implemented by the actors whose decisions can advance the possibilities of success of promising proposals). On the other hand, setting up this virtuous circle requires first and foremost the development of certain design capabilities: the communication and strategic skills necessary to recognise, reinforce and transmit adequately the ideas and solutions generated at a social level. And to transform them into original – and potentially successful – proposals.

More precisely, designers and design researchers should contribute to this far-reaching innovation process by organising their capabilities in four steps:

1. Focusing and giving visibility to promising cases (highlighting their most interesting aspects)
2. Building scenarios of potential futures (showing what could happen if these cases were to spread and consolidate, becoming mainstream ways of doing)

07   In a multi-local society, communities and places are junctions in a network: points of connection in short networks, which generate and regenerate the local social and production fabric; and long networks, which connect that particular place and that particular community with the rest of the world. This connection of the 'long global networks' with 'short local networks' provides support to organisational forms and production and service systems based on the subsidiarity principle. That is: to do on a larger scale only what cannot be done on a smaller scale, i.e. at a local level.

3. Developing enabling systems (conceiving specific solutions to increase the promising cases efficiency and accessibility)
4. Promoting creative contexts (collaborating in the development of new governance tools)

Below, I briefly outline these third and fourth steps and their main design research implications.

Enabling solutions

We have just seen that a positively oriented process of social innovation is emerging,[02] generating some practical experiences of sustainable ways of living. At the same time, we noted that an expansion of this emerging social innovation process into a mainstream tendency is only a possibility at the moment.

Let us consider, for instance, the cases of grassroots social innovation that we have seen. Looking at them closely, we realise that they emerge in very specific conditions and, above all, that they are the result of the enterprise of very special people. People who have been able to think and act by breaking out of the cage of dominant thought and behaviour. Although this almost heroic aspect is the most fascinating side of these phenomena, it is also an objective limit to their diffusion (and often also of their lasting power): exceptional people are not so common and, above all, they are not eternal.

To help these ways of doing things last and spread we must therefore start with these experiences, and the organisational model they have invented and brought to life, and propose products and services specifically conceived to increase their accessibility. In other words, we have to imagine and enact enabling systems, i.e. systems that provide cognitive, technical and organisational instruments so as to enable individuals and/or communities to achieve a result, using their skills and abilities while regenerating the quality of the living contexts in which they happen to live. For example: the intention of a group of parents to start up a micro-nursery could be facilitated by an enabling solution that includes a step-by-step procedure indicating what must be done, a system of guarantees that attests to the suitability of the parent organiser and the house, and health and educational support for problems that cannot be solved within the nursery itself. Similarly: a solidarity purchasing group could be supported by special software designed to manage shopping and guarantee relationships with producers; a co-housing project could be facilitated by a system that puts potential participants in touch, helps find suitable buildings or building plots, and that helps overcome any administrative and financial difficulties ... The list of examples could continue, showing in a very clear way the role that design (mainly intended as design of services and communication, and strategic design) could play to support these cases of social innovation and to make them more accessible, effective and replicable.

In my view, the opportunity for designers to support these cases opens a new, extensive field of design research. In fact, these promising cases can be seen as new kinds of services: collaborative services, the effectiveness of which, and indeed their very existence, is due to the existence of groups of people willing to collaborate and to participate in innovative forms of social networks. How to deal with this kind of initiative, how to support them, and how to promote the possibility of their being replicated without losing the very delicate social qualities on which they are based, is an open and very challenging question that should be investigated.[18, 19]

At the same time, it is clear that this kind of case-by-case intervention cannot be enough. The dimension of the problem requires something more than that. It requires the creation of conditions for these good ideas to really spread into larger social networks. To make this more feasible, something has to be done on a larger scale; in a wider context.

New governance tools

To consolidate and spread, the cases of grassroots social innovation we have introduced above have to find favourable contexts and innovative forms of relationship between their local level and higher ones, i.e. with regional, national and international levels.

In practical terms, it has been observed that the contexts that facilitate creative attitudes present certain common characteristics: they have to give access to appropriate technologies, to promote the diffusion of knowledge, skills and abilities, and to enhance social and political tolerance.[03, 20, 21]

In this perspective, the governance tools needed have to promote horizontal links between peers, while connecting different vertical levels of the public administration organisational structure. In doing so, they must be capable of stimulating and keeping alive the creative contexts that are the 'natural habitats' of the creative groups and of the diffuse social innovations they are able to conceive and establish.

How can design research participate in conceiving these new governance tools? In my view, what design research can (and should) do is to help to introduce a new spirit and advanced forms of organisation into the governance toolkit. I obviously refer to the ideas and practical models that are emerging in contemporary network society, as mentioned above (such as the open source and peer-to-peer systems). In this perspective, new, flexible and adaptable forms of governance have to be evaluated and practical experiments have to be made. The results should produce a new governance toolkit: an open governance toolkit to give creative groups of people access to physical and virtual spaces where they can share ideas, communicate, help each other and collaboratively build a new body of common knowledge.

Active wellbeing

In parallel with the development of enabling solutions and new governance tools, another line of research is needed. This specifically relates to the idea of wellbeing, and particularly to the role of the subjects searching for it, that hypothesises a change from a mainly passive role to a mainly active one.

The starting point of this proposal is the consideration that the current mainstream idea of wellbeing arose with the enthusiastic discovery that artefacts could work for us like modern mechanised slaves. From here, and from the memory of frequent hardship in pre-mechanised daily life, came the idea of wellbeing as the minimisation of personal involvement: the idea that when faced with a result to achieve, the best strategy was always the one that required the least physical effort, attention and time and consequently the least need for ability and skill.

This vision of wellbeing, which is of course still largely dominant, is starting to change. The proposed cases of social innovation show us that something new is emerging: a wellbeing where the 'user' is actively involved. Where he/she is, in some way, the co-producer of the results he/she wants to achieve (and is able to do so because he/she has many of the necessary intellectual and practical resources). Finally, a kind of wellbeing where the involved subject, facing a problem, is not only 'part of the problem', but

08 |

also 'part of the solution'.08 | [02, 06, 22]

Designing for this new user's profile means conceiving and developing the enabling solutions we have seen above. That is, to consider and evaluate people's capabilities in terms of sensibility, competence and enterprise, and to design systems that enable them to fulfil their potential, using their own skills and abilities in the best possible

09 |

way.09 | [23]

What we want underline here is the opportunity for in-depth research on these topics. In particular, research on the conceptual and practical tools that are needed to deal with subjects considered not only in terms of needs and wishes, but also for their

08 | It should be added that cosmopolitan localisation and creative communities generate a new idea of wellbeing from the point of view of expectations in terms of products and services as well. In fact, the emerging wellbeing is based upon an awareness of the way and the extent to which some local and social qualities can contribute to it. For example, the awareness of how a sense of security resulting from a still active social fabric, the healthiness of places, the beauty of landscape etc. can contribute to wellbeing.

09 | This approach implies the introduction of the concept of capability, intended as the possibility for a person to achieve a result using his/her own personal resources and the set of solutions to which he/she has access. This concept of 'capability' is taken from Nussbaum's and Sen's theories. The most interesting aspect of this concept is that it leads us to talk about people's wellbeing moving our attention away 'from goods, to what goods enable human beings to achieve'.[23]

capabilities. The result should be the evolution of user-centred design, towards something that could be defined as 'actor-centred design'. To move from the idea of 'designing to solve problems' to one of 'designing to enable people to live as they like, while moving toward sustainability'.

Designing networks

The research directions introduced up to now are based on the existence of a diffuse creativity in a context that, if appropriately stimulated and directed, could evolve towards the scenario of the multi-local society. We have said that this perspective implies a deep transformation of the user's role. But a similar, parallel change also has to take place on the designer's side. In fact, if it is true that we live in a society where 'everybody designs',[09, 10, 24] designers should accept that they can no longer aspire to a monopoly on design and, at the same time, they have to be able to recognise what could be their new, and in my view important, specific role.

In this new environment of diffuse creativity, designers have to learn how actively and positively to participate in the social processes where new and, hopefully, promising ideas are emerging. That is, they should actively and positively participate in the social innovation processes that have been introduced briefly in this paper, above. To do this, a new line of research is needed. What must be developed are the knowledge and the tools that are necessary to collaborate with a variety of interlocutors. More precisely: to be the design specialists in a world of design amateurs and to interact with others as experts, but in a peer-to-peer mode; to promote the convergence of different actors towards shared ideas and potential solutions.

More generally, and going back to the beginning of this paper, this design research stream should make it possible for designers to operate as intelligent actors in complex designing networks. 10 | That is, to operate in a positive way in the emerging, interwoven networks of individual people, enterprises, non-profit organisations, local and global institutions that are using – and hopefully will use more and more in the future – their creativity and entrepreneurship to take some concrete steps towards sustainability.

10 |

---

10 |

The notion of designing networks emerged in the final consideration of the EMUDE research results.[03] The theatrical and practical background was also given by other important lines of research, such as the ones developed by Pierre Lévy, on collective Intelligence,[25] or by Hilary Cottam and Charles Leadbeater of open services in the framework of the wider phenomenon of the open source movement.[17]

References / Bibliography

[01]	Manzini E, Jégou F (2004) Design degli scenari. In: Manzini E, Bertola P (eds): *Design Multiverso, Polidesign, Milan, 87*
[02]	Young Foundation (2006) *Social Silicon Valleys. A Manifesto for Social Innovation.* http://www.discoversocialinnovation.org/Social%20Silicon%20Valleys.pdf (accessed 6 June 2007)
[03]	EMUDE (2006) *Emerging User Demands for Sustainable Solutions, 6th Framework Programme (priority 3-NMP).* European Community, internal document
[04]	Sachs W (1998) *a cura di, Dizionario dello sviluppo.* Gruppo Abele, Turin
[05]	Manzini E, Vugliano S (2000) *Il locale del globale. La localizzazione evoluta come scenario progettuale.* Pluriverso N1, Milan
[06]	Manzini E, Jégou F, (2003) *Sustainable Everyday. Scenarios of Urban Life.* Edizioni Ambiente, Milan
[07]	Appadurai A (1990) *Disgiunzione e differenza nell'economia culturale globale.* In: Featherstone M (ed.): *Cultura globale.* Seam, Rome
[08]	Meroni A (ed.) (2007) *Creative Communities. People Inventing Sustainable Ways of Living.* Edizioni Polidesign, Milan (also available from www.sustainable-everyday.net with CreatiVe Commons licence)
[09]	Beck U (1997) *Che cos'è la globalizzazione. Rischi e prospettive della società planetaria.* [Was ist Globalisierung? Irrtümer der Globalisierung – Antworten auf Globalisierung] Carocci, Rome
[10]	Giddens A (1991) *The Consequences of Modernity.* Polity Press, Cambridge
[11]	Castells M (1996) *The Information Age: Economy, Society and Culture. Vol I, The rise of the Network Society.* Blackwell, Oxford
[12]	Pine BJ II, Gilmore JH (1999) *The Experience Economy. Work is Theatre & Every Business a Stage.* Harvard Business School Press, Boston, MA
[13]	Rifkin J (2000) *The Age of Access.* Putnam, New York
[14]	Lessig L (2001) *The Future of Ideas: the Fate of the Commons in a Connected World.* Random House, New York
[15]	Stalder F, Hirsh J (2002) Open Source Intelligence. *First Monday* 7(6), http://www.firstmonday.org/issues/issue7_6/stalder/ (accessed 6 June 2007)
[16]	Tapscott D, Williams AD (2007) *Wikinomics. How Mass Collaboration Changes Everything.* Portfolio, New York
[17]	Cottam H, Leadbeater C (2004a) *Open Welfare: Designs on The Public Good.* Design Council, London

[18]   Cipolla C (2004) Tourist or Guest – Designing Tourism Experiences or Hospitality Relations? In: Willis A-M (ed.): *Design Philosophy Papers: Collection Two*. Team D/E/S Publications, Ravensbourne, Australia

[19]   Manzini E (2005) Creative Communities and Enabling Platforms. An Introduction to a Promising Line of Research and Actions on Sustainable Production and Consumption. In: Doyle D (ed): *Taking responsibility*. Hedmark University College Publishing, Allkopi, Norway

[20]   Ray PH, Anderson SR (2000) *The Cultural Creatives, How 50 Million People Are Changing the World*. Three Rivers Press, New York

[21]   Florida R (2002) *The Rise of the Creative Class. And how it's Transforming Work, Leisure, Community and Everyday Life*. Basic Books, New York

[22]   Cottam H, Leadbeater C (2004b) *Health. Co-creating Services*. Design Council – RED unit, London

[23]   Nussbaum M, Sen A (1993) *The Quality of Life*. Oxford University Press, Oxford

[24]   Giddens A. (2000). *Il mondo che cambia. Come la globalizzazione ridisegna la nostra vita.* [Runaway World. How Globalization Is Reshaping our Lives] Il Mulino, Bologna

[25]   Lévy P (1994) *L'intelligenza collettiva. Per un'antropologia del cyberspazio.* [L'Intelligence collective: pour une anthropologie du cyberspace] Feltrinelli, Milan

Gui Bonsiepe

Information designer and design educator. Studied and taught at the hfg ulm. Moved to Latin America in 1968 and worked in various government programmes for industrial development (Chile, Argentina, Brazil) and as a freelance designer. 1987–1989 interface design at a software house in Emeryville, California. 1993–2003 Professor of Interface Design at the Köln International School of Design. Author of numerous publications about design in peripheral countries. Books: *Teoria e pratica del disegno industriale* (Feltrinelli, Milan 1975). *A 'tecnologia' da tecnologia* (Edgar Blucher, São Paulo 1985). *Dall'oggetto all'interfaccia* (Feltrinelli, Milan 1995; English edition *Interface/an approach to design* (Jan Van Eyck Academy, Maastricht 1999). Lives in Brazil and Argentina.

Richard Buchanan

Richard Buchanan is Professor of Design and former Head of the School of Design at Carnegie Mellon University, where he is currently Director of Doctoral Studies. He teaches in the traditional fields of Communication Design and Industrial Design and is also well known for extending design thinking into new areas of application such as Interaction Design and Organisation Design. His numerous publications include *Discovering Design: Explorations in Design Studies* (co-edited with Victor Margolin, University of Chicago Press, Chicago 1995); *The Idea of Design* (co-edited with Victor Margolin, MIT Press, Boston 1996); and *Pluralism in Theory and Practice* (co-edited with Eugene Garver, Vanderbilt University Press, Nashville 2000). He is co-editor of *Design Issues*, an international journal of design history, theory and criticism published by the MIT Press. He is a former President of the Design Research Society, an international learned society based in the United Kingdom. Professor Buchanan received his AB and PhD from the Committee on the Analysis of Ideas and the Study of Methods at the University of Chicago.

Paul Chamberlain

Professor Paul Chamberlain is a graduate of the furniture school at the Royal College of Art, and was co-founder and director of London based FLUX Design. His research explores the role of artefacts in multidisciplinary user-centred research. He works with diverse academic specialists and commercial partners with the aim of realising new knowledge that informs and is demonstrated in commercial outputs. He explores the multisensory aspects of design in the areas healthcare, disability and ageing, which includes investigating educational and therapeutic environments, furniture and medical devices.
He is Director of the LAB4LIVING research centre, a collaboration between Design and Health at Sheffield Hallam University. His work has achieved international recognition through publications, exhibitions and awards.

Nigel Cross

Professor Nigel Cross is a leading international figure in the world of design research. He has an academic and professional background in architecture and industrial design, and has conducted research into computer-aided design, design methodology, design epistemology and design cognition since the 1960s. His current research focuses on creative cognition in design, based on studies of expert and exceptional designers. He is a long-time member of the academic staff of the UK's pioneering, multimedia Open University, where he has been responsible for, or instrumental in, a wide range of distance education courses in design and technology.

Books by Professor Cross include *Designerly Ways of Knowing* (Springer, London 2006), *Analysing Design Activity* (co-edited with Christiaans and Dorst; Wiley, Chichester 1996) and the third edition of his successful textbook *Engineering Design Methods* (Wiley, Chichester 2000). Professor Cross is also Editor-in-Chief of *Design Studies*, the International Journal of Design Research. In 2005 he was honoured with the Lifetime Achievement Award of the Design Research Society. He is President of the Design Research Society, and of the International Association of Societies of Design Research.

Joep Frens

Joep Frens was born in 1974 in Amersfoort, the Netherlands. After obtaining his Master's degree in Industrial Design Engineering from Delft University of Technology (the Netherlands) he went to Switzerland to pursue a career in research at the Swiss Federal Institute of Technology (ETH) in Zurich. He returned to the Netherlands as a PhD student. In 2006 he received his doctorate from Eindhoven University of Technology for his thesis 'Designing for Rich Interaction: Integrating Form, Interaction, and Function'. He is now assistant professor at the same university. He teaches several courses at bachelor and master level and continues to do research on designing for interaction.

Wolfgang Jonas

Wolfgang Jonas was born in 1953. He studied naval architecture at the Technical University Berlin, did research on the computer-aided optimisation of streamlined shapes, and gained his PhD in 1983. Consulting engineer for companies in the automotive industry and the German Institute for Standardisation (DIN). He has been teaching (CAD, industrial design) and research (systems theory and design theory) since 1988 at the University of Arts Berlin and the University of Wuppertal. 1994 lecturing qualification (Habilitation) in design theory. 1994–2001 Professor of Process Design at the University of Art and Design Halle / Burg Giebichenstein. 2001–2005 Professor of Design Theory at the University of the Arts Bremen. Since 2005 Professor of Systems Design at the School of Art and Design, University of Kassel.
Focus of interest: design theory as meta theory, design methods in a systemic perspective, scenario planning. Numerous publications on theoretical and practical aspects of designing, for example: *Design - System - Theorie: Überlegungen zu einem systemtheoretischen Modell von Designtheorie* (Die Blaue Eule, Essen 1994) and *Mind the Gap! On Knowing and Not-knowing in Design* (with Jan Meyer-Veden, HM Hauschild, Bremen 2004).

Klaus Krippendorff

Klaus Krippendorff (PhD) is Professor of Communication at the University of Pennsylvania's Annenberg School for Communication. He has authored: *The Semantic Turn, a New Foundation for Design* (Taylor & Francis, New York 2006); *Content Analysis* (2nd ed., Sage, Thousand Oaks 2004); *Information Theory* (Sage, Beverly Hills 1986) and numerous articles on communication theory, cybernetics, social science methods and analytical techniques. He edited the report *Design in the Age of Information* (1997), among others. With epistemology in mind, he inquires into how language brings forth reality; as a critical scholar, he explores conditions of entrapment and possibilities of emancipation; as a second-order cybernetician, he develops recursive conceptions of the self and others in conversations, and as a designer (grad.), he attempts to shift the meaning and human use of technological artefacts into the centre of design considerations, encouraging a redesign of design.

| Ianus Keller | In 1995 Ianus Keller (born 1970) received his master's degree in Industrial Design at the Delft University of Technology. In 1994 he participated in the Apple Interface Design Project, where he was invited to present the team's results at the Apple Avanced Technology Group at Cupertino, CA, USA. From 1995–1999 he worked for the Dutch design company Landmark Design & Technology in Rotterdam, and at the Internet consultancy Virtual Affairs in Amsterdam. |

In November 1999 he started his PhD project and his Cabinet. While he was working on his PhD project, he acted as a teacher and adviser in different design-related classes. In 2003 he co-ordinated an interface design project similar to the one he had done a decade earlier, for the Microsoft Research Design Expo, Seattle, WA, USA.
At the Faculty of Industrial Design Engineering, his Cabinet is a showcase for research. It is regularly shown in presentations. In 2005 his Cabinet won the international design competition at the Third International Conference on Appliance Design in Bristol, UK. As an independent designer and consultant, he participates in juries and brainstorming sessions. He is often invited to speak at cultural and academic institutes.

| Ezio Manzini | Ezio Manzini is Professor of Design at the Politecnico di Milano. He deals with strategic design and design for sustainability, with a focus on scenario-building and solution development. |

Some results of his recent works have been published in the books: *Sustainable Everyday* (with François Jégou, Edizioni Ambiente, Milan 2003); *Design Vision: a Sustainable Way of Living in China* (with Benny Ding Leong, Ningnan, China 2006); and in several papers. Some of these can be found on: http://www.sustainable-everyday. net/manzini/

| Anna Meroni | Anna Meroni, architect and designer, has a PhD in Industrial Design. She works as researcher in the research unit DIS, Design and Innovation for Sustainability of the Department INDACO (Industrial Design) of the Politecnico di Milano, where she is Assistant Professor of Service and Strategic Design and co-director of the International Masters in Strategic Design, organised by the consortium POLI.design. Her topic is system strategic innovation: she is involved in several international research activities, in the organisation of symposiums and events, and writes about strategic innovation for design journals. |

| Ralf Michel | Born in 1964 in Niederwald, Germany. Designer, curator, publicist. Ralf Michel studied social science in Frankfurt and Cologne, and design at Köln International School of Design. As design editor, he also wrote for the Swiss magazine *Hochparterre*. Michel advised the Swiss Federal Office of Cultural Affairs on revising design sponsorship; he was a founding member of the Swiss Design Association and served on its board. He has curated exhibitions and published pieces on various aspects of design, including its significance for society. Since 2000, he has been lecturing at Zurich University of the Arts. Until mid-2007, he was responsible for developing and managing the Swiss Design Network (SDN). In this capacity, he has held design research symposia and published works on design research. Ralf Michel is a founding member of BIRD (the Board of International Research in Design). Since 2007, he has been vice-director of the design and technologies research institute at Zurich University of the Arts, where he is also involved in research projects. Ralf Michel is co-editor of *Schriften zur Gestaltung der Zürcher Hochschule der Künste* (Papers on the design of the Zürcher Hochschule der Künste), which are also published by Birkhäuser. |

Beat Schneider	Born in 1946 in Nidau bei Biel. He attended grammar school in Basel before studying philosophy, art history and theology at the universities of Basel, Mainz and Heidelberg. Beat Schneider obtained his doctorate in theology and religious studies. He has also done both journalistic and theoretical work and published works on cultural and art history (including *Penthesilia*). He has written a critical history of cultural and art history and, more recently, *Design – Eine Einführung. Entwurf im sozialen, kulturellen und wissenschaftlichen Kontext* (An introduction to design: design in a social, cultural and academic context, Birkhäuser, Basel 2005).

He has lectured at the Bern School of Design, given in-service teacher training, and taught at the University of Bern. Since 2000, he has been working as a lecturer in culture, art and design at the Bern University of the Arts, where he has been Head of Research since 2001.

Beat Schneider was the first President of the Swiss Design Network (SDN): the national skills network for design research of the Swiss universities for art and design. From 1974 to 1990, he was a member of the Bern city council and the Grosser Rat of the Canton of Bern. |
| Pieter Jan Stappers | After an education in experimental physics (MSc 1984), Pieter Jan Stappers switched to Industrial Design Engineering at Delft University of Technology, and followed a research path that led from human perception, spatial imagery, Virtual Reality (PhD in 1992), to design tools and participatory design techniques. His current activities as Professor of Design Techniques (as of 2002) encompass coordinating Delft's new Master's programme of Design for Interaction, being informal director of ID-StudioLab, and heading the research subprogramme on tools and techniques for the conceptual phase of design. Key elements in his work are 'research through design', 'experiential prototypes', and context mapping, which can be found on his website http://studiolab.io.tudelft.nl/stappers/. |
| Susann Vihma | Susann Vihma is Professor of Design Semiotics at the School of Visual Culture, University of Art and Design Helsinki, where she is responsible for doctoral studies. She is also a lecturer at the University of Lapland (Design Semiotics and Design History). She is head of the research project SeFun 2004–2007 (funded by the Academy of Finland, www.uiah.fi/sefun) and is constitutive member and head of the Nordic network of design research Nordcode (www.nordcode.hut.fi) financed by Nordforsk. Among her publications are *Products as representations* (UIAH, Helsinki 1995) and the textbooks on design history *Ornamentti ja kuutio* (in Finnish, 2002) and *Designhistoria* (in Swedish, 2nd ed. 2003).

For more information, see http://www.uiah.fi/page.asp?path=1,1450,1452,19545,19547,19890 |

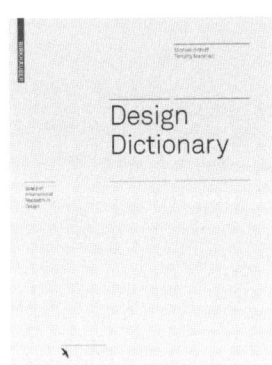

Design Dictionary

The ideal reference work on the international language of design.

This dictionary provides a stimulating and categorical foundation for a serious international discourse on design. It is a handbook for everyone concerned with design in career or education, who is interested in it, enjoys it, and wishes to understand it. Some 50 authors from Japan, Austria, England, Germany, Australia, Switzerland, the Netherlands, the United States, and elsewhere have written original articles for this design dictionary. Their cultural differences provide perspectives for a shared understanding of central design categories and communicating about design. The volume includes both the terms in use in current discussions, some of which are still relatively new, as well as classics of design discourse. A practical book, both scholarly and ideal for browsing and reading at leisure.

Michael Erlhoff, Tim Marshall (eds.)
In cooperation with the Board of International Research in Design
approx. 416 pp.
16.8 x 22.4 cm
Softcover
ISBN 978-3-7643-7739-7

Designerly Ways of Knowing

The concept 'designerly ways of knowing' emerged in the late 1970s alongside new approaches in design education. Professor Nigel Cross, a respected design researcher, first articulated this idea in his paper 'Designerly Ways of Knowing' published in 1982. This book is a unique insight into an expanding discipline area with important implications for design research, education and practice.
This book traces the development of a research interest in articulating and under-standing the idea that designers have and use 'designerly' ways of knowing and thinking. The following topics are covered: nature and nurture of design ability; creative cognition in design; natural intelligence of design; design discipline versus design science; expertise in design.
As a timeline of scholarship and research and a resource for understanding how designers think and work, this book will interest researchers, teachers and students of industrial and product design, design practitioners, and design managers.

Nigel Cross
In cooperation with the Board of International Research in Design
approx. 128 pp. 30 b/w ills.
16.5 x 23.5 cm
Softcover
ISBN 978-3-7643-8484-5